Chicano Engli
Context

Carmen Fought

First published 2003 by
PALGRAVE MACMILLAN
Houndmills, Basingstoke, Hampshire RG21 6XS and
175 Fifth Avenue, New York, N.Y. 10010
Companies and representatives throughout the world

PALGRAVE MACMILLAN is the global academic imprint of the Palgrave Macmillan division of St. Martin's Press, LLC and of Palgrave Macmillan Ltd. Macmillan® is a registered trademark in the United States, United Kingdom and other countries. Palgrave is a registered trademark in the European Union and other countries.

ISBN 0–333–98637–7 hardback
ISBN 0–333–98638–5 paperback

This book is printed on paper suitable for recycling and made from fully managed and sustained forest sources.

A catalogue record for this book is available from the British Library.

Library of Congress Cataloging-in-Publication Data
Fought, Carmen, 1966–
    Chicano English in context / Carmen Fought.
        p.   cm.
    Includes bibliographical references (p.) and index.
    ISBN 0–333–98637–7—ISBN 0–333–98638–5 (pbk.)
    1. Mexican Americans—Languages.   2. English language—United States—Foreign elements—Spanish.   3. English language—Variation—United States.
    4. Spanish language—Influence on English.   5. Bilingualism—United States.
    I. Title.

PE3102.M4 F68 2002
427'.973'0896872—dc21   2002074837

10 9 8 7 6 5 4 3 2 1
12 11 10 09 08 07 06 05 04 03

Printed and bound in Great Britain by
Antony Rowe Ltd, Chippenham and Eastbourne

Contents

List of Tables

List of Figures

Acknowledgments

In writing this book, I have been blessed by a tremendous amount of support from many sources, all conspiring to make it a pleasurable process and one which I look back on with joy.

My fieldwork experience was an exceptionally positive one, with few frustrations and many rewards. This is due completely to the tremendous assistance I received. At Westside Park, Dr Anita Johnson saw to it that all doors were opened to me, and shared with me her own insights and experiences. Marsha Litter and Debbie Berger helped me find my place as a participant-observer at the school. Finally, of course, I must thank the many varied individuals in the Latino community of Los Angeles who agreed to participate in this research. In particular, I thank the students at Westside Park for talking with me openly and sharing with me some of the best and worst moments of their lives. I found them generous, kind, complex, sometimes naïve, often hopeful. I feel fortunate to have had the opportunity to meet them. I wish them all long, healthy lives. The parents from the Down's Syndrome network and their children were also incredibly generous with me. They introduced me to new foods, new music, and new people, and made my fieldwork a rewarding experience in and of itself.

I have been fortunate to have far more than my share of mentors among my colleagues in linguistics. Ronald Macaulay, John Rickford, Otto Santa Ana, and Walt Wolfram have all given generously of their time and wisdom. I hope it is clear in my own work how much respect I have for each of them and for their contributions to the field of sociolinguistics. Additionally, I want to thank Ronald for reading and commenting on a draft of this book. I am also thankful to the two anonymous reviewers who commented on my original proposal. Their suggestions opened up new and interesting possibilities to me, which I have pursued as much as possible.

I owe a tremendous debt of gratitude to my family and friends, whose support has been so crucial in the writing of this book. My friend Patti Thorp-Robinson was there when I first started my Ph.D. and has given me her full support since then, through all the ups and downs. I am also grateful to Sheryl Wilson for saying 'How bad would it be if you just trusted yourself?' And I am thankful to Martha Crunkleton in so many ways that I cannot begin to summarize them here. I hope that since she is a wise woman, she will know what I want to say.

My family has showered me with love and support in this endeavor, as in all things. My brother Carlos is a constant source of support, humor, and inspiration. My mother, a.k.a. my 'Spanish-speaking research assistant,' has had such a large part in who I am that I imagine her voice speaks through every page. Her love has been a constant through my entire life. My husband, John Fought, has accepted my mood swings, distracted responses, late hours at the library, and requests for editorial help with great equanimity. All this in addition to helping me extensively with Chapter 3, and doing all the laundry for more than a year. His patience, humor, and love give me strength.

I also wish to thank the students who worked as my research assistants, especially Lea Harper, Laura Staum and Rebecca Wilson, for their efficient and insightful participation. Their assistance, as well as the transition into book form of this material generally, was funded by a grant from the Pitzer Research and Awards Committee. Additionally, I want to thank the *Journal of Sociolinguistics* for permission to use passages from my article 'A majority sound change in a minority community: /u/-fronting in Chicano English' (*Journal of Sociolinguistics* 3:1, 1999, 5–23) in an adapted and revised form, as part of Chapter 5. Finally, I am grateful to Jill Lake, my editor, for making the publishing process as easy as possible, and for giving me this opportunity to say something. I have said it as I thought best, and if there are any failures in this regard, they are purely my own.

Introduction

I.1   What is Chicano English? Setting aside the myths

From the beginning, the study of Chicano English (for which I will use the abbreviation CE) has necessarily included defining exactly which linguistic varieties this label encompasses.[1] As early as 1974, however, Allan Metcalf provides a very reasonable definition of Chicano English. He describes it as:

> a variety of English that is obviously influenced by Spanish and that has low prestige in most circles, but that nevertheless is independent of Spanish and is the first, and often only, language of many hundreds of thousands of residents of California.   (1974:53)

Though his particular focus of study was California, if we extend his definition to include other regions, particularly the southwest, it represents fairly accurately the facts about Chicano English. It is a non-standard variety of English, influenced by contact with Spanish, and spoken as a native dialect by both bilingual and monolingual speakers. Santa Ana (1993) discusses the importance of reserving the term 'Chicano English' for the variety used by native speakers, as I will also be doing throughout this book:

> Chicano English is an ethnic dialect that children acquire as they acquire English in the barrio or other ethnic social setting during their language acquisition period. Chicano English is to be distinguished from the English of second-language learners...Thus defined, Chicano English is spoken only by native English speakers. (1993:15)

1

In theory, one could use the label 'Chicano English' to encompass any dialect spoken by people of Mexican origin in the USA, including both varieties that are identical to those of Anglos in the area, and varieties spoken by adult immigrants for whom English is a second language, but I have chosen not to do so.

Nonetheless, some of the studies of Chicano English published in the early 1980s seem to have misplaced elements of Metcalf's early definition. For example, Penfield and Ornstein-Galicia describe Chicano English as 'a variety or dialect of English spoken predominantly by bilingual Chicanos' (1985:1), though they provide no evidence that bilinguals are more likely to speak Chicano English than monolinguals. Several of the early works also include discussion of whether Chicano English is actually a dialect of English separate from simply the non-native English of second language learners, often concluding that the answer is not yet known. A few of the authors suggest that Chicano English fades as its speakers 'learn English'. For example, Gonzalez (in Ornstein-Galicia 1984) comments:

> Even if we agree with Sawyer (1969, p.19) that Chicano English is '...simply an imperfect state in the mastery of English,' it would behoove us to look at the various 'imperfect states' that Chicano English goes through in arriving at Standard American English. (1984:35)

Gonzalez's perspective, which resurfaces later in the article, is that Chicano English is just a stage on the way to full acquisition of standard English; presumably if enough speakers were successful in acquiring this 'target' of Standard American English, Chicano English might disappear from the community.

Fortunately for me and my future as an author, Chicano English has not disappeared. It is alive and well in Los Angeles, among other places. It is a dialect in its own right, separate both from Spanish and from other local varieties of English such as California Anglo English (CAE)[2] or African-American English (AAE). It is changing, as all dialects do, but shows no signs of being abandoned by the community as a whole in favor of more standard varieties of English. It is an important cultural marker, a reminder of linguistic history, and a fertile field for the study of language contact phenomena and linguistic identity issues. It may even, in the area of intonation, carry a tiny seed of influence from Nahuatl. Like other dialects, it is not a single monolithic entity, but a range of ways of speaking that have certain features in common.

Chicano English can vary on a continuum from less to more standard, and from less to more influenced by other dialects, and it encompasses a wide range of stylistic options. Having said what Chicano English is (briefly, since in fact this entire book is devoted to the answering of that question), I will now turn to what Chicano English is *not*, since so many myths about this dialect persist.

Myth 1: Chicano English is spoken by people whose first language is Spanish, and whose Spanish introduces mistakes into their English

A co-worker of mine asked me recently, 'Why do so many Mexican-American students seem to have such a hard time learning English, even if they were born here in the USA?' She then gave me the specific example of a Mexican-American student who worked in her office. I happened to know that the student she was talking about was a native speaker of English, specifically of Chicano English. Similarly, in a class where I showed a clip from the film *Mi Vida Loca* (1994) and commented on some features of Chicano English in one girl's speech, a student raised her hand and said, 'But she only sounds like that because she speaks Spanish.' I asked her 'How do you know that she does? Have you seen the movie?' And she replied, 'No, I haven't seen it, but you can just tell from how she talks.' The comments of my co-worker and the student in my class illustrate the greatest myth that the public has about Chicano English: that it is a non-native version of English spoken by people whose first language is Spanish, and whose Spanish introduces 'mistakes' into their English. As the citation from Gonzalez (1984) illustrates, even the early linguistic literature on Mexican-Americans sometimes reflects this type of confusion; as late as 1993, Santa Ana describes this issue as still 'not settled' (1993:3) among linguists. Many people hear CE and assume that what they are hearing is the 'accent' of someone who speaks Spanish as their first language.

The problem with the theory that Chicano English reflects the influence of a bilingual's other language is that many speakers of Chicano English are *not* bilingual: they may scarcely know any Spanish at all, like the Chicanos that Santa Ana refers to as 'monolingual-English speakers who cannot order a *taco* in Spanish to save their lives' (1993:24). These speakers have in reality learned English perfectly, like children of all ethnic backgrounds who grow up in English-speaking countries, but the local variety of English they've learned is a non-standard one, and one which happens to reflect the historical contact with Spanish. Metcalf was absolutely right. Chicano English is both influenced by Spanish and separate from it. It is one of the English dialects available in the United States for native speakers to learn, like Appalachian English, or AAE, or the English spoken by professors at Harvard University, or by used car dealers in Houston. Chicano English cannot possibly be just a non-native variety spoken by second-language learners of English if it is spoken by people who *only* know English.

Not surprisingly, this myth has repercussions in the educational system. At the high school where I did most of my fieldwork, I helped out in the office.[3] One of the things I was occasionally asked to do was to administer the Bilingual Syntax Measure, a test designed to help the school classify certain students as 'LEP' (Limited English Proficient).[4] The test focuses on a number of English morphological forms, such as – *ed* for past tense, irregular verbs, plural –*s*, and so on. The test was administered to any student whose parents had reported, in a survey sent home by the school, that Spanish was spoken at home. I dutifully administered the test and recorded the scores. Often, students who were completely fluent in English and fairly poor in Spanish were classified as LEP because of the non-standard forms they used in responding to the questions. Monolingual Mexican-American students, some of whom would have had equally low scores, were never tested. When I naively tried to convey all of this to the principal of the school, she looked at me with the expression that professionals in the 'real world' reserve for academics, and explained patiently that the money the government provided for LEP students was important to the school, and that the question of exactly why their English was low-scoring was somewhat irrelevant. Nonetheless, someone looking at the scores (and here I picture some faceless administrator in the state government) would probably conclude (mistakenly) that bilingual Mexican-American children are likely to be hindered in learning English properly, because of their Spanish.

There is more to say about the relationship of bilingualism and CE. When I began my fieldwork, I was interested in determining what the differences were between monolingual and bilingual native speakers of Chicano English. In other words, among speakers of Chicano English who were born and grew up in the United States, how might the English of those who also spoke Spanish sound different from that of the monolinguals? With the unarticulated assumption that there must be some difference, I searched and searched for the answer to this question. I produced vowel charts and performed interesting linguistic analyses involving expensive computer software. In the end the software did not help at all. While there may be some features characteristic of the bilinguals, which I will discuss briefly in Chapter 4, they are subtle, ambiguous and infrequent. From a short stretch of speech, one cannot distinguish bilingual and monolingual Chicano English speakers (assuming we are talking about individuals born in the USA in both cases, not adult immigrants who speak English as a second language).

This finding surprised me a little (though perhaps it shouldn't have) but I accepted it. However, I find that many of my students are extremely reluctant to give up on the notion that they can pick out the bilingual speakers in a crowd. Partly in response to this, I have assembled a tape of short segments (in English) spoken by four male Chicano English speakers from my fieldwork in Los Angeles. Two of the speakers are bilingual (fluent in English and Spanish), and two speak only English. I play this tape for the students in various classes and have them try to guess whether each speaker is bilingual or monolingual. Invariably, the class does very poorly in this guessing exercise. What the students seem to be going by is social class. The tape includes an individual who works as a paralegal and speaks a somewhat middle-class version of Chicano English. The students mainly guess that he is monolingual, presumably because he sounds a little more standard than the others; however, he is an extremely fluent bilingual. At the other end of the scale is a speaker from a very low income family, who happens to be monolingual. But because he clearly speaks a vernacular dialect, the students tend to guess that he is bilingual. This link between social class and expectations of bilingualism is interesting in its own right. But for now, the main point is that there are no clear phonological or other features used by mono- lingual vs. bilingual native speakers of Chicano English which allow the two groups to be easily distinguished.

Myth 2: Chicano English is the same as 'Spanglish'

In general, codeswitching (the interspersing of elements from two or more languages in bilingual/multilingual communities) tends to generate a large number of myths, both inside and outside the communities where it occurs. Even though the process of mixing lexical items and structures from two languages is a perfectly natural one in bilingual societies, it is often regarded by non-linguists as sloppy, inaccurate or leading to the degeneration of one or both languages. The attitudes toward codeswitching in the Los Angeles community I studied were surprisingly positive, and are discussed in more detail in Chapter 8.

While codeswitching certainly occurs in this community, where it is most commonly referred to as *Spanglish*, it is a separate phenomenon from Chicano English and should not be confused with it. A person may speak Chicano English for an hour without using any Spanish words at all. Also a person who is a fluent bilingual may codeswitch between Spanish and a more standard variety of English; a few of the older middle-class speakers in my sample did exactly this. Nonetheless, speakers inside and outside the community tended to view codeswitching as the characteristic way of speaking of Mexican-Americans, and often weren't aware of Chicano English as a separate dialect of English that need not involve any Spanish words or structures. It is true that Chicano English speakers may choose to throw in an occasional Spanish word – what Poplack (1980) calls 'emblematic' switches – intended to highlight ethnic identity. These occur even among speakers who are basically monolingual (not surprising, since even monolingual Anglos, especially in California, will use expressions like *loco* or *Hasta la vista*). In fact, the younger speakers I talked to tended to do mostly this emblematic type of switching when speaking English; the slightly older speakers were more likely to do the traditional type of switching involving significant mixing of elements from both languages.

Though Chicano English is definitely *not* Spanglish, it is still true that codeswitching is a part of the linguistic competence of the community. Interestingly, one of my speakers, Patricia, 16, who is monolingual, pointed out to me that codeswitching allows monolingual English speakers to follow the gist of a conversation that is mainly in Spanish. Another speaker, Jorge, 18, talked about codeswitching as the linguistic factor that distinguishes Chicanos (that is, Mexican-heritage individuals born and raised here) from people born and raised in Mexico. As I mentioned, the attitudes of the speakers toward codeswitching were very positive overall. Even though the young speakers I interviewed did not seem to do as much codeswitching as has been described for other Latino populations, they commented on it favorably, and seemed to see it as a part of their community. In a sense, then, one might say that communicative competence in Chicano English includes the acceptance of mixing Spanish and English in the same sentence, whether or not one does it.

Myth 3:   Chicano English is a dialect spoken mostly by gang members and not used by middle-class Latinos and Latinas

As with other non-standard dialects, such as AAE, there is a tendency for those outside the community to associate Chicano English, particularly when it falls at the more non-standard end of the continuum, with gang members. Contributing to this effect are a number of movies with

Latino casts that focus on the gang lifestyle, and which are exactly the movies where CE is most likely to be heard (see Chapter 8). This is one of the myths about which linguists as well as others must be particularly careful. Complications arise in this regard because any factor that is important to the construction of identity in a community will have repercussions in the area of language. Where there are gang members in a community, this membership is obviously a salient factor in the construction of identity by these young adults, and to some extent in the construction of identity by the other young adults in the community, who may see themselves as standing in opposition to the sub-culture represented by the gangs. In such a community, gang membership must be taken into account when conducting a sociolinguistic study of variables. Even the difference between two gangs may be represented linguistically, as in Norma Mendoza-Denton's study of Norteñas and Sureñas, which was conducted in Northern California (Mendoza-Denton 1997). In Chapters 5 and 6, I will discuss the role of gang membership in sociolinguistic variation for the Southern California community that is the focus of this study.

Nonetheless, in our excitement over how neatly gang membership aligns with a particular linguistic variable, we may unintentionally reinforce a stereotype among the general population that CE is the language of gang members. In reality, as I mentioned earlier, CE encompasses a continuum of styles and of varieties, from less to more standard. If we count as CE any variety that includes some sub-group of the phonological, syntactic and semantic features that will be discussed in later chapters, then this dialect is spoken by millions of people in California and the southwest who come from a very wide range of socioeconomic, educational and occupational backgrounds.

Myth 4: Chicano English is merely incorrect grammar

Although I will not spend much time discussing this particular myth, Chicano English, of course, suffers from the same misperceptions and prejudices as other non-standard dialects such as AAE, Appalachian English and so on. Even those who do not attribute the differences in Chicano English specifically to Spanish often judge its structures as 'incorrect' relative to Standard English. There is (most unfortunately) no understanding in the general public of the fact that non-standard dialects have rules and patterns just as standard ones do, and that the distinction between them is social and political rather than linguistic. As with speakers of other non-standard dialects, Chicano English speakers, apart from those who also are fluent in a completely standard dialect, can experience tremendous discrimination in educational and professional settings (which will be discussed further in Chapter 8). Until linguists find a way to be more successful in getting crucial scientific information about non-standard dialects into the light of public awareness, speakers of Chicano English will be affected by these prejudices.

I.2   The scope of this work

Although people of Latino origin make up the second largest (and the fastest growing) minority in the USA, there has been very little socio-linguistic study of language and language change in Latino communities. In contrast with a much larger body of research that exists on AAE, the research on Chicano English and other English dialects associated with Latinos has been sparse. In the early and mid-1980s, there were a few studies (Peñalosa 1980; Duran 1981; Ornstein-Galicia 1984; Penfield and Ornstein-Galicia 1985) of the speech of Mexican-Americans that attempted to document Chicano English for the first time. As noted above, there was a great deal of uncertainty, reflected in some of these studies, about whether there even existed a dialect distinct from the non-native speech of individuals learning English as a second language. Often, when features of 'Chicano English' are discussed, it is not made clear whether these features were found among native or non-native speakers, or both. With respect to the list of phonological features in Peñalosa (1980:121), for example, almost all of them occurred among the non-native speakers I interviewed, but only a few were used by the native speakers in my sample. Additionally, in looking at the language of Mexican-Americans, there has been a much stronger focus on Chicano Spanish than Chicano English. For instance, Peñalosa's book has a chapter on each; the chapter on Chicano Spanish is 38 pages long, while the chapter on Chicano English is only eleven pages.

Since these early studies, there have been a few interesting articles published on Chicano English (for example, Wald 1993, 1996; Santa Ana 1993, 1996), but as yet there has been no modern, comprehensive study of this dialect. This book seeks to address that gap, at least partially, looking at the structure of Chicano English (its phonology, syntax and semantics) and how it reflects and constitutes the social and cultural identity of its speakers. The book is entitled *Chicano English in Context* because context, an important factor in the study of any dialect, is particularly crucial to Chicano English. Context here encompasses many things. Perhaps most salient is the historical context, both the history of Mexican immigration to the United States, and the linguistic history of a dialect that grew out of the contact between English and Spanish (in individuals and communities). There is the contemporary context of life in Los Angeles, a multilingual and multicultural city, and the particular social context of Mexican-American culture in all its forms, including norms for the construction of gender, age and ethnic identity.

Finally, there is the linguistic context, including the surrounding dialects of English such as AAE or California Anglo English, the latter encompassing a mixture of geographical dialect features from the speakers' source regions (mostly the Inland Northern and Inland Southern dialects). The other significant element of the linguistic context is, of course, the presence of Spanish in the community. Because Spanish has been so significant, both historically and synchronically, in the development of Chicano English, I have devoted an entire chapter of the book (Chapter 7) to Spanish fluency and the role of bilingualism in the community.

The book is based primarily on data from my fieldwork among young adult native speakers of Chicano English in Los Angeles. I chose to work with a sample of adolescent and young adult speakers because they are likely to be the leaders in sound change (Labov 1994:156). However, I will also comment on the characteristics of slightly older speakers of Chicano English, as well as on the differences between native Chicano English and the type of English spoken by non-native immigrants, whatever one might choose to call it. Where studies of other dialects found in Spanish-speaking communities (such as Puerto Rican English in New York City) are relevant, I will cite them. However, I will not attempt here to address the similarities and differences between these dialects and Chicano English, leaving that to future researchers.

The book presents data of many types from this one community, as a representative case of the forces (both linguistic and social) at work in Latino communities. Although each community will be different, the description of CE in Los Angeles should provide a sense of the language patterns and the basics of the dialect that might be found in other communities encompassing large Mexican-American populations. In addition, though I bring in the results of other studies from time to time as they are relevant, the problems discussed above limit the usefulness of much of the previous research, and my main focus will be on the new data collected here. Since this is the first modern work on this topic, I have endeavored to provide the 'basics' of Chicano English, such as a description of its phonology, a sketch of interesting syntactic features and so on. This macro-level overview is complemented by detailed analyses of particular sociolinguistic variables, some of which represent sound changes in progress in this community. This is important in its own right, because there are so few studies of sound change in dialects spoken in minority ethnic communities, even AAE (Fought 2002). Nonetheless, it is impossible in a single work to cover everything of interest in a dialect like CE. I hope that this book will inspire more sociolinguists with interest in these issues to conduct further fieldwork and help fill in the gaps that exist with respect to the linguistic characteristics of Mexican-American communities.

1
Fieldwork in the Los Angeles Chicano Community

1.1 History of Mexican immigration to Los Angeles

It needs to be strongly emphasized that as long as metropolitan Los Angeles (LA) has existed, there have been native speakers of dozens of different languages there; a large number of these are, of course, native speakers of Mexican Spanish. California was a part of Mexico until 1848; before and since that time there has been significant population movement between southern California and all parts of Mexico, particularly after World War II. At any given time, then, there are many recent arrivals from Mexico, especially in the Latino neighborhoods, and still more who came to LA years ago. Many Californians of Latino ethnicity have lived in Southern California their whole lives, and so have their parents, and so on, for varying numbers of generations. As a result, some Chicano English speakers come from families that have been in America as long as or longer than the Italian Americans on the Eastern seaboard, or the Polish Americans in the Midwest.

The Latino population of the United States

Latinos make up the fastest growing minority in the United States, and are now or soon will be the largest as well. Between 1990 and 2000, census figures show that the US Latino population (the census uses the term 'Hispanic') increased by more than 50 percent, from 22.4 million to 35.3 million. This represents 12.5 percent of the national population. The largest segment of this minority, people of Mexican origin, increased by 52.9 percent, from 13.5 million to 20.6 million. Because census questions relating to Latinos have changed over the decades, it is not easy to trace the long-term growth of this population in detail. The Latino population also has a distinctive demographic profile: it is

Table 1.1   Latino population by birthplace

Year	Native born (million)	Foreign born (million) (%)	Total
1990	14.0	7.8 (35.8)	21.9
1980	10.4	4.2 (28.6)	14.6
1970	7.3	1.8 (19.9)	9.1
1940	1.4	0.4 (23.0)	1.8

younger than other groups. Its median age in 2000 was 25.9 years, compared with 35.3 years for the entire population.

In recent decades, legal immigration from Mexico has been limited, averaging less than 100,000 per year during most of this period. There was a spike in the four years from 1989 to 1992, however, with about 2.24 million immigrants arriving during that period. Illegal, undocumented immigration also occurs across the Mexican border, but numbers are naturally not known. Table 1.1 gives a breakdown of the Latino population by birthplace: native (US) born versus foreign born, based on available immigration and census enumerations.

As can be seen from the figures in Table 1.1, native born Latinos have outnumbered immigrants historically by a large margin, a fact that would appear to have many social and linguistic implications. In 2000, 76.1 percent of Latinos in America (27.1 million) lived in seven states: California, Texas, New York, Florida, Illinois, Arizona and New Jersey. Just over half of them lived in either California (11.0 million, 31.1 percent) or Texas (6.7 million, 18.9 percent) combined. Moreover, much of this population is concentrated in counties on or near the Mexican border, although there are also important enclaves in metropolitan areas elsewhere in the country.

Greater Los Angeles

The census reports 4.2 million Latinos living in Los Angeles County in 2000, of whom 3 million are of Mexican origin. The main portion of metropolitan Los Angeles forms a rough parallelogram measuring about 50 miles (80 km) NW–SE from San Fernando to Santa Ana and about 40 miles (65 km) SW–NE from Long Beach to Pomona. Los Angeles County includes the city of Los Angeles and a number of other cities, some quite well known in their own right, such as Beverly Hills, Burbank, Glendale, Long Beach, Pasadena, Pomona, Santa Monica and Torrance. These areas vary in their ethnic compositions. The city of Los Angeles itself, for example, is 46.5 percent Latino, while East Los Angeles, an unincorporated place within the city, is 96.8 percent Latino, the highest proportion of Latinos in any American city outside Puerto Rico.

Culver City

Culver City, the main location for my fieldwork, was developed by Harry H. Culver, a real-estate entrepreneur, between 1913 and its official founding in 1917, when it had a population of 550 and an area of 1.2 square miles. The area around it was then still grazing and agricultural land, traversed by streetcar lines linking Los Angeles and the newly developed seaside resort of Venice. It was already used by the rapidly growing motion picture industry for location shooting. With Culver's cooperation, industry pioneer Thomas H. Ince located his studio in Culver City in 1918; after his death in 1924 it became the DeMille studio. The film *King of Kings* was produced there. Hal Roach purchased land and built a studio in 1919. This studio, through business alliances, became RKO Pathe and then Selznick International. Many films associated with 'Hollywood' were actually made in Culver City, such as *King Kong, Gone with the Wind*, and, more recently, *ET*. It remains a center of the film and television industries, as the headquarters of Sony Pictures and many other companies are located there.

The streetcar lines are long gone, but Culver City is near the intersection of two major freeways, the 10 or Santa Monica Freeway (to the North) and the 405 (to the West). By 1940 its population had grown only to 8,976 (in an area of 3.2 square miles). Its population in 1980 was 38,189; this has changed little since then, reaching 38,816 in 2000. The demographic breakdown reported by the city is shown in Table 1.2.

The advantage of using Culver City, which is above the median of LA County in income, as a main location for fieldwork is that it includes Latino residents from a larger range of socio-economic categories, from very low income to middle class. This makes the area more representative in some ways of the Latino population as a whole.

Table 1.2   Population of Culver City, 2000

Ethnicity	%
White	52
Latino	23
Asian	13
African American	11
Other	1

1.2   The history of Chicano English

As was noted above, Latinos in the USA are concentrated along the border with Mexico, in territory that was first explored and colonized by Spain, and was ceded to the USA by Mexico after the war of 1848. Thus, from the beginning of Anglo-American settlement in this region, the English-speaking and Spanish-speaking populations have been in close contact. Both groups have continued to grow since then by both natural increase and migration. For a very long time, then, like other cities near the Mexican border and having a substantial Latino population, Los Angeles has had native speakers of English of Latino ethnicity, as well as foreign-born Latinos in various stages of learning English. The history of settlement within the urban area is such that Latino native speakers of English have been in close contact with native Spanish speakers, and with Anglo speakers of English as well.

Chicano English, therefore, is an important dialect to study because it is a contact dialect, one that emerged from the setting described above in which two languages, English and Spanish, were present. The early Mexican immigrants who arrived in Los Angeles (and in other parts of the southwest) learned English as a second language. Like adult learners of any language, they spoke a non-native variety which included phonological, syntactic and semantic patterns from their first language, in this case Spanish. But the children of these immigrants generally grew up using both Spanish and English (possibly in different settings or with different people). As the community began to stabilize, so did a new dialect of English.

This type of setting, involving languages in contact, is similar in certain ways to the types of settings in which pidgin and creole languages develop (as first discussed by Wald 1984:21). Generally, a pidgin is the second language of a group of adult speakers, exhibiting a great deal of interspeaker variability, simplification and so on. However, when the succeeding generations of children grow up speaking the pidgin as their first language, it quickly becomes more elaborated and grammaticized, as well as more stable, so that a fully developed creole is linguistically indistinguishable from languages that developed in other types of settings. Similarly, the non-native interlanguage of adult Mexican immigrants, which is still a very common variety in the Chicano community of Los Angeles, exhibits great individual variation and the presence of somewhat idiosyncratic 'errors'. This interlanguage provided the historical basis for the more stable and consistent dialect which developed among the younger generations, namely Chicano English.

Chicano English itself is not truly a creole, of course, since among other things, a creole generally emerges from a setting where multiple languages are involved, and pidgins and learner varieties are not the same thing. However, particularly within the phonological component, the various non-native English patterns of the immigrants were inherited by their children, modified somewhat, and can still be seen in the new (native) dialect. To a lesser degree, there may be syntactic and semantic elements that also reflect the influence of Spanish. Chicano English now has independent phonological and syntactic norms of its own, which will be discussed later. It is important to reiterate the inaccuracy of the idea that Chicano English is simply English influenced by Spanish.

An interesting issue in tracing the history of Chicano English is the role of other dialects in its development, including African-American English (AAE) and local Anglo varieties. As will be seen in Chapter 4, many of the syntactic patterns that distinguish Chicano English have possible origins in AAE. It has been suggested that regional dialects associated with the local Anglo culture have not influenced Chicano English as much as national norms (Peñalosa 1980:28). This is another intriguing question which I will address later in the book. Finally, one might ask whether Chicano English may be exerting an influence on other dialects with which it is in contact, and what this might mean for the future development of dialects in the LA area.

The speakers in this study

As mentioned in the introduction, my goal is to use a single community of CE speakers, studied in detail, to illustrate patterns typical of this dialect. The research presented here was conducted in Los Angeles in 1994. The speakers participated in individual (and occasionally group) sociolinguistic interviews, which I conducted myself. The study focuses on young Mexican-American adults between 15 and 32 years of age, many of whom are bilingual. Most of them live in Culver City, although a few live in other parts of LA, such as Echo Park. A large percentage of them attended Westside Park,[1] the local continuation school for kids who have had learning or disciplinary problems at the regular high school (Culver High, where I also conducted some interviews). Others came from a network of families of people with disabilities, accessed through their acquaintance with my family.

In addition to the core group of young adult speakers, I included some older speakers who came from Mexico as adults, in order to use them as a reference group for the Spanish spoken in the area. (A few of my younger speakers were themselves born in Mexico, though most of them came to the USA at an early age.) One or two of the young adults are from Latino backgrounds other than Mexican, but integrated completely into the Mexican-American community in terms of peer networks, and so on. There are also a few non-Latino speakers whom I interviewed to get a sample of the English spoken by Anglos of the same peer group. In reporting the results of the study, I have assigned pseudonyms to all of my speakers, as well as to the school.

After the study had been completed, and in fact after this book had already entered the preparation stages, some colleagues suggested to me that it would be interesting to know about a slightly older generation of native Chicano English speakers, Mexican-Americans in their 40s and 50s, and how their dialect might compare. So in 2001 I arranged for a research assistant to collect some additional interviews with older speakers in the community, through her personal contacts. Though these speakers were not included in the sociolinguistic analyses of Chapters 5 and 6, they provide an interesting perspective on the evolution of Chicano English, as well as a different perspective on cultural and linguistic issues in the community.

Not everyone in this community speaks Chicano English. As I mentioned in the Introduction, I will use 'Chicano English' only to refer to the distinct dialect spoken by native speakers, excluding varieties identical to those of local Anglos, and varieties spoken by adult second language learners of English. Even so, this leaves a wide range of styles that can fall under this dialect label, as is the case with any dialect, including standard ones. Some middle-class speakers in a Mexican-American community may speak a variety that is grammatically fairly similar to more standard dialects, but retains a special phonology or sound system (other middle-class speakers might not speak Chicano English at all). I found that among the older speakers in my study, most of whom were professionals, this grammatically standard, phonologically distinct variety was very common.

It is an interesting question whether someone who does not use any non-standard grammatical features at all can be said to speak 'Chicano English', assuming that their phonology includes at least a few of the elements which will be described later as characteristic of CE. The same question of a 'standard' variety arises with respect to AAE. If a speaker clearly 'sounds black' but does not use any of the grammatical variables associated with AAE, is it still AAE? This question cannot be answered in an objective, technical way. Like many other issues of language, this one is mostly a matter of attitude. We might, for example, attempt to answer it in some sense by playing tapes of speakers whose grammar is standard but whose phonology includes features of a dialect associated with a particular ethnic group and see if they are judged by listeners to be 'non-standard.'

There is little research on the roles played by non-standard phonology vs. non-standard syntax in folklinguistic perceptions of 'dialect.' Judgments of 'accent' (that is, phonology) can often be made very quickly, long before particular grammatical features turn up in conversation, so we might expect the relative importance of these components to differ. In any case, all dialects encompass varieties that are farther from or closer to the standard. In this book, I will treat those speakers in this study who did not use any marked syntactic features, but who can be clearly identified as Mexican-American from their phonology, as speakers of Chicano English. Nonetheless, the question of what counts as 'standard' or what counts as 'Chicano English' remains an open and intriguing one, worthy of more explanation.

Terms for ethnic self-identification

I have been using the terms 'Mexican-American' 'Chicano' and 'Latino' in this study. It is my intent to use ethnic terms that are viewed positively by the members of the ethnic community in question. In asking individual speakers about the meanings and connotations of the various terms, I have found a surprisingly wide range of opinions. The vast majority of my US-born young adults identify themselves as simply 'Mexican.' Since my study includes people actually born in Mexico, I felt that using this term to apply to the entire group, including those born here, might confuse readers not familiar with the community. I will use 'Mexican' with this broader meaning only in the context of reproducing closely something said by an informant where this was the term the speaker used, for example, 'says she only dates Mexicans.'

The main term about which some speakers expressed dislike was 'Hispanic,' which was often described by the speakers as a 'white person's word.' A few speakers also had mixed feelings about 'Chicano,' which was sometimes associated with radical politics, or surprisingly even with gang members. Others thought 'Chicano' was a neutral term, and to some it had an important and positive ethnic significance. Both 'Mexican-American' and 'Latino' were viewed positively, although almost nobody mentioned the former term unless I asked about it. There was a great deal of disagreement about what these words actually meant. Some people felt that 'Latino' could refer to people of any Spanish-speaking background, while others thought that it referred specifically to people of Mexican background. Having established that a majority of my speakers are in fact of Mexican background, I will continue to use the terms 'Mexican-American' and 'Latino' to refer to the ethnicity of my speakers, more or less interchangeably. I will use 'Chicano' mainly in particular contexts, such as when a speaker was emphasizing US-born ethnicity.

For the white speakers that I included, and in referring to other studies of the majority communities of California, I use the term 'Anglo.' The speakers of this group referred to themselves as 'white,' but I wanted to use a term that emphasized ethnicity rather than race, since it is the social construct (ethnicity) that might be expected to correlate with linguistic variables. The term used most often by my Latino speakers for this group was, to my surprise, 'American.' This term was used as often as the term 'white' in English, and in Spanish the comparable term (*americano*) was even more frequent. However, I find this usage somewhat disappointing in its suggestion that my Latino speakers, most of whom were born here, may subconsciously accept that others have a greater right to call themselves American than they do. I have chosen to use 'Anglo,' the term most often found in current linguistic literature, even though the speakers I interviewed do not generally use it.

Bilingualism across the city

As noted above, Los Angeles county has a Latino population of more than 4 million according to the 2000 census. I am myself a native of Los Angeles, and have my own recollections of what it is like to grow up there to draw on. Nonetheless, when I returned to LA from Philadelphia to conduct my fieldwork, I attempted to make more systematic observations of the use of Spanish and English in the larger community, trying to view it as an outsider might. Los Angeles is a city where the Spanish language and Latino culture permeate the environment. It is impossible to live and work there without at least occasionally hearing Spanish spoken. Many of my speakers are bilingual, speaking Spanish in varying degrees and fluent English. For most of them, the dialect of English they speak is Chicano English.

I overheard numerous instances of the use of Spanish around Culver City, the area where I was living (and where most of my speakers live). The first time that I went to the bank, I saw a man walk up to the teller window and speak in Spanish. The teller asked him in English to wait, and came back with a Spanish-speaking co-worker who handled the rest of the transaction in Spanish. I observed one other interaction in Spanish in the 20 minutes or so that I was waiting in line. On a trip to the supermarket, the man working at the fish counter helped me in accented (non-native) but perfectly understandable English. The woman after me in line began by saying to the man, 'Speak Spanish?' He replied, 'Sí', and the transaction continued in Spanish. I saw many interactions like this every day. At no time did I witness a case where someone asked for Spanish-speaking assistance and did not receive it. Many of my Spanish-dominant informants have also confirmed this pattern. Mercedes, for example, who knows some English, says she tries to ask for what she needs in English at the store, and so on, and if she is unsuccessful in her communication, resorts to Spanish.

Local television, as is so often the case, provided an excellent mirror for the community. With reference to English, I noted that the local newscast included many reporters with Spanish surnames, who pronounced the Spanish place names in their stories with accurate Spanish phonology. There was also a Latina newscaster who had distinctly non-standard phonology in her English, though it was difficult to determine whether it was due to non-native acquisition of English or to native use of Chicano English. Incidentally, the preferred ethnic term in the media seems to be the one I have used here: 'Latino.' For example, one newscaster interviewed an individual who was identified with the caption 'Latino activist.'

There are numerous local commercials that use Spanish phrases or play on bilingual themes as well. My favorite was for a fast food place called *La Pizza Loca* ('The Crazy Pizza'). Their special of the month was billed via a rap-style jingle as 'DOUBLE! . . . DOBLE!' (two cokes and two pizzas for a low price). The ending slogan was something along the lines of 'No matter how you say it, it's a great deal.' This ad struck me as different from other ads where the producers include food terms or a few stock phrases in Spanish. It used Spanish, not as a colorful garnish aimed at non-speakers to add 'ethnic charm,' but rather as an integral part of the entire pitch. The slogan seems to target an audience of bilingual speakers who *could* actually say it either way. It might even be concluded that the use of a rap theme suggests they are targeting a community of *young* bilingual speakers. There was also a bilingual promotional spot for a special report segment on the local news program. The theme was traditional Mexican medicines and cures, and how impoverished Latinos are turning more and more to *curanderos* (folk healers) rather than expensive doctors. The segment was titled 'Home Remedios' (= 'Home Remedies'). Many special programs of this type revolve around issues that concern Latinos.

My own exposure to Latino culture was extended by the speakers I interviewed. One shared with me a home-made drink called *tejuino* made from fermented corn. It has a sweet-and-sour taste completely unlike any other beverage that I am familiar with. I was also lucky to have my fieldwork coincide with Cinco de Mayo (Mexican Independence Day). I attended a holiday assembly at the local elementary school, where the daughter of one of my Latino contacts was a student. All the announcements were made twice, in English and Spanish, and children of every ethnicity participated. Many songs were performed entirely in Spanish by classes of children of mixed ethnicities. I also overheard the kids in the audience whispering to each other as they often do, and both English and Spanish could be heard in this context. In addition, the teachers used both English and Spanish to shut them up ('¡A callar!' 'Shh! Be quiet!'). In sum, Los Angeles provides numerous opportunities for the use of Spanish, and takes for granted that a large number of its residents are at least partially bilingual.

1.3   Field methods

This section will serve as an introduction to the field methods I used for collecting the interviews in Los Angeles. The many ways in which this community differed from nearby Anglo communities – in its social structure, in its status as part of a language contact area, and so forth – affected both the field methods and the subsequent methods of analysis. Having completed the data collection, and I imagine this may be true for other researchers, I now know a great deal about the dynamics of the community that would have been helpful at the beginning of the process. I made a number of adjustments in response to my early interviews, though, and kept the general approach flexible and responsive.

Making contact with the networks

As was mentioned above, a majority of my speakers came from two basic social networks within the area of Los Angeles.[2] (The only speakers who do not fall into one of these two categories are a small number of students I spoke with at the main Culver City high school, and the older speakers interviewed later.) The first network is that of parents of people with disabilities (mainly Down's Syndrome) in the Los Angeles area. The other (much larger) group of speakers came from Westside Park school. Westside Park is small enough that all the people I interviewed there know each other at least vaguely, and in this sense it forms a group for which the term 'network' is appropriate, more so than might be expected at a larger high school.

The Latino parents have their own parents' organization which meets separately from the larger and more general Los Angeles Down's

Syndrome Parents' Group. The parents I contacted were friends or acquaintances of my mother, most of whom I had met on one or two occasions, with a few that I knew quite well. Some are officers in the parents' group, while others participate only occasionally. Since the main focus of the study is on young adults, however, I spent more time interviewing the children of these contacts than the parents themselves. I had not met any of these younger speakers previously, except for one that I had last seen when he was a small child. While I did not set out specifically to interview any of the children with Down's Syndrome, they participated in short segments of interviews with their parents and siblings, and always added a note of energy and humor to the interview. In addition, though I did not interview any speakers under the age of 15 individually, I have several speakers in this age range who participated peripherally in interviews with others.

I contacted the members of the parent group directly, and they introduced me to their young adult children if they had any. I generally interviewed these speakers at their homes. The young adults were interviewed individually, although some of them also participated in group interviews with parents and/or other siblings present. A few parents were interviewed as couples in addition to individually. All of these interviews lasted at least one hour; some lasted quite a bit longer. While at these homes, I often participated in activities other than interviewing. In one case, the parents put on records of traditional Mexican singers, so that I could hear their Down's Syndrome son do his very showy imitation of them. Another family brought take-out food and treated me to lunch. I have referred previously to the informant who took me to a Cinco de Mayo assembly. It is appropriate here to mention (again) the tremendous generosity of all these families towards me. It is difficult to imagine a more welcoming situation for an ethnographic fieldworker.

The data collected from Westside Park required a different approach. The school will be discussed at greater length below, but I will provide here the information most relevant to field methods. I became a participant-observer at the school, with the help of the principal and the main administrative assistant, both of whom I knew from when I lived in Los Angeles. I spent many hours in the school office, helping with any tasks that came up, particularly with translations for school–parent conferences where the parent was monolingual in Spanish. The school office is located in such a way that the students are constantly passing through. Some of them work in the office during a designated period. Another common office activity is using the telephone to call friends, for which permission is usually granted by the administrative assistant in exchange for a quarter.

I did not attempt to select specific students for interviews in any way except by ethnicity (Latino).[3] In the first days of my fieldwork, when a Latino student came through the office, or was standing around waiting for a class period to begin, or had just finished meeting with someone, one of the staff would introduce me to the student. The introduction could be made by the principal, the counselor or the administrative assistant. It followed a general pattern in which they usually asked me 'Have you met . . . ?' filling in the name of the student (since I had already talked to some students informally in the office). They would then introduce me and say that I was doing a project in which I was talking to people about what it was like to live in LA. I would ask the student if he or she had some time to talk to me right then. Only in a single instance did someone say that he had to attend a class but would be willing to talk to me later (which he did). Once the student indicated a willingness to talk with me, we would go somewhere on the campus, often some picnic tables outside, or a lounge area with sofas that was used at certain times for job training classes but was otherwise empty. The teachers knew that I was conducting a research project on campus, and if a student agreed to talk to me during all or part of a class period, the instructors excused them with a note from me on their attendance slip.

After I had been at the school a week or two and conducted some interviews, I began to look for students who had been mentioned specifically by other students, especially in answer to the question, 'Who around here might have some interesting stuff to tell me? Who do you think I should talk to?' Usually the administrative assistant would help me by pointing these people out. (It quickly became evident that just about every student would wander through the office sooner or later.) I would then introduce myself to the student, give the brief explanation about studying life in Los Angeles, particularly among Latinos, and so on, and say that I had heard they might be an interesting person to talk to. I also continued to talk to any students who happened to be hanging around, and after the first week or two, I usually introduced myself rather than going through a staff person, since by then everyone in this small school had heard that I was around and knew what I was doing. After a certain point in my time at the school, students I did not recognize began saying, 'Hey! Don't you want to interview me?' (Needless to say, I generously granted an interview to everyone who asked.)

In addition to these two main groups, I spoke with a small number of students at the main high school. This school setting was completely unlike that of Westside Park. While I obtained permission from the principal to talk to students, I did not make contact through the administration. Instead, I attended a meeting of Alianza Latina, one of the clubs for promoting activities of interest to Latino students. At the meeting I attended, for example, they showed a videotape of a school assembly at which a Zoot Suit-style dance was performed by members of the club. I had asked the teacher who serves as club sponsor if I could make an announcement about my project at the meeting. I explained briefly what I was doing, and asked any students who would be willing to talk to me to stay for a few minutes after class. I then made appointments to meet these students and interview them individually at various locations around the campus (a bench outside, a corner of the library, and so on).

In all cases, I began the interviews by explaining the presence of the tape recorder (to help me 'keep straight' who told me what stories), and by assuring speakers that their information would be kept private. This is important with all linguistic consultants, but some of the speakers I interviewed were gang members, for whom it could be a matter of life and death. I told the students that if I published something that included information from the interviews, I would change everybody's name. One woman said that the members of a rival gang also knew her as 'Frankie's [pseudonym] little sister,' and I assured her that I wouldn't use his name either. Despite my belief in the importance of anonymity, I also had a good number of students who said that they didn't care whether I used their names (presumably implying that they were not afraid of anybody). One student (a gang member) specifically wanted me to keep his name rather than assigning him a pseudonym. We agreed to the compromise that I would keep his first name the same, but assign him a fictitious last name, and that he was to promise not to tell anyone that I had done so.

Background data on Westside Park school

Because of its large representation among my speakers, the Westside Park school merits some discussion. In general, it is the landing place for students who have had serious academic or personal trouble at the main high school, including repeated truancies, violence, failing grades, pregnancy and so on. One interesting detail is that some students from the main high school *request* transfer to Westside Park, usually because they know someone who is a student there, and feel that it would be better for them. Transfer is sometimes requested by the parents as well. Generally speaking, if the principal of Westside Park gives her permission, these transfers are accepted. In some special cases, students may even transfer in from outside the district.

The school has a student body of about 110–20 and a staff of six teachers, plus the principal, counselor, administrative assistant and other support staff. The student body at the time I worked there was about 55 percent Latino, with about 25 percent African-American students, and the rest divided between Anglo students and those of other ethnicities (Korean, Vietnamese, Tongan and so on).[4] The two most important administrative figures are the principal, who assists students in setting up a plan to help them meet their goals and who monitors and guides their progress, and the counselor, who encourages the students to talk about the many problems they face, at home and at school, and also teaches independent study courses. Both individuals help students deal with academic and social problems. Incidentally, the counselor, though not a Latina herself, is fairly fluent in Spanish and very familiar with Latino culture.

Westside Park can be described as a tight-knit community. The teachers and staff generally have a friendly relationship with the students, knowing their individual histories very well. The students, in turn, treat them with respect, but also often with a familiar teasing that signals their trust. They talk to the staff about problems in their home life, even about very serious concerns like drug abuse by themselves or their parents. The counselor occasionally attends their social functions, and the school itself organizes certain functions, like the annual Thanksgiving meal, prepared entirely by the students.

Clearly the school fills a crucial role in the community. LA is a difficult and often dangerous place to live. While at school, the students are protected and find a group of supportive people with whom they can share their problems and concerns. Their presence or absence at the school is monitored very carefully, and at the time of enrollment, the parents are asked to be responsible for seeing that the child gets to school. In addition, the school's academic structure, which helps the students to set their own pace for completing assignments, has many benefits. Students with learning disabilities can take the time they need to complete a particular task. Students who have fallen behind have the opportunity to work harder and make up more course units in a shorter time. The responsibility is placed on the student, although the staff monitors each student's progress closely. Since the school's founding in 1979, the number of students graduating has increased almost exponentially. Some years ago the principal fought for and won the right for Westside Park graduating seniors to participate in the general commencement ceremony with the students from the main high school. This is a place where the students are treated with dignity. Though not all of them graduate, a fair number of them have received high school diplomas after it seemed that they would never make it.

Schools as sites for research

In conducting sociolinguistic interviews, the researcher is constantly fighting the observer's paradox, trying to counter the effects of his or her own presence in order to obtain the most natural sample of vernacular speech possible. In a school setting it is often easiest to make contact with the students through a teacher or administrator. This type of contact, however, may put the interviewer in the category of an authority figure from the perspective of the student, and therefore lead to the use of a more formal speech style. It is the very essence of the observer's paradox that the interviewer can never be sure how casually an informant was speaking in an interview (without additional data of a very different type). However, I have reasons for believing that with respect to Westside Park my initial strategy of contact through the counselor and principal was a valid one. In addition, I attempted to further minimize the degree of formality of the situation in a number of respects.

Relationships between the staff and students at Westside Park are unlike those at most high schools. The school's small size and the fact that the students have all come there in order to deal with difficulties they had at other high schools make Westside Park less of an institutional setting than other schools. Presumably because of the special at-risk status of most students there, the staff members interact with the students in a way that falls between 'teacher' and 'friend.' While the nature of individual relationships varies, depending on the particular staff member and the particular student, my introduction as someone who was an old friend of the principal would not necessarily lead to my being perceived as an authority figure, and on the other hand would in some sense affirm my trustworthiness.

In addition, my visible participation in the office work, alongside several student helpers, allowed me to become familiar to the students in a general sense. Unlike the majority of high schools, the office at Westside Park is a place where the students feel comfortable 'hanging around' and often come for a variety of reasons (many of which are positive ones, in contrast to most high schools). My presence there allowed me to chat informally with several of the students, and it assured that, with the exception of a small number of cases at the beginning, the students I interviewed had seen me around, rather than my being a total stranger.

As often as possible, I participated in other activities that involved 'hanging around' at the school. I ate lunch in the office with some of the student workers, and went to events such as a student softball game. One of my informants mentioned that her parents owned a Mexican restaurant, and encouraged me to come eat there. I went, along with the school counselor, and we had an excellent meal. The restaurant was fairly small and not too crowded, so the student, who was waiting tables, sat with us and talked to us for part of the dinner. This event also provides a good example of the friendlier than usual relationship between the staff and students, particularly since the student was talking about whether or not her mother was going to leave her abusive husband, the student's stepfather.

Finally, in the individual interviews I provided a considerable amount of background about myself in order to minimize the perception that I was a complete outsider. I mentioned that I was familiar with the school, and knew the staff, because my mother had worked in the office a number of years earlier. As part of presenting my interest in talking to people, I said that I had grown up in LA but had been living in Philadelphia for several years, and had just returned to Culver City. I commented that I had a sense of things having changed in LA over the years I was away, but that I wasn't sure exactly how, and then asked if the student thought things had changed recently. This was a topic on which almost everyone had an opinion. Some students asked more questions about my background, such as where exactly I grew up, did I attend Culver High, and so on, which allowed the interview to begin in a more bi-directional fashion than usual, and also indicated that I had generated some curiosity by my presence.

Among the factors that had to be considered in my fieldwork were those involving personal safety. It would not have been safe, for example, for a woman from outside the community to hang around alone at the Projects, no matter how tempting such a site might be as a focus for community activity.[5] In addition, obtaining access to gang members for an outsider is complex. My association with the school, a place where they felt safe and comfortable on the whole, provided them with the assurance that I was not a threat, and also allowed me to talk to them in a setting that was not dangerous for me in any way.

Although there is no simple way to assess how successful I was in obtaining casual speech, the methods I used seem to pay off in several respects. First of all, some of the students talked to each other about the interviews, and I would hear comments like: 'I was over at my friend Patricia's house – you talked to Patricia, right? She told me she talked to you.' If the students had felt uncomfortable in the interviews, the friends they talked to might not have been willing to be interviewed, and at the very least, probably would not have mentioned the other speaker to me. As noted above, several students volunteered to be interviewed. In addition, I collected a large volume of personal narratives, including, as one might expect from a school that contains many gang members, a good number of danger-of-death stories. The students responded to and introduced topics of a very personal nature, talking about friends who had died, getting pregnant unexpectedly and, occasionally, using drugs. None of these topics seems consistent with a very formal level of speech, or a high level of self-consciousness regarding the interview.

A final factor that suggests casual speech in the interviews is the use of taboo ('four-letter') words. Although I did not do tabulations of this usage, my sense is that a majority of the students used four-letter words frequently in their interviews. This was true of students of both genders, although it was more common among the boys. Typically, the taboo words were used in English, although occasionally I had students who used them in the Spanish portion of the interview. Christian, for instance, used the word *jodido* ('fucked'). Ramon used *chingar* ('to fuck') and also switched into English, so that he could say, *pero si se porta como un asshole . . .* ('but if he acts like an asshole . . .'). In addition, the students used many local slang terms such as *homeboys* (members of the same gang), *bud* (marijuana), *jack* (assault or rob), and *g-ride* (ride in a stolen car), that referred to illegal activities. While the use of these various lexical items does not absolutely guarantee that the students were speaking casually, if they were treating the interview as formal, I would have expected them to edit their language somewhat.

While I did, as might be expected, have a few speakers who spoke less than others and seemed more hesitant, overall I believe the participant-observer approach through the school worked well.[6] I will end this section with an anecdote from my interview with Chuck. Toward the end of our conversation, Chuck told me that he was going to tell me something, but that I had to swear I would not tell anyone. Since I knew Chuck spent a good deal of time with the gang members, I assumed it would be something involving gang activities, possibly criminal in nature; I assured him that whatever he said to me would be kept in confidence. He lowered his voice and told me, 'I like to listen to

Phil Collins.'[7] I consider this to be crucial evidence of my success in generating a situation of trust in the interviews.

The role of the interviewer

One primary goal of the sociolinguistic interview is to generate a large sample of speech from the informant, so that the appropriate linguistic analyses can later be carried out. To this end, it is recommended in some sociolinguistic field methods courses that the interviewer speak as little as possible. In fact, a test recommended in such courses at the University of Pennsylvania is to fast forward through the tape of an interview stopping at random 10 times to listen briefly. The more times that one hears the informant talking (rather than the interviewer) the more successful the interview, at least in terms of volume of speech collected. While I certainly encouraged my speakers to talk at length, I probably also took more conversational turns of my own than some researchers might have done, not accidentally, but as part of a developed plan specific to the community.

The Latino community in Los Angeles, and particularly the young segment of the population that includes gang members, is one where *exchange* and *obligation* play a very important role, perhaps more than in most Anglo communities.[8] With the parent network, the informants began with a perceived obligation to provide me with help, through their loyalty to my mother. Among other things, I provided them with news of my mother and brother, as well as with small gifts such as a box of cookies for the younger children or something of this nature. As was mentioned earlier, many of them generously provided me with food, invitations or other non-interview-related favors. With the children of these parent contacts, I offered a specific kind of understanding through the fact that I was also the sibling of a person with Down's Syndrome. All of these interviews were long, covered a wide range of topics and included many personal narratives. In no case did I observe any signs that the people in question were treating the situation as that of a formal interview.

At Westside Park, I made a more deliberate effort to contribute my own experience to the interview. Among the gang members particularly, information is a key element in exchange and obligation, as they themselves explained.[9] Therefore, I tried to begin my interviews at Westside Park by offering some information about myself, as discussed above. If someone asked where I lived, or where I had grown up I told them. Occasionally they asked for more details about what I was doing beyond the brief description that I always gave at the beginning, and I expanded my explanation. I was careful to keep the main focus off language, although sometimes I would mention that the fact that a lot of people in LA spoke two languages was interesting to me. I allowed the students to ask me as many questions as they wished, keeping my answers reasonably short, but without making any obvious attempt to turn the conversation back to questions about them.

Erica, for instance, asked in the middle of something else, 'What do you do, like, what do you work for, are you like a writer?' When I told her, among other things, that I lived in Philadelphia, she responded 'Nah-ah!' and asked, 'How is it over there?' and 'Do you like it better over there or over here?' I realized that the majority of these students had never been outside California, sometimes not even outside Los Angeles, and that they had a great deal of curiosity about other places. When these types of topics came up, I told them about Philadelphia or about other places I had visited, and I could see the interest it provoked in them. I tried to allow the interviews to be a source of information for them as well as for me.

At any point, if I had specific information that I felt could be helpful to them, I provided it. Amanda, for example, wished to apply for a driver's license but did not know what documents she needed, and I told her which ones I thought they were, and where she could call to check. Rita mentioned that she had allergies and asthma, and was encouraged when I told her that I had mainly outgrown my own allergies, and that a doctor had told me this was quite common. Sometimes if a student was trying to evaluate possible career choices, I gave them some idea of the type of schooling and skills that I thought would be required for each. To my surprise, several students expressed a strong interest in my own career, asking what I did on a daily basis, what kind of classes I had taken and so on, and I tried to convey some idea of what I did and why I liked it. Although this process generally may have led to my speaking more than is usual in a sociolinguistic interview, I had no difficulty stemming from this method in collecting a sufficiently large sample of speech. One part of the interview in which information exchange often played a crucial role was when the speaker was bilingual and I wished to switch the conversation to Spanish. I will discuss this aspect of the interviews in Chapter 8.

2
The Social Context of the Chicano Community

2.1 Social structures and gender roles in Latino families

The majority of the young adult speakers I interviewed lived with their parents. Of course, one would expect that most high school students would not be living on their own, but even those in their 20s and 30s tended to be living in their parents' home. Only two of my speakers lived elsewhere. Interestingly, one of them was a 17-year-old high school student, Marina, who lived with her boyfriend. The other was Rafael, 28, who shortly before I interviewed him had moved to an apartment in order to be closer to his workplace. Both his older sisters (Paulina, 32, and another that I did not interview) still live at home. The most common pattern in the community seems to be living at home until one is married, and even then some people remain with the family. I heard several examples of married people living at their parents' home, often in some semi-separate space, such as an upper floor with a separate entrance or an 'in-law' house.

This pattern highlights an issue that I believe has not been sufficiently explored in previous studies of language use in Latino communities: the complex role of the family. Often, Latino families are perceived as being more close-knit than many Anglo families. In some ways, this is true. But rather than relying on a stereotype, it is more instructive to look specifically at what distinguishes the Latino family, and what variations on the general picture can be found across the community. In this section, I will present a qualitative view of the structures and cultural patterns in the families of the speakers I interviewed.

To begin with, as mentioned above, a large percentage of Latino young adults live at home, even if they have an independent income, and sometimes even if they are married. Of my sample of young adults (ages 15–32) 95 percent lived at home. Though I do not have comparable numeric data for the Anglo community in the same city, Keefe and Padilla (1987), who also studied Latinos and Anglos in Southern California, found that the Anglo Americans in their sample were less likely to have children living at home than the Mexican Americans.

Another factor that emerged in many of my interviews was the strictness of the rule systems established by the Latino parents. It might be expected that parents of teenage children would have rules for them, especially in a place with a crime rate as high as that of Los Angeles. Many of my Latino informants, however, described systems based specifically on the traditions of Mexico and much stricter than what seems to be common in the Anglo communities with which I am familiar. Marta told me: 'A lot of Hispanics, like, Mexican families, they're really strict, especially with the girls.' A good example of this is Daisy, 23, who said that she has never been allowed to go anywhere with a boy. Her parents insist that if a boy is interested in her, he can come and talk to her on the steps of the house. Daisy accepts this arrangement willingly, and she told me that if a potential suitor were really interested in her, he would accept the situation as well. Avery said of his 15 year old sister that the only place she is permitted to go without her parents is to church. As Marta noted above, the general tendency is for the strict rules to apply particularly to girls, which highlights an important element of the construction of gender in the community.

These specific facts tied to the nature of traditional Latino families could have important linguistic significance. If children are spending more time at home, both daily and over their lifetimes, their parents and siblings may contribute more to their linguistic environment than in a community where the peer group receives more emphasis. The family structure may also be a crucial element in bilingual acquisition, which will be discussed in detail in Chapter 7. Also, Chicano English is a dialect which has been influenced by Spanish and which has its origins in the dialects of non-native speakers. Therefore, the intensity of continued contact of monolingual Chicano English speakers with speakers of 'learner' varieties of English could influence and reinforce certain patterns in the structure of Chicano English.

It remains crucial, however, to look at the full range of possibilities that define family and social relationships in the community. While there are many children of Mexican-born parents who accept a traditional role, particularly a traditional gender role, within the family, at the other extreme are the gang members. Here, within the same community, are speakers for whom peer influence is extremely strong. This is not to suggest that the gang members remain completely detached from traditional values as regards the family. On the contrary, some of them find themselves in a constant struggle between a desire to please their parents and the parents' attempts to impose rules on them (often to keep them from the gang).

The intersection of gang loyalty and family loyalty can be seen strikingly clearly in Ana. Although Ana's parents are from Guatemala, the traditional ways they espouse are the same ones common to many Latino cultures, and Ana's close friends are mostly of Mexican background, so her situation can be considered typical of the community. Ana claims that her parents think they 'own' her. She is a core gang member, who told me 'I guess I don't hang around with too much of a good crowd.' She admits that she is not close to her parents, and would rather talk to her friends when she has a problem. Ana may have been 'jumped in' (initiated into the gang with a beating), and has probably been called on in other ways to defend herself physically; the gang lifestyle by nature involves elements that are at odds with the traditional construction of femininity.

On the other hand, because her mother is working, she is expected to cook dinner for her father before he arrives home, and seems to take this traditional responsibility very seriously. When I asked her what her dream for the future would be, she said she wanted to be married, have her own house, and have her parents close by so that she would be able to take care of them. Her attitude toward her parents seems to carry the force of tradition, particularly in terms of her construction of gender, despite her conflicting feelings about them and her close ties to the gang.

It would be a mistake to characterize the Latino parents in this community as homogeneous regarding the parental role. Not every family follows the traditional pattern. In particular, those speakers whose parents were born in the USA often described a very different type of relationship from the traditional one. Patricia, for example, says that her mother knows where the parties are going to be on a particular weekend before Patricia herself does. She refers to her mother as 'cool' and more like 'a friend.' When I asked Chuck if he could talk to his mother about things, he said yes, and added 'She's my homegirl.' Both of the parents in question were born in the USA.

The role of the family also encompasses the role of the siblings. Very few of my speakers were only children. Many of them mentioned a particular brother or sister to whom they were close. Some also pointed out that one could trust a brother or sister more than a friend. In many cases, an older sibling talked about feeling responsible for a younger brother or sister, in terms of setting a good example, and so on. Some speakers complained about older siblings who were too protective. This relationship tended to hold particularly between male and female siblings, with the male in the protective role, even when the brother was actually younger than the sister. Because of the close nature of the traditional family, as discussed above, the sibling relationship structure around a speaker should be considered carefully when looking for language models.

Finally, it is generally assumed that Latino families are larger and encompass a more extended network than most Anglo families. The number of siblings among my young adult speakers was 4.3, which is higher than the Anglo average. Keefe and Padilla (1987) for example, list 2.8 as the average number of children in an Anglo family from their Southern California sample. Often these larger families include an extended network. Though I will not go into detail on extended networks here, this will be an important factor to consider when looking at bilingual acquisition in Chapter 7.

Interestingly, Christian, who has only one younger sister, told me he wishes that he had a larger family, and said that his mother had tried to have another child but had miscarried. His actual words when he told me were 'We tried having another daughter.' This suggests that there is a positive value on having a large family in the community, and not only among those who immigrated from Mexico. I was surprised by the number of teens, and boys particularly, who placed a positive value on the relationships they had with parents and siblings, as well as on someday having a family of their own. In my experience this is not often a topic that is discussed among Anglo teenage boys.

2.2   Social class differences among Chicanos

Numerous studies have highlighted the important role of social class in analyzing and understanding sociolinguistic variation. Though the socio-logical literature on social class presents a wide range of approaches to the issue, sociolinguistic researchers have tended to use a multi-index scale with a fairly consistent set of indicators in assigning speakers to a class (for example, income, education and occupation). However, most of these are studies of majority Western communities of white speakers, so their results may not generalize to ethnic minority or non-Western communities.

Rickford (1986) reviews the approaches to social class that have been taken by sociolinguists over the years. He points out that a typical scalar model may have been developed for use in communities that are organized very differently from the specific community under study:

> [These] scales are usually not tailored to the local speech community, and might miss or misrepresent the realities of social stratification therein. . . . To apply a Warner, Hollingshead or similar scale indiscriminately to any and every speech community, without doing the local ethnographic footwork, is to misuse it, and to leave oneself open to other problems, such as where to draw the lines between social groups.   (1986:216)

He notes that even applying the scales with full consideration for the specifics of the community does not resolve certain problems inherent in the model per se. Rickford illustrates this point with reference to his work in a village of Guyana, where he found that 'the local stratification system involved only two primary groups . . . Estate and Non-Estate Class' (1986:217). He discovered that language patterns in these two groups represent completely different views of the relationship of language to the social order, particularly with regard to whether or not use of standard language can help one get ahead in the world.

Besides functioning differently in different communities, it is also known that social class may play less of a role for some segments of the population than others, for example in the case of adolescents. Eckert's various studies of adolescents in Detroit (1987, 1989, 1991, 2000) found that the categories of 'jocks' and 'burnouts,' in interaction with gender, were what determined linguistic variation for these speakers. Eckert states clearly that while these categories may correlate to a degree with parents' social class, the two are not identical, and social class is an inferior predictor of variation in these cases. Since the speakers on which my study focuses are mainly adolescents, as well as members of a minority group, new approaches to social class and social structure may be needed to adequately characterize the community.

Adapting social class measures to the Latino community of Los Angeles

The traditional multi-index scales used by most sociolinguists for determining social class – which combine rankings for factors like education, occupation and income (as in Labov 1966) – are not entirely practical for an analysis of the Latino community in Los Angeles. A majority of my informants are high school teenagers, most of whom have no income or occupation of their own, and all of whom are still completing their education, so presumably they would have to be classified by their parents' social class. Given the factor of upward mobility, this raises some problematic issues. Of the traditional measures, occupation is probably the most useful in this community, and it was a topic of discussion brought up by the speakers, indicating that they see it as having an important role. Still, the range of occupations represented by these young adults and their parents is narrower than that of the majority (Anglo) community, with blue-collar work making up a proportionally larger percentage (Keefe and Padilla 1987:36–7).

Even if the traditional multi-index scale cannot be applied, some appropriate way of identifying social class distinctions will be needed, since social class will be one of the factors used in the sociolinguistic studies of Chapters 5 and 6. The method I used to assess social class among my speakers is based on the sociological literature on social class, but incorporates factors with particular relevance to this community.[1] However, there remains a need in the field of sociolinguistics for more studies of social class and its role *vis-à-vis* other types of social categories, particularly as these relate to language; I do not claim that this system would necessarily generalize to other types of communities.

In general, the system I used for determining social class has the following properties:

- I used only information that seems relevant to the community in that it comes up spontaneously in interviews. For example, there were numerous references to someone's living in 'the Projects', an area which both indicates a low socioeconomic level for its residents, and functions as a sort of ethnic center.
- I made finer subdivisions in the category of occupation, since, as was mentioned above, my speakers and their parents tend to be concentrated in a more limited range of occupations. This category will be given significant weight in the assigning of social class, since education and income are not practical or applicable measures for the reasons that were discussed. There is some parallel with Guy *et al.* (1986), where occupation was used as the sole determiner of social class, as well as with Macaulay (1976).
- Where I had information about a particular young adult that indicated social mobility in comparison with the parents, I took this into account. The most obvious example would be a speaker with a job of his or her own, or living in his or her own apartment.

- Where I had data relevant to social class that was unique to a particular speaker, I kept a record of it. While the objective measures that could be compared across speakers were given primacy, individual details such as a speaker mentioning that her aunt is a physician or that he knows how to ski were recorded also and used supplementally, particularly at the stage of determining class divisions.

The specific factors I used in determining social class,[2] all of which were brought up in the interviews, included: (a) the occupation of the speaker if the person was no longer in high school; for students, the occupation(s) of the parent(s); (b) the type of neighborhood in which the speaker lived, noting particularly whether he or she lived in the Projects; (c) whether the parents rented or owned their house or apartment; (d) whether the speaker lived at the parents' home or on his or her own; (e) any miscellaneous data that came up in the interview and that might index social class.

Numerical rankings and social class groups

Each speaker had a final numerical score which was used as their social class value. These values ranged from 0 (generally people whose parents were unemployed and who lived in the Projects) to 14, and are shown in Table 2.1. I will not present the details of the calculations of social class here; for a complete discussion of how the final class determinations were made, however, see Fought (1997). My interviews did not encompass the type of detailed information about social standing in the community that would permit me to attach meaningful class labels to these rankings based on community opinion. I have elected arbitrarily to make five initial class distinctions at those numerical junctures which seem to provide some external evidence for a break, sometimes taking into account the miscellaneous additional information on social class gleaned from the interviews. (As an example, David's aunt is a doctor, so I have grouped him with the class group above him rather than below him.) The number ranges and corresponding categories are 13–14 (middle class), 8.5–12 (lower middle class), 6–8 (working class), 4–5 (lower working class), 0–3 (low income).

However, as I mention above, the divisions are based on numerical breaks and are somewhat arbitrary, I will give a brief description of the typical speakers in each group. The middle-class group encompasses mainly speakers who are professionals of some type or whose parents are professionals; for instance, Mario is a paralegal and James' mother is a nurse at UCLA. The lower-middle-class group includes people who

Table 2.1   Social class rankings

Pseudonym	Job score	Class group
James Santana	14.0	mc
Mario Iglesias	14.0	mc
Paulina Mendez	14.0	mc
Rafael Mendez	14.0	mc
Ana Flores	13.0	mc
Chuck Ruiz	13.0	mc
Sol Esquival	13.0	mc
Daisy Olmedo	12.0	lmc
Amanda Quinto	12.0	lmc
Erica Otero	12.0	lmc
Richard Carter	11.5	lmc
Tony Lopez	11.5	lmc
Jamie Diaz	10.0	lmc
Ramon Ibanez	9.5	lmc
David Herrera	8.5	lmc
Carlos Olmedo	8.0	wc
Marta Ugarte	8.0	wc
Salvador Garcia	8.0	wc
Roberto Olmedo	6.0	wc
Sancho Campos	5.0	lwc
Ricky Torres	5.0	lwc
Jesus Ybarra	4.5	lwc
Suni Padilla	4.5	lwc
Christian Fernandez	4.0	lwc
Oscar Marino	4.0	lwc
Antonio Quintero	3.0	lowinc
Avery Valdes	3.0	lowinc
Marina Elenda	3.0	lowinc
Rita Diego	3.0	lowinc
Helena Baker	2.0	lowinc
Magda Huerto	2.0	lowinc
Reina Perez	2.0	lowinc
Veronica Nido	2.0	lowinc
Jorge Gomez	0.0	lowinc
Patricia Avila	0.0	lowinc
Sylvia Barcos	0.0	lowinc

Notes: mc = middle class; lmc = lower middle class; wc = working class; lwc = lower working class; lowinc = low income group

have jobs that have somewhat fewer requirements and pay slightly less (such as Daisy, who is a bank teller) or whose parents have such jobs.

The working class category includes mainly people who have 'blue-collar' or other less-prestigious jobs, such as grocery clerk (Carlos). Their jobs differ from those represented in the lower-working-class group in that they involve less physical labor; the lower-working-class includes mainly people whose parents are gardeners, day laborers and so on. Living area might also make a difference in whether someone fell into the range of scores for the working or lower working class. Finally, the low income group includes mainly people who live in low-end neighborhoods, such as the Projects, and whose parents either hold the same types of jobs as those in the lower working class, or are unemployed.

I have assigned recognizable categories such as 'lower-middle-class' to these five class groups in order to make the discussion easier to follow, and because they have some correspondence with the occupations represented by the speakers. In particular, I have used labels that include 'middle-class' for speakers whose occupation corresponds to those associated with the middle class in the sociological literature, and similarly in the case of working-class occupations. However, the subdivisions of these groups may not be comparable to labels in other studies involving social class, and no claim is made about whether these labels correspond in any way to the perceptions of speakers in this community. I also leave open the possibility of combining some categories when these class distinctions are correlated with the sociolinguistic variables in Chapter 5.

2.3   The dynamics of conflict and oppositions within the community

The Latino community of Los Angeles is undeniably complex. Among other issues, I discovered attitudes and opinions suggesting that there exist certain patterns of opposition or conflict within the Latino community, not only as regards social class, but also in a more general sense. Latinos in Los Angeles are a minority group (at least in some parts of the city) with a strong ethnic identity, often defined in contrast with the majority Anglo culture by the media, researchers, Chicano activists and others. Members of the dominant Anglo culture often perceive minority ethnic communities as solidly banding together in the face of racism and injustice. However, the picture of the community provided by my speakers suggests that, not surprisingly, the situation is more complex than what is represented in the media.

A surprising number of my speakers brought up the topic of conflicts within their own ethnic group. One important division in the community is between people born into the community (that is, here in the United States) and immigrants (Mexican nationals). In particular, recent immigrants seem to have a different status from those who have lived in Los Angeles for a long time, and US-born Latinos often refer to the former as *wetbacks*. This is a traditional term of disparagement for Mexican immigrants. It refers to informal immigration across the Texas–Mexico border, which coincides with the Rio Grande/Rio Azul.

The presence of this opposition has also been noted in other studies. Santa Ana, for instance, reports that 'a social division between later generation Chicanos and Mexican immigrants is commonly acknowledged in the barrios' (1991:176). Vigil notes that his barrio youth informants 'hold somewhat disparaging attitudes toward 'chúntaros' and 'wetbacks'...[and] have become increasingly antagonistic toward recent Mexican immigrants' (1938:42).

The students I interviewed who were themselves recent immigrants from Mexico belonged to different social networks from the students who were born in Los Angeles. For example Oscar, from Westside Park, hangs around with two students of Salvadoran background, one of whom is also an immigrant. He has little contact with Mexican-American students. Suni and Antonio, from the main high school, hang around with other members of Alianza Latina, a club which Suni told me was formed specifically to address the interests and needs of immigrant Latino students, including those who do not speak much English. In contrast with the other Latino club on campus, which conducts meetings in English, meetings of Alianza Latina are conducted entirely in Spanish.

In fact, the dichotomy between these two clubs led to an overt conflict. Coincidentally, at the very first meeting of Alianza Latina that I attended, this incident was one of the topics discussed. Alianza members had put on a show at a school assembly, performing traditional Mexican dances as well as an impressive Zoot-suit style dance number, of which I saw a video. At a later assembly, the other club sponsored a Chicano musical group which performs only in English. Apparently some Mexican immigrant students booed and made noise during this performance because they wanted to hear traditional Mexican music in Spanish, such as *quebraditas*. Later some members of the two groups met behind the school with the intention of having a fight. At the meeting I attended, Suni, who is the president of Alianza, berated and criticized the members of the group for their behavior, and explained that the school was planning to cancel a social event that the club had been hoping to sponsor. I was astonished to find such a high level of tension between groups that I would have assumed had a great deal in common.

Several students at Westside Park also brought up the topic of conflict between those born here and immigrants. Chuck, the child of American-born parents, told me 'there's like Chicanos and Mexicans over here,' and used the derogatory term *border brothers* to describe the immigrants, as well as a Spanish term that I was unfamiliar with: *vanamachos* or *banamachos*. He draws a specific parallel between these conflicts and inter-racial conflicts:

> The *vanamachos* hhh, that's what everybody calls them and shit. You know the border brothers or whatever, and then . . . Like, my home-boys be jacking [robbing] them or whatever you know. It's like, if they're . . . almost like . . . like the way that, that they feel about niggers, like how they say, you know, that you know, 'Oh fuck it' you know . . . If you want to do something and, and he's a nigger, and you want to do him wrong, well, fuck it, he's a nigger. It's like the same thing with, with . . . 'Oh well,' you know, 'I want to take his money, and you know, he's just a border brother so fuck it.' It's like that.

A bit later in the interview he adds:

> Sometimes you're cool with them and s- it's just like the blacks. Sometimes they're cool with them and this and that, but . . . That's just the way that, I don't know, that's the way they are. Like if they're different, you know, they're like separate. I don't think it should be like that.

Beyond what these comments reveal about attitudes toward Mexican nationals, the strong racial epithets used about African-Americans here are indicative of the tremendous racial tensions between blacks and Latinos at the time of my fieldwork. Other speakers also mentioned the idea of Mexican-Americans and Mexican immigrants as two separate groups. One example of specifically linguistic interest is the fact that Jorge said he approved of codeswitching because it distinguishes Chicanos from Mexicans living in Mexico.

There are other themes that intersect with these tensions in the Latino community of Los Angeles. The first concerns the Chicano identity and degree of assimilation. As in many minority communities, being conventionally successful for Latinos in LA most often involves adopting the habits of the majority Anglo culture in speech, dress and so on. Some Latinos are willing to adapt in this way, while others feel that ethnic pride is more important, and that honoring one's heritage implies not 'selling out,' that is, assimilating completely. Chuck, for example, expresses frustration over the fact that most of the middle-class Mexicans he knows show a high degree of assimilation: 'Successful Mexicans . . . they're like *white*, you know . . . that just makes me mad.' Vigil mentions the use of *engabacheado* ('anglicized') as an insult among his informants (1938:42). Among my speakers I mainly heard the form *gabacho/gabacha* (a generally derogatory term for Anglo). Marina, for instance, told me that she considers herself 'Mexicana' rather than 'Chicana,' explaining that she does not think of herself as *gabacha*. The implication is that for her, the concept of 'Chicano' goes with assimilation.

Yet another possible source of tension within the community is the salient division between gang members and non-gang members that was discussed earlier. As might be expected, individuals who belong to the non-gang group often spoke negatively about gangs and gang members and their effect on the community. Somewhat surprisingly, a large number of gang members expressed similar views about themselves. In any case, most non-gang members attempt to have little contact with gang members (with some salient exceptions, which will be discussed later). In contrast with the situation reported above regarding immigrants, gang members do not generally seem to pick on or target non-gang members for violence. Everyone I spoke with at Westside Park said there was no danger for non-gang members from the gang members. The division is still present under the surface, however, and can cause trouble in individual cases. The rivalries between gang and non-gang girls will be discussed later in the chapter.

These three types of conflict may well be related. Part of the resentment of immigrants toward native-born Chicanos may be due to the fact that most gang members in the area are native born, so that a negative stereotype of native born Latinos is perpetuated among the immigrants. Similarly, the process of assimilation or non-assimilation to Anglo norms may further exaggerate existing gang/non-gang divisions and resentments: since gang members are required to dress and act in certain ways, they have less freedom to incorporate Anglo elements in their dress, and so on, than non-gang members.

Finally, there is the question of the role of conflict in relations across social classes, which was the original motivation for this discussion. Vigil claims that socioeconomic conditions are part of the immigrant/native born conflict:

Much of this intraethnic friction revolves around economic and cultural sources. Competition for scarce job resources, especially between members of the depressed underclass and desperate immigrants, generates a part of the animosity. However, it appears that linguistic and cultural differences play at least an equal role in pitting one group against the other.   (1938:42)

Leaving aside for the moment the intriguing question of the role of language barriers in the conflict, it seems logical that in a community where there is poverty and competition for jobs, intraethnic tension would surface. Much of the tension might occur between groups of speakers who would fall into the same social class as determined by a socioeconomic index.

From a slightly different perspective, García (1984) suggests that '[t]he latter group [new immigrants from Mexico] tends to inherit the low rung on the socio-economic ladder, taking the low-status jobs' (1984:87). In addition, Peñalosa (1980) notes that 'Chicanos raised in Spanish,' which by his definition includes the immigrant speakers, are more likely to experience job discrimination at the white-collar level. These occupational effects could logically create resentment by the (working- and lower-class) immigrants toward the more 'successful' (middle-class) native born Latinos, as well as some distancing on the part of the native born Latinos. If such class resentments exist, they might explain the high level of tension between immigrants and natives in the community. This situation also ties in with conflicts over assimilation. The speakers from higher social classes will generally show more assimilation than those from the lower classes, since such assimilation tends to be a prerequisite for success. This adds animosity over ethnic disloyalty to the class conflict.

Social class divisions also tend to be involved in the gang/non-gang distinction. Most of the gang members in this study tend to be from the working or lower classes, a trend that is confirmed by other studies (Vigil 1938:27). While there are also plenty of Latinos in these classes who are not gang members, as well as the occasional middle class gangster, resentment toward gang members could easily heighten any already existing tensions between middle-class and working- or lower-class speakers.

Finally, a factor that, as far as I know, has not been studied extensively in Latino communities is the generation gap. Some sense of opposition or lack of understanding between younger and older individuals is probably present in all communities the world over. However, in the Chicano community of Los Angeles, the complaint by teenagers that 'my parents don't understand me' has a particularly literal interpretation in cases where the parents may not be completely fluent in English and the child may have low fluency in Spanish.[3] The conflict between Mexican immigrants and Chicanos born here, which was found to be so salient in the community, can easily occur within a single family. Even where the parents are not Mexican immigrants, there can be other types of differences between the generations. For instance, the older generation of speakers born in the USA may have more ties to the political and social movements of the 1960s and 1970s which seem to be of little interest to the teenagers I interviewed.

I have spent some time discussing these conflicts and tensions because they may have important implications for linguistic behavior. With regard to social class, it would not be surprising to find that the speakers pattern somewhat dichotomously, for example, with the more assimilated upper and lower middle class acting one way linguistically, and the working and lower classes acting another. The same may be true of gang membership versus non-gang status. There could be sociolinguistically significant differences in language patterns between immigrant vs. native born speakers as well, although such indicators might be overridden by the more dramatic effects of the speakers' language backgrounds (that is, native speaker of English vs. second language learner).

Nonetheless, it is important to emphasize that the presence of these tensions within the community is in no way unusual or unique among Latinos. All ethnic groups, including the dominant majority Anglo culture, have intraethnic conflicts of various types. My intention here is to combat the stereotypes of Latinos and other members of ethnic minority groups as being unidimensional and homogeneous. All communities feature certain oppositions and complexities within their social structures that must be taken into account when doing ethnographic fieldwork.

The importance of culturally specific categories

The same elements that make ethnic minority communities interesting in terms of their potential contributions to understanding the relation of language and culture also require the sociolinguistic researcher to focus carefully on the nature of the social data collected. When dealing with any community, it is best to try to identify the social factors that are relevant to that particular group, as opposed to limiting the research to established sociological categories like 'social class,' 'ethnicity' and so on. The social variables that are most often used in studies of majority communities, for example social class, may be organized differently in a minority community, as discussed above. Additionally, the traditional categories (age, social class and sex) may be insufficient to represent the social structure of the community.

There has been an increasing focus on the use of ethnographic techniques in sociolinguistics. As Eckert (1991) observes:

> The use of ethnography in the study of variation allows the researcher to discover the social groups, categories and divisions particular to the community in question, and to explore their relation to linguistic form.   (1991:213)

Eckert's own work has shown the importance of non-traditional social categories, namely the groups of *jocks* and *burnouts* (cf. Eckert 1987, 1991, 2000). Mendoza-Denton's (1997) study of Latina teenagers found that a number of local categories were involved in the pattern of use of tense /ɪ/, such as *fresas*, Latina jocks or Norteñas (one of two important gang groups). Such use of community-specific categories is not new. As early as Labov's (1972a) study in Harlem, for example, there was evidence that gang membership can play an important role in sociolinguistic variation. However, there continue to be sociolinguistic studies in which general sociological categories are applied without attempting to identify community-specific factors that might also be relevant. Additionally, many ethnic minority communities are bilingual, raising the question of whether bilingual and monolingual speakers differ in their implementation of sound changes in English.

Several culturally specific social categories proved particularly significant among the speakers at Westside Park. These ways of identifying themselves and other students came up again and again in the interviews and around the school. In many ways the most intriguing of the community-specific categories, and certainly the most salient in the media, is the category of *gang members* (also *gang-bangers*, *gangsters* or *cholos/cholas*). Its salience in the eyes of the general public, however, particularly for those outside the community, makes it important to clarify exactly how gang membership fits into the social context of the community.

As I discussed in the introduction, CE is spoken by people from a wide range of socioeconomic and educational backgrounds. The majority of the speakers I interviewed in order to be able to describe CE were *not* gang members, and this applies to the wider community of CE speakers as well; the idea that CE is mainly spoken by gang members is simply incorrect. Kids in gangs represent one small segment of the Mexican-

American community in Los Angeles. The same is true of teen parents, who will be discussed here, but represent only a very small percentage of the Latino teens in the community. I will spend some time discussing these social categories because they are often not well understood by those outside the community, and because they do, in fact, have a social significance that will be crucial in assessing sociolinguistic variation in the community. However, it should be clearly understood that these speakers represent small subgroups of the population as a whole, and they should be viewed from this perspective only.

Among the CE speakers who participated in this study are bank tellers, social workers with Master's degrees, paralegals, computer software developers, administrative assistants and editors. Within the group of young people around whom the sociolinguistic studies in Chapters 5 and 6 center, gang members are represented disproportionately in comparison with the general population, because of the alternative nature of the high school where I conducted my fieldwork. Nonetheless, even in this sample they represent less than a third of the students I interviewed. CE is an English dialect with important cultural significance and widespread distribution among Latino speakers in LA as a whole, not simply particular subgroups.

2.4   The structure of the gang member sub-group

Gang members

Having emphasized that gang members are not representative in any way of the Latino community as a whole, I will now try to give a sense of the organization of the gang member sub-group. I learned a great deal about gang life through the many stories told by my informants. The gangster identity among students at Westside Park includes members of several different gangs. The vast majority are members of 'Culver City' (or CC) which is logical since they live in that area. There are, however, members of other LA gangs at the school, and I interviewed speakers who belonged to three of them – 18th Street, Inglewood, and 8th Street/Watts. In addition, Richard, one of the Anglo speakers I interviewed, told me he used to belong to a Latino gang in Pomona (Pomona/12th Street). Everyone I asked, from students to administrators, confirmed that there is no problem between members of different gangs at the school. Unless some specific issue comes up between individuals, the members of the less common gangs get along well with the CC members, and are not in danger. Both boys and girls can be gang-bangers in Los Angeles, and in the groups I encountered, both are members of the same gangs, rather than having separate 'girl gangs.'[4] Generally, I found that the boys are more likely to be involved in the core gang activities than the girls.

In general, the main rivalries seem to be between the Latino gangs and those associated with people of other ethnicities, particularly African-Americans. Several students explained to me the concept of *red light*, which helps in understanding the situation. Apparently, a few years ago, the older gang members, called *veteranos*, many of whom are in jail, agreed that there should be a truce among different Latino gangs (a 'red light' to stop the violence among them). They condemned 'brown on brown' killing, and urged the rival Latino gangs to make peace with each other, which they mostly did. Though the situation could change rapidly, a majority of the stories I heard were about trouble between gangs of different ethnicities. There are African-American students at the school, but this does not seem to cause any problems. Many of them are not gang members, and those that are do not seem to be from the gangs in serious rivalry with the Latino gangs. It also appears that the school offers a place where a truce is always in effect. In addition, there does not seem to be any problem between Latinos who are gang-bangers and those who are not, with the rare exception of those who cause some particular type of trouble for the gang.

There are many lexical items associated with gangs and gang life; I will mention only the most crucial here. The word *cholo* (or *chola* in the feminine) is used by most people to refer to a member of a Latino gang. I often heard this word used, additionally, as a type of fond insult. For example, at the baseball game I attended, when a gang member would step up to the plate, sometimes his friends would call out, 'Choloooo!' with the kind of laughing intonation that signifies friendly teasing. This term could be heard quite a bit around the school. Another relevant term is *jumped-in*. When a new guy wants to become a member of a gang, the procedure, if the other members are ready to accept him, is for him to be beaten up seriously by a member of the gang, with others as witnesses. Most often the person doing the beating is a friend. The other possibility is to be *walked-in*, which means to be accepted as a member without the beating. This may happen when someone has already done some type of work for the gang, and thus 'paid his dues.' Among the girls, the *walked-in* option is more frequent than among the guys. However, it is possible for a girl to be *jumped-in* by the other girls. Another expression I heard often was *throwing signs*. Generally, gang members have a way of positioning their hands to indicate the first letter or letters of their gang name. Culver City's was a fairly obvious 'C' shape. Making this shape in the presence of members of a rival gang who might be passing by represents a hostile challenge.

At a conference, I was once asked how I knew which speakers were gang members. At Westside Park, gang membership is not kept secret in any respect. The teachers, students and administrative staff all know which students are gang members and which are not. Among other things, the gang members favor distinctive styles of dress and (for girls) of make-up.[5] It is interesting to note that when I asked about what they liked or disliked in a guy, several girls brought up looking 'like a gang member' as something that either they or their parents did not approve of. Sometimes more specific details were provided like 'wearing big pants' or 'having a shaved head.' Interestingly, having a tattoo was generally rated negatively even by girls who liked gang members, although many male gang members do have them (Reina's brother, for instance, has 'Projects' tattooed on his stomach).

Even without these external clues, it was usually clear from the interview when the person was a gangster, since references to gang fights, and so on, came up frequently among these students. Some references were more oblique, such as Ana's saying 'I don't hang around with too much of a good crowd.' In this community there is an extremely high probability that such a comment is about gang membership (and I knew from other sources that in her case it definitely was). Erica, in discussing why she would consider a career as a parole officer, told me 'I understand how it is, like, the type of people they work with. Cause like I hang – I just – you know, like gang, or whatever, I know a lot of people, like, so I understand.' Also, most non-gang members found an opportunity in the interview to set themselves apart from the gangsters, by saying things like 'I don't know a lot of cholos.' The school counselor, who knows the intimate details of most of these students' lives, helped me to confirm any ambiguous cases.

People who 'know' gangsters

Before leaving the topic of gang affiliation, it is worth pointing out what relationships non-gang members have to the gangs. First of all, several students were described to me as 'not a gang member but he *knows* them.' Others said of themselves that they 'don't *know* a lot of cholos.' It was clear from looking at several of these cases that *know* means something specific in this type of context. Everyone at this small school knows everyone else in the usual sense, that is, knows their name and a little about them. This specialized use of *know* means something like 'be friendly with,' 'occasionally spend time with,' 'know about the activities of.' (I have also heard *hang with* to describe this relationship, although that term seems to extend to closer contacts like friendships as well, and it is not restricted to gang members.) In one case, I heard 'he knows them [CC gang members], but doesn't bang'.

People described in this way seem to fall into three groups: (a) people who are friends or family of gang members and might have grown up with them in the same neighborhood, but are not themselves interested in being in a gang; (b) people who spend most of their time with the gang, sometimes participate in its activities, and may someday become members; or (c) people who pride themselves on having some amount of information about gang activities, want to keep on the good side of the gang members, but do not participate in gang-type activities. All three types of people who *know* gang members contrast with a separate group, which I will describe below, of people who seek no contact with the gang.

The situation of having family members in a gang is particularly common among girls, who are less likely overall to be in a gang themselves. The following narrative, told by Reina, 17, illustrates how people who are not gang members can still be deeply connected with the gang lifestyle:

Me and my brother, we almost got sha- shot. [CF: Oh, really?] Cause we went to go drop off his girlfriend at work. [CF: Mhm, which brother, the older brother?] The older one. And we stopped at a red light. It was in Santa Monica, then some gangsters from Santa Monica stopped us, and they got off the car. And the one that had the gun stood by my side, and kept asking me if I was from, you know, Culver City. And I told him I wasn't from anywhere. And they already knew my brother. Then my brother goes, 'You know what? At least – if you don't respect me, at least respect my sister.' He goes, 'You're- you're the one- I'm the one that you wanna get not her. Don't do nothing to my sister.' And they just stopped, and th- and they were like, 'Naaah, nah, it's all right, it's cool, it's cool.' And then they're like, 'We're gonna let you go, just don't tell anybody this happened.' And they- they were about to shoot, but like, my brother told 'em, you know, disrespec- you're disrespecting my sister. And they just left, and before they left one of the guys got off and asked for my number! And they got me mad! And I- and I said, 'I'm not gonna give you my number after you tried to shoot me!' And then he goes, 'Oh, I'm sorry, I'm sorry' and then he left. But like, before I would, um . . . . Before I think

> I w- I- told- they used to tell me I used to look like a gangster . . .
> before. And I used to get chased, by some, like gangs.

Despite the fact that Reina makes it clear that she herself is not a gang member, by saying she's not 'from anywhere,' her affiliation with the gang through her brother leads to her involvement in gang-related incidents such as this one. In addition, this was not the only time in the interview that she mentioned an instance of someone telling her she looked like a *chola*. My own observations confirm that Reina chooses the type of clothes, make-up and so on, that are associated with gang membership.

In addition, the principal spontaneously brought up a term she had heard used to describe a different group of students who hang around with gang members: *wanna-bes*. She volunteered this label when I asked what groups she thought there were at the school, and I later found the same term used by Klein in his book on American gangs (Klein 1995:46). At Westside Park, the group known as *wanna-bes* includes people in both the second and third categories mentioned above. Those in the second category may be respected by the gang, and may support or *back up* the gang in certain ways, as will be discussed below. Those in the third category are generally looked down on and rejected by the gang. Two individual speakers that I interviewed can be used to illustrate the difference between *wanna-bes* who will probably become gang members, and those who are essentially *lames* (as discussed in Labov 1972a), who will never be jumped in, even though they think of themselves as connected with the gang.

The clearest example of a *lame* is David, 17. David is not a member of the Culver City gang, but would very much like to be, and hangs around with them as much as possible. He is not well respected by most members of the school community. The gang members have been reluctant to jump him in because they do not trust him. Some time before I interviewed him, he had been beaten up by gang members for what was described to me only as 'telling gang stuff.' There was a more recent incident in which he was with another student who also was not a gang member, but, like David, was *backing up* the gang, which I heard mentioned often. Rita, for instance, said about a friend of hers: '*no era de* [he wasn't from] Culver City, but he backed them up.' This term generally means that even though a person is not a gang member, he is known to be associated with them, and will not deny it if approached by a rival gang. It can also imply that the person has assisted the gang in some way, perhaps by hiding a weapon for them or something of this nature. By getting shot by rival gangsters, Chuck earned respect from the gang members.

Nonetheless, Chuck told me explicitly in the interview, 'I'm not *from* anywhere.' Chuck impressed me as articulate and intelligent, an impression confirmed by the staff at the school, and he told me he would like to be a writer. He described the conflict between his own interests and ambitions to be successful and the opinions of his *homeboys*:

> It's funny, though. Like I'm all into this Chicano activist shit and . . . like . . . my- my homeboys, like, it's not something that they look up to, you know, it's like . . . [CF: Oh really?] I don't know, it's like, the whole, the whole like, idea for everybody around here is that like you know, if you go fuck around and read and education and this and that it's like, it's just, you're not supposed to do it, it's like, you know. Like you're s- you're just a dork or something, but I mean you know, they're my homeboys you know, I mean, they don't think, like, I'm a dork, but . . . [CF: Mhm.] But like they, they clown me for shit like that you know. Which, it seems funny to me. That's th- you know, that's discouraging too, to some other fool that wants to do the same thing that I want to do. And then there's nobody else to show him that, hey, fuck it.

Chuck wants to choose his own activities, get an education, and so on, yet feels pressure from his gangster friends to abandon these plans.

There were many ways to differentiate the *lames* from the other *wanna-bes* in conversation. David, for example, boasted in his interview about the dangerous life he led. In contrast with the actual gang members, however, his stories of danger involved incidents such as driving around a parking lot trying to get away from someone whose car he had bumped. David clearly wanted to impress me with his ersatz danger of death stories and his knowledge of gang culture. The real gang members, on the other hand, never boasted about dangerous situations. Even Chuck, who was not technically a gang member when I interviewed him, summed up his story about being shot by saying, 'That was, like, a bad night.' I would not have been able to predict from the interview whether or not Chuck would eventually become a gang member. I had a strong impression, however, that David would never be jumped in. Two years after the conclusion of my research I spoke with the principal of Westside Park. She did not know what had become of David, although he was presumably not a known member of the gang, but Chuck had in fact been jumped into the CC gang, and was in jail for participation in a drive-by shooting.

Taggers

The *taggers* have an interesting social role, which has not been as clearly defined by sociologists as that of the gangs. Most important is the fact that they are completely separate from the gang members, even though there may be superficial similarities. The gangs in Los Angeles have a long tradition and can include people whose families have lived there for generations (Klein 1995). Taggers often are adolescents who have moved to the area more recently. I did not encounter any cases of female taggers, although the people I asked about this believed that in principle it would be possible for a girl to be a tagger. The term comes from *tagging*, the practice of writing graffiti, usually including nicknames and symbols. Taggers focus their energy on this activity, rather than on more violent ones. In contrast, I was told that gang members seldom tag, but that if they do (signing their name or their gang letters) it has a more serious significance, for example claiming a new territory. At the present time, there is no real trouble between gangsters and taggers, who occupy completely different roles in the social structure.

Recently, some taggers have coalesced into groups that are much more like gangs. These individuals are referred to as *tag-bangers*, but nobody I interviewed talked about this topic. An interesting analysis of the transition from tagging to tag-banging can be found in Klein's book (1995:208–12). The principal of Westside Park suggested that these groups provide a way for kids who are not in a gang to be anti-social, and that Anglo kids are often taggers or tag-bangers, since there are no white gangs in the area.[6] As far as I could determine, nobody I interviewed was a tag-banger, but I did interview several taggers, all of whom were from relatively higher social classes. Since most gang members are from working-class or lower income backgrounds, it may be that having a family with higher social status makes it difficult for someone to be accepted into a gang (although this may be less true for women than for men). Where a person lives might also be a factor, since gang members usually are centered in a particular *barrio*. Just as with Anglo adolescents, tagging may provide Latino adolescents who do not meet the usual pattern for gang membership with an outlet for rebellious behavior.

Since taggers are completely separate from the gangs, I would not expect their language use to be similar to that of gang members. However, it is possible that their role as a secondary organization in the community might be marked linguistically in some way that distinguishes them from other non-gang members. The attitude that taggers have toward gang members could also be crucial. For example, if they admire the gang members, having at some point possibly wished to be in a gang themselves, this might be reflected in the use of gang-oriented linguistic features. On the other hand, if they tag because they disapprove of the violent behavior of gangs, one would expect them to pattern more like non-gang members.

People with no gang affiliation

Finally, there are many young adults who have, and want to have, no association whatsoever with the gangs. In many places, there is no particular significance associated with a young adult not being a gang member because that choice would never present itself in the community in which they live. However, all the young speakers I interviewed, including those outside the school, have had to make a choice determining whether or not they would be a gang member. This is not to say that they have been specifically solicited by a gang. Yet, the strong gang presence in LA is a fact of life; all of these speakers have met someone or know of someone who is in a gang. I stress this point because I believe that the social factor of 'gang status' must be taken into account for all speakers. It is part of the linguistic identity constructed by the non-gang members, just as it is for the *cholos* themselves. Every boundary has two sides; linguistic behavior aimed at maintaining boundaries is influenced by those outside as well as those inside the group.

Only one student, Richard, who is an Anglo, offered an actual term for non-gang members. In describing what would happen if some gangsters saw a group of non-gang members on the street he says:

> If you're walking down the street and there's a group of just- straight-just- you know, schoolboy- just- nobodies, and there's a group of gangbangers, they might, you know, harass them because they know they can get away with it.

Richard appears to be searching for the right term for the group, and comes up with 'straight,' 'schoolboy' and 'nobody' in that order. None of the other students used these actual terms, although I have a feeling that the adjective 'straight' may have a wider distribution. The term 'nobody' also seems a logical extension of the term 'from nowhere' meaning not a member of a gang (though possibly affiliated with one). Since I cannot be sure how common any of these terms are in the Latino community, I have referred to the speakers in question simply as non-gang members, although even the suggestion that there might be a term for non-gang members confirms the importance of this social role.

2.5 Other affiliations

Parents (or moms)

Distinct from any gang-related identity, although sometimes intersecting with it, is the category of *parent*. Though both genders can, of course, be parents, in practice the identity is more often associated with girls. This is not a category that one would assume a priori to be important among high school students. I knew that there would be students at the school who had babies; in fact, there is an established infant care center at the school itself, which allows students with babies to continue going to class. But I was unprepared for how often the parent identity came up as part of a description of an individual. There were also frequent references to *the moms* as a group.

This identity is highlighted in part of an interview with Rita, who is complaining about some of the infant care center workers:

> I'm the only one that sticks up for myself. All the other moms just ignore them . . . There's some mothers that used to bring their kids here last year that don't bring them no more this year because of the way they are . . . All the moms, this was like two weeks ago, they said, 'We should all not bring our baby one day, see what they do.'

The students who have babies are required to use one of their class periods in the day care center, spending time with their child and occasionally helping with other kids, although there is a full-time staff. For the most part, as mentioned above, this category applied to girls, but there were also some boys at the school who had acknowledged parental responsibilities. I noticed at least one who was listed as having a class period in the infant care center, although I was not able to interview him.

I talked to several girls who had babies or were pregnant. None of them were married, though one of them was living with her boyfriend. Some girls had contact with the baby's father, while others did not. The one guy that I talked to who was a dad did not bring up the child himself in the interview, but talked a little about it after I asked (carefully) if he had any children. The girls who had young babies all described it as a positive experience. They were willing to go on in great detail about how cute or smart their child was, just as older parents do. Some were more ready than others to discuss the drawbacks as they saw them, such as having fewer friends, not being as free to go out, or having more trouble finishing schoolwork.

For young people of both genders, being a parent was cited several times as having had an influence on their gang status, often by the individuals themselves. In all cases, the result of parenthood was less contact with gang activities. Reina commented about several of her brother's friends, 'Some of them are changing . . . because they have kids.' She said that they get jobs, go to fewer parties, and so on. She later brought up Patricia's brother Frankie, who had been killed recently, and who according to Reina was also 'trying to change.' Though Reina didn't mention this, I know from my interview with Patricia that Frankie was also married and the father of a baby, to whom he was very devoted.

Rita, who was cited above, told a poignant story about an evening when she was supposed to go out with a girlfriend on a double date, but couldn't because the baby had a fever. That night the friend who had gone in her place was shot and killed. She told me that she believes her daughter saved her life. She also said:

> Now I'm more responsible. . . . People tell me that I messed up my life. But I didn't, I mean, as a matter of fact my life just begun. My life got better, with my baby.

Gang members who are also parents have particularly complicated social roles where the demands of gang life and the responsibilities of parenthood may sometimes be in conflict. Since this conflict plays an important role in the speakers' construction of identity, it may also be reflected in their use of language.

Mexican nationals

Not only at Westside Park, but also throughout the community, the distinction between Latinos and Latinas born in the USA and those who immigrated from Mexico or another country seems to be very significant, as was discussed earlier. Recent immigrants are often looked down on in the community by those who were born in Los Angeles, although the status of those who have lived in the USA a long time is less clear. The terms used by US-born Chicanos to refer to immigrants include the long-established derogatory term *wetbacks*, the less offensive term *Mexican nationals*, *border brothers*, and in Spanish, *vanamachos* or *banamachos*.

At Westside Park, some students who fell into this category were also called *the nerds*, although the group referred to by this term included at least one US-born Latina as well. This may reflect the fact that the more recent immigrants bring with them a high cultural value on studiousness, as part of their traditional upbringing, in contrast with, for example, the negative attitude toward education of the US-born gang members, mentioned by Chuck in the quote given earlier. I interviewed some students who were recent immigrants from Mexico and found that they generally belonged to completely different social networks from the native-born students. There may be other social categories at Westside Park that I was not able to observe, but these are the ones that emerged as most salient in how students identified themselves and others.

General information about speakers outside Westside Park

The social backgrounds of the speakers I interviewed outside the school (including those from the main high school) both paralleled and contrasted with the backgrounds of the Westside Park students. Not surprisingly, the young adults in these other networks could generally be described as more 'successful' in a conventional way than those at Westside Park. The speakers who were still in school had not had any serious academic or disciplinary problems. The older ones had jobs: at a bank, at a supermarket, at a newspaper. None of them was involved in gangs. I did have one speaker, Mario, who admitted to having been involved with gangs and drugs when he was younger, but who now works as a paralegal (one of the highest-prestige occupations among those I interviewed) and is no longer connected to the gang. The age range for these young adults was also broader than for those at Westside Park; the speakers from other networks ranged in age from 16 to 32, excluding the older Spanish-dominant speakers. None of the young adults outside Westside Park was a parent.

2.6   The role of networks

Personal networks

As with most school communities, the Westside Park community includes a series of smaller social networks. I was able to learn a good deal about these social groups from my observations of students in and around the office and campus, from conversations with members of the staff, and from talking with the students themselves. I also kept careful track of instances of students mentioning each other in the interviews.

As an example, I interviewed four members of a core group of Culver City (CC) gang girls. Their status was confirmed for me by one of the members, Amanda, who told me:

> Okay it's me and [Erica] – you talked to [Erica] right? – [Ana] and [Patricia], we're like all friends, we're like good friends, all four of us. We ki- we- we hang around each other every day, we go out every weekend, we're at each others' house all the time, we're with each other every day.

Note that this explanation was brought up spontaneously by her as part of a narrative and was not in response to a question on my part about school groups.

Figure 2.1 shows the distribution of the young adults I interviewed into smaller networks. It includes the speakers from outside Westside Park school, who form a set of separate networks. Not included on the chart are speakers older than 32 (including Spanish-dominant or monolingual parents), or speakers younger than 15. I also included one speaker whom I did not interview, Mariana, since she formed a clear part of the *nerds* group and her name came up often. Speakers who were born outside the USA are marked with an asterisk. People who have a gang affiliation other than CC are so labeled, as are people who have been CC members, but whose status is now uncertain, so that they appear outside the main circles. People who are said to know or hang with CC gangsters appear outside the circle but are connected to it by lines. All other lines indicate ties between individuals, such as mutual naming in interviews or repeated observation of those individuals together at the school.

Not surprisingly, many of the networks are related to gang membership. There are the core Culver City girls, as mentioned before, and the Culver City boys. Reina, whose brother is in the gang, falls outside the core CC group, but nonetheless has ties to them. As an example, she mentioned Patricia's brother's death (a story that came up in many of the interviews) and described him as a friend of hers. While there were, as I expected, no direct ties between the taggers and the gangsters, the wanna-bes, David and Chuck, had ties to both these groups.

Two other areas of interest in the networks are the moms, and the ties of some speakers to 'the black kids.' Interestingly, the moms network includes people who are and are not in a gang, though of the moms I interviewed, only one, Sol, was not a gang member. I got the impression from her that she does not have close ties to the other moms. She was

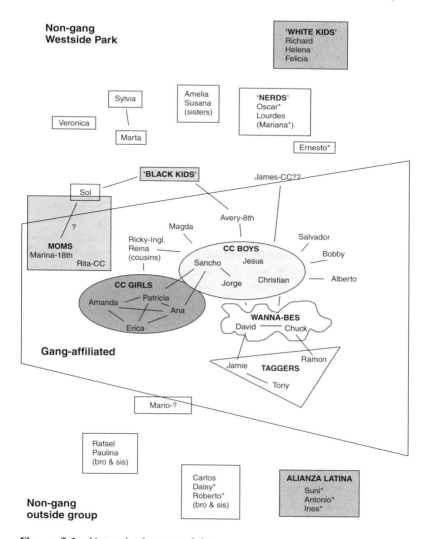

Figure 2.1 Network of young adults

described to me as hanging out mainly with 'the black kids.' Sylvia was pregnant at the time of the interview, but did not yet hang out with the moms, although she may by now be a member of that group. The same was true of Lourdes. As will be discussed later, different individuals among the moms have stronger or weaker ties to this group.

Only Sol and Avery, of the students I talked with, were associated in any way with the African-American network at the school. Both of them were described as spending time with this group, and both confirmed it to me in their interviews. In principle, the amount of contact that CE speakers have with African-American English (AAE) speakers is a highly relevant social factor, and I expected, for example, to code for this factor in the sociolinguistic analyses. I came to this community, however, at a time of high tension between young Latinos and African-Americans, as can be seen in Chuck's discussion of Mexican nationals above. Particularly for the gang members, it was extremely rare for them to have black friends, and not reliable to ask them about it. Many people cited others (never themselves, of course) as using extremely strong racial epithets with respect to African-Americans. In general, individual contact with AAE was not a significant factor among these particular CE speakers.

The group I have labeled 'nerds' includes two immigrants and Lourdes, whose parents are from El Salvador. This difference in national background would not in and of itself exclude anyone from participation in the networks of Mexican-American students; the parents of Ana, a core CC girl, are from Guatemala, for example. I did not hear any of the students call this group the nerds; it is a term the principal brought up. But I did confirm that these three speakers always spend time together. The few 'white kids' at the school also tend to hang around with each other. It is important to remember that the label 'white kids' applies to the network and not to individual speakers. Felicia, who is Tongan, also hangs out with this group.

The fact that some speakers, like Veronica, appear in relative isolation does not mean they are not part of a larger network, but only that their network includes people I did not interview, usually because they are from other schools in the area. There are two exceptions, however. Ernesto was specifically described by the counselor at the school as a 'loner' who seldom spent time with any other students. He is an immigrant from El Salvador, and the logical group for him to join would be that of the nerds. But this group is easy to spot, because they always have lunch together in the same place, and I never saw Ernesto with them. Mario is the other exception. He is a former gang member, which is why he appears on the gang/non-gang line. He told me specifically that he does not like to 'get too close to people.' Many of the friends he grew up with are dead, and Mario insists that he now does not have any friends, by choice. The only exception is his girlfriend, to whom he is very close. (We discussed the possibility of my interviewing her, but in the end, she was not willing to talk to me.)

I have not grouped all of the speakers from the parent group network together, since though their parents know each other, the children generally do not, although it is possible, for example, that Daisy and Paulina may have met briefly at some point. This brings up the possibility, not reflected on the diagram, that some of the speakers I interviewed might be part of the same network without my knowledge.

One interesting thing about these networks, particularly at Westside Park, is that they contain speakers of different social classes. Some complex issues related to social class were discussed earlier. As can be seen in Table 2.1, three of the CC gang girls, Erica, Ana and Amanda are from middle-class families, while Patricia and Rita are from the lowest income level in the community (in fact they live in the Projects). Yet all of these girls are part of the same network. Guy (1988:54) describes network studies as reflecting the microsociological level of the more 'macroscopic' class studies, and takes for granted that personal networks only occur within a class. Though Milroy (1987) does not state explicitly that networks can occur only within a class, the networks that are the focus of her study are completely homogeneous with respect to social class. In addition, in citing examples of other studies, Milroy says:

> Network studies have in fact been carried out by social anthropologists in societies of many kinds, ranging from middle- and working-class groups in Edinburgh, to shanty-town communities in Mexico City and rural or migrant communities in Africa. (Milroy 1987:178)

Though these groups do clearly represent very different cultures, none of them would be likely to include people from different social classes. The possibility that social networks in a community might include members of different social classes raises many intriguing questions. If the class and the network represent different value systems, for example, how does an individual speaker resolve these conflicting loyalties, linguistically and otherwise?

Personal conflicts

Studies looking at networks naturally focus on the people that a particular informant spends time with and counts as friends. Often, informants are asked to name their five closest friends, for example. But another interesting area to explore might be whom the informant dislikes and does *not* want to spend time with. It could be enlightening in some communities to have speakers name five people in the local community that they really hate. Particularly among adolescents, rivalries and prejudices are always present and can be informative with respect to community structure.

At Westside Park, I found that there were certain dyads of students who were known not to get along. In all the cases that I heard of, the students were girls. My suspicion is that with the level of inter-gang violence available to the male gang members, small-scale personal rivalries are less common. Girls who are gang members play a subordinate role in the gang structure and are less likely to be involved in real violence than the boys. Whatever the reason may be, there were two cases in particular that were talked about by the girls themselves, as well as by other people, in the interviews. One was the conflict between Patricia and Veronica. The other was the conflict between Erica and Sol. In each of these cases the first of the pair is a gang member, and the second is a clearly unaffiliated non-gang member.

Patricia and Veronica both live in the Projects. They both live with single mothers who were born in the USA, and they are both monolingual in English. Superficially, they would seem to have much in common. However, I interviewed Veronica shortly after Patricia had begun attending Westside Park, and she was quite distressed that Patricia would be coming to the school. Veronica told me that her grandmother had offered to lend her a car for the day, but Veronica refused because 'there's this girl here that I don't get along with, and she might mess it up.' In the past the tension between them had escalated to the point of a physical confrontation, as described in the following excerpt from Veronica's interview:

CF: [asking about Veronica and Patricia] Did you ever get in a fight?
V: Yeah. [pause] Hm, yeah, she comes to this school and I hate to see her. She just barely checked in. And I can't stand to see her here.
CF: How, how did it get started . . .
V: Cause, cause some other girl lied, about something that I didn't even say. And then, when, w- like before we had fought, she had came up to see me and I told her I didn't say it, and then a couple days later, she came up to me and heard that, that I did say it, and I was like, fuck it, I go, 'I know you're not gonna believe me,' so I just said I said it. And then we started fighting. Even though I didn't say it.
CF: That's too bad.
V: Cause I knew she wasn't gonna believe me, so why am I gonna sit there and look stupid?

Even though Veronica did not mention her name, I knew the referent was Patricia because she had arrived at the school very recently ('she just barely checked in'), and because the counselor also mentioned the fight to me.

Erica is a student who has had similar conflicts with two other girls (that I know of). One is Alicia, whom I did not interview and with whom Erica had a fight at the school. Another is Sol, whom I did interview. An encounter between Erica and Sol actually took place while I was at the school. Sol came in looking very upset and went into the principal's office. It turned out that Sol had been standing in the school parking lot. Erica regularly drives to school, and she had apparently hit Sol with the car (accidentally) while backing up, and then driven away without stopping. Sol was not really injured, but she was very, very angry. Fortunately, the principal and counselor were able to talk to both parties and defuse the situation somewhat, although Erica decided not to come to school for a few days.

Again, the gang versus non-gang pattern is repeated: Erica is a gang member, while both Sol and Alicia are clearly non-gang. I cannot say with certainty that such conflicts are a *result* of gang/non-gang tensions, however there seems to be this type of gang/non-gang pairing in most of the cases I heard about. An analysis of which people in a community do not get along can supplement the study of network ties and might in some cases reveal important social divisions in the community that are not otherwise evident. Having given some sense of the social context in which these CE speakers construct their ethnic and linguistic identities, I will now turn to the basic systems and structures of CE itself.

3
Phonology of Chicano English

3.1   Introduction: features of Chicano English phonology

The most salient differences between Chicano English and California Anglo English (CAE) are in the phonology, rather than in the grammar, although pinning down exactly what is different about the Chicano English sound system is not easy.[1] Its basic inventory of phonemes is very similar to those of other dialects. Some segments might be realized slightly differently in CE, but often these differences are subtle. Moreover, intonation and stress patterns are highly significant even when there are very few differences at the level of the segment. As with other communities, phonetic elements vary from speaker to speaker and within the speech of a single individual. There are also quantitative differences, particularly in the application of certain rules, such as the reduction of unstressed vowels. In this chapter, I will give an overview of the distinctive characteristics of the Chicano English sound system, and how these relate both to the sound systems of neighboring dialects (like CAE), and to the sound systems of non-native speakers of English (NNS). This description is intended to be broad in scope, a starting point to which other researchers can add new information and patterns as they are studied.

Before investigating the nature of the English variety spoken in the Latino community of Los Angeles, it would be helpful to know something about the phonology of other English dialects in the area, particularly the matrix dialect of the majority Anglo community. Unfortunately, as Santa Ana notes (1991:4), there is very little documentation of California Anglo dialects, geographical or social, especially related to phonology. In deciding which features of Chicano English phonology to highlight as distinctive, I have used for comparison the phonology of some Anglo speakers I interviewed from the same community, as well as my own pronunciations as a native speaker of California Anglo English.

It is also particularly crucial to distinguish the phonology of Chicano English from that of non-native learners of English in the community. As discussed in the introduction, there is a persistent myth that Chicano English and a 'Spanish accent' are the same. The sound systems of native and non-native English speakers are actually quite different, as will be shown. A more reasonable hypothesis would be that Chicano English speakers have inherited a subset of the non-native features of the 'accented' English spoken by older generations. However, even this assessment turns out to be too simplified. In an early article, Godinez (1984) shows that the vowels used by Chicano English speakers do not shift uniformly in the direction of the Spanish language equivalents. Many elements of CE phonology do reflect the influence of Spanish, but some may come from contact with other dialects or from other sources.

The phonetic overview presented here is based mainly on phonetic transcription and analysis by myself and another linguist. Later in the chapter, I also provide charts of acoustic measurements of the vowel space for a couple of speakers, and more such measurements are provided in Chapter 5. However, further study of the some of these features with speech analysis software would be productive. I have focused mainly on the speech of the young adults who form the core of my sample. I have also noted, though, which features are used more or less frequently by the slightly older generation of speakers in my sample, who ranged in age from 45 to 66. Since most of these speakers are from the middle class, they do not constitute an exact parallel for the younger speakers, many of whom were from working-class or low income backgrounds, but they can give some sense of how CE has evolved. I have not attributed the examples I give to particular speakers, since so many of the items turned up over and over across many speakers, but all of them were drawn from transcriptions of the interviews. I have also included, in Appendix A, phonetic transcriptions of passages of speech from two CE speakers, Reina and Chuck, as an illustration of how the various phonological features that will be discussed work together. I will begin by describing the features that distinguish CE from the dialect of local Anglo speakers, as well as the features that distinguish CE from the learner speech of non-native speakers of English. In the latter part of the chapter, I will look at features that CE and the California Anglo dialect might have in common, in contrast with other dialects of English.

3.2   Vowels

Less frequent vowel reduction

Overall, Chicano English speakers show less frequent vowel reduction than Anglos from the same area. This feature was first studied in depth by Santa Ana (1991). He found that not only did CE speakers tend to reduce vowels in unstressed syllables less often than Anglos did, but also that the direction of movement for unstressed vowels was sometimes quite distinctive in CE.[2] Particularly with the high vowels, /u/ and /i/, there was very little centralization, and in the case of /i/, little reduction of any type in unstressed syllables. Among the Latinos and Latinas I interviewed, this lack of reduction in high vowels was a very salient feature of their speech. Examples of pronunciations I heard very often were:

> *together* realized as [tʰugɛðɚ] or
> *because* realized as [bikəz]

In CAE, the first vowel in *together* or *because* would usually be [ɨ] or something similar. Generally speaking, the preposition *to* is seldom realized as [tʰuw] in casual speech among Anglos; it is more likely to be rendered as [tʰə]. However, CE speakers often had [tʰu] or [tʰʉ], even in unstressed occurrences of *to*.

Frequent lack of glides

Another feature noted by Santa Ana (1991:155) is a lack of glides among CE speakers in many places where Anglo speakers would have them, a feature that I also found to be very prevalent. In particular, the high vowels, realized as [ij] and [uw][3] by most Anglos, often lack glides among CE speakers. Also, the diphthongs [ej] and [ow], although they tended to be realized with a glide more often than the high vowels, were variable in this respect. Examples of vowels without glides included:

> *least* realized as [lis]
> *ago* realized as [əgo]
> *LA zoo* realized as [əlezu]

Particularly among the high vowels, the lack of gliding seems to be accompanied by a slightly higher articulation of the vowel in question, as well as a slight lengthening, although I have not marked this in the transcription.

With the diphthong [aj] there was no loss of the glide among CE speakers, but the nucleus often tended to be a bit higher than the nucleus typical for Anglos in this diphthong, as in

time realized as [tʰɐjm]

For most of my young adult speakers, the diphthong [aw] was very similar to the diphthong used by Anglos. For a few speakers, the nucleus might be raised slightly. However, the non-native speakers in the sample, and a few of the older generation of native speakers, had occasional loss of the glide in [aw]. For example, the word *counselor* was realized several times as [kʰanslə˞] by both these groups. For the older generation, lack of glides with [ow] was also more prominent. Joaquín, for example, told me a story in which someone came to a sudden realization, and said 'Oooooohhh!' This long, drawn out version of the vowel made it easy to discern that there was absolutely no offglide at all.

Tense realization of /ɪ/

The neutralization of /i/ and /ɪ/ is a typical feature of non-native learner English for people whose first language is Spanish, as will be discussed below. None of my CE speakers showed a complete lack of phonemic contrast between these vowels. However a phonetic realization of /ɪ/ as /i/ did sometimes occur. The most common environment for this realization was the morpheme *-ing* (where it is often accompanied by an alveolar realization of the nasal). This process was noted by Garcia (1984), and later was studied in detail by Mendoza-Denton (1997). Examples would include:

working realized as [wə˞kin]
embarrassing realized as [ɪmbɛɹəsin]

This variable turned out to have important sociolinguistic significance in the Northern California community Mendoza-Denton studied, correlating with the significant local ethnographic categories she identified. Additionally, some of the more vernacular sounding CE speakers have a realization of /ɪ/ in other places which is slightly more tense than CAE [ɪ], and sounds intermediate between [ɪ] and [i]. However, this is fairly infrequent and the reverse pattern (substitution of /ɪ/ for /i/) never occurs; overall CE would have to be characterized as a dialect in which /i/ and /ɪ/ contrast, but where /i/ has a wider distribution than in CAE.

Interestingly, tense [iŋ] or [in] is a variant which occurs in the local Anglo dialect as well, possibly as a result of contact with CE. Garcia (1984) suggests that the variant is both less tense and less frequent among Anglos. My impression from listening to my students is that it is now more frequent than it was (even in comparison with my own dialect, for example). It has also spread to contexts besides the morphological suffix. A native California Anglo student in my introductory linguistics class was mystified when I wrote the IPA symbol [ɪ] on the board with *king* as the example word. She came up to me after class and said 'But that word is [kiŋ]!,' pronouncing it unmistakably with a tense vowel. It is not clear yet whether there was always a moderate level of use of this variable among the Anglos, with quantitatively more in CE, or whether its presence in CE has actually caused an *increase* in the use of this feature among young Anglos.

Other vowels

There are a number of other phonetic realizations of vowels that are characteristic of CE. Though some of these features may be less widespread than those discussed above, they were used by many of the CE speakers, especially the more 'vernacular' sounding speakers. For California Anglo speakers, the vowel in *mom* or *caught* would generally be realized as the low back vowel [ɑ].[4] However, for many CE speakers this vowel is fronted, more like the [a] of Spanish. As with many of the other features that have been discussed, this feature is variable. Examples include:

> *daughter* realized as [daɾɚ]
> *talk* realized as [tʰak]
> *law* realized as [la]

Another vowel that can be realized slightly differently in Chicano English is [ʊ], the vowel in *book*. A number of CE speakers had a high central rounded version of this vowel, as in the following examples:

> *look* realized as [lʉk]
> *looking* realized as [lʉkiŋ]

Others also have an unrounded variant of this vowel, as in [lɨk], which parallels a common realization of [ʊ] in CAE, part of the tendency in this dialect to front back vowels. Even though he does not comment on it explicitly, some of the charts in Santa Ana (1991) suggest that his speakers have this centralized realization of [ʊ] as well.

Interestingly, for other CE speakers in my sample, this same vowel appeared as a variant of phonemic schwa, as in:

money realized as [mʉni]
luckily realized as [lʉkəli]
gun realized as [gʉn]

Occasionally, I also found [ɛ] as a realization of schwa, as in:

brother realized as [bɹɛðɚ]

Finally, the vowels preceding [ɹ] in CE often had a different quality than the corresponding ones in the Anglo dialect. This was particularly true of [ɛ] which tended to be centralized in this position, as in the following example:

there realized as [ðɚ]

Though this list does not encompass all the possible phonetic variation in the CE vowel system, it provides a sense of the most salient features that distinguish it from the systems of other English dialects. Those local vowel features that are specifically shared with California Anglo speakers will be discussed separately.

3.3   Consonants

The 'standard' American English inventory which will be used for comparison with CE is shown in Table 3.1.

Since the transcriptions here are broadly phonetic, glottal stops are included. In both CAE and CE, as in most varieties of American English, there is a glottalized articulation of syllable-final voiceless stops (discussed in more detail below). This complex is often called an 'unreleased' stop. In the transcribed examples, this type of articulation is indicated by an upper corner after the oral stop symbol, for example [t']. Although the American 'r' is sometimes considered to be vocalic, I have followed the IPA practice of using a 'consonantal' symbol [ɹ] for the onglide, and [ɚ] for the syllabic realization of this phoneme. In general, this consonant inventory is the correct one for CE as well.

Stops for interdental fricatives
In CE, apico-dental stops [t̪ d̪] are frequently found as substitutes for the interdental (or apico-dental fricatives) [θ ð]. Examples included:

Table 3.1 'Standard' inventory for American English

	Labial	**Apical**	**Dorsal**	**Glottal**
Stops	[p b]	[t d]	[k g]	[ʔ]
Flap		[ɾ]		
Nasals	[m]	[n]	[ŋ]	
Fricatives	[f v]	[s z]		[h]
		[ʃ ʒ]		
		[θ ð]		
Sonorants		[l ɹ]		

something realized as [səmt̪ʰɪn]
then realized as [d̪ɛn]
there's realized as [d̪ɛɹz]
think realized as [t̪ʰɪŋk]

This is of course a very common feature in many non-standard dialects, including AAE (Bailey and Thomas 1998). My impression is that it is not a feature of working-class Anglo dialects in California, but as I mentioned, there is very little data on these dialects. I know the Anglos I interviewed who were from lower socioeconomic classes did not use it. Some CE speakers seemed to have this substitution almost categorically, and it also was found among very 'standard' sounding CE speakers who used few or none of the CE syntactic features.

Consonant cluster reduction and other loss of consonants

As with all dialects of English, there is a tendency in CE to reduce consonant clusters. An example provided earlier was:

least realized as [lis]

With respect to t/d deletion (the loss of a final /t/ or /d/ after a consonant), CE parallels AAE somewhat, in that this reduction process occurs quantitatively more than in most Anglo dialects (Bailey and Thomas 1998). I also found as Wald (1984) did, that CE speakers often had reduction before a pause, an environment in which it is disfavored by most Anglo dialects. Santa Ana (1991, 1996) studied t/d deletion in CE in detail and these studies provide a complete analysis of the linguistic factors affecting this variable process, particularly with respect to the influences of sonority, which I will not present in detail here. I do want to note, however, that while numerous studies of t/d deletion in other dialects have found that the process is significantly more frequent in unstressed syllables, Santa Ana (1991) found no effect of syllable stress on t/d deletion among his CE speakers. The significance of this will be discussed more below. I also had a few instances where the entire cluster was deleted, as in the following example:

> *hardware* realized as [hɑwə]

This process was fairly infrequent, however; the example given is from one of the older speakers.

More characteristic of CE is the loss of final consonants that are not in a cluster, as in the following examples:

> *met some* realized as [mɛsəm]
> *night #* realized as [naj]

This process can be found in AAE as well (Bailey and Thomas 1998), but it is extremely common in CE, and my impression is that a quantitative study would show it to be more frequent than in any other English dialect. There were stretches of speech by some CE speakers where four or five final consonants in a row were deleted. A good example is the following:

> *...wouldn't get lost* realized as [wʊn gjɛ las]

Again, this is variable across speakers and would probably be a productive feature to study from a quantitative sociolinguistic perspective.

Glottalization of final voiceless stops

Where final voiceless stops occur in CE, there is a strong tendency among some speakers to glottalize them, that is, to progressively tense and close the vocal bands as the oral stop closure is made. Often they are also preceded by creaky voice in the vowel. Sometimes there is full substitution of a glottal stop for the expected consonant, [p, t, k]. Presumably these cases also contribute to the perception of 'lost' final consonants in CE. Alternatively, there are rare instances of the glottalized final stop being released as an ejective, with a characteristic sharp burst of aspiration before the ensuing pause.

3.4   Prosody in Chicano English

Prosodic features are among the most distinctive elements that define CE. CE speakers often seem to be using a rhythm and melody that are quite distinct from other varieties of English, even when a particular speaker has few of the typical phonological and grammatical elements of CE. In one of the early studies, González comments that 'intonation continues to be a problem even among adults with an otherwise flaw-less command of English' (1984:39). The infelicitous wording here reinforces the myth that CE is just a stage on the way to acquisition of standard English. There is nothing 'flawed' about CE intonation, but we can see from this quote that it has always been distinctive and may have an important role to play in conveying ethnic identity among otherwise very standard-sounding speakers.

In general, intonation and other prosodic features have received less attention from linguists than have other aspects of phonology, a fact often mentioned in the literature. Theoretical and practical study of these phenomena remains far behind what has been done in segmental phonology. There are some generalizations about intonation contours, for instance, but there is little information about how they work as a system. In particular, the relationships between specific intonation patterns and their functions in ordinary discourse remain unclear for any one variety, and still more so for the range of regional and social variation found across the Spanish and English speech communities. Pending future advances in this field, it is therefore possible here only to make some general observations and conjectures, based both on my data and on a survey of the sparse literature concerning Mexican and Chicano intonation and other features beyond the segmental level. I follow Hirst and DiCristo (1998) in discussing stress patterns and other segmental issues (including syllabification) as well as long-span features such as intonation, under the heading of prosody.

Stress patterns

It has been reported (Santa Ana 1991) that CE sounds impressionistically as though it is syllable-timed (like Spanish) rather than stress-timed (like most dialects of English).[5] Of course, both English and Spanish have stress differences such that some vowels are longer or shorter depending on their phonetic environments. However, the preponderance of the influence is different in the two languages, and CE is intermediate in some ways. Setting aside for a moment the question of whether it is completely accurate to call CE syllable-timed, stress patterns are a very salient element of CE, and clearly different in many ways from the patterns of the local Anglo dialects. These differences take place at a number of levels.

To begin with, CE speakers occasionally place the stresses within a word (and particularly a compound word) distinctly from Anglo speakers, as in the following example, said by Rita, which received two strong stresses:

/   ˘   /   ˘
morning   sickness

The dominant stress here, of the two, was on *sick-*. In my dialect, this compound would have a strong stress only on the first syllable, and if a secondary stress was present on *sickness*, it would be a very weak one. Another example comes from Avery, who said *Thanksgiving Day* (at the end of a sentence) with the following stress pattern:

˘   /   ˘   ˘
Thanksgiving   Day

In my dialect, the stress would most likely be on *Thanks-* and *Day* in this context. These stress shifting patterns occurred more often among the slightly older speakers (for example, Joaquín said *finances* with the stress on the second syllable), and most frequently of all among the NNS. A tendency of this type was also noted by Penfield (1984), who suggests that noun compounds in CE are often stressed on the second word, rather than the first as they would be in most other English dialects (which would account for the 'morning sickness' example). Penfield also notes that in CE, verb + particle combinations are more likely to be stressed on the verb, unlike in other dialects (in other words *to <u>sit</u> up* rather than *to sit <u>up</u>*).

More commonly, over a phrase, the main stresses may not be located where speakers of other dialects would expect them. Examples can be found in the following utterances from Avery:

Some girls don't think what they're gonna <u>go</u> through.
It's alright for <u>her</u> to talk to <u>her</u> homeboys, but it ain't alright for me to talk to <u>my</u> homegirls?

The primary stress in the first sentence was on *go*, with a secondary stress on *some*. In my dialect, the primary stress in this utterance would normally be on *through*. In the second sentence, the primary stresses were on both instances of *her* and on *my*; given the meaning of the utterance (which is about rules for flirting outside a relationship) I would have had stresses on the first *her* and on *me*. The stress on *my* would indicate for me some contrast with other homegirls. I can imagine that some speakers of standard dialects may find this stress pattern marginally acceptable, but I think it also parallels very closely a usage by a non-native speaker, which I will discuss below, and which suggests that this may reflect the influence of Spanish.

Returning to the question of whether CE is syllable-timed, Santa Ana (1991) provides some interesting evidence. He found that CE contrasted with other dialects of English in that there was no effect of syllable stress on the process of t/d deletion. Presumably this suggests that the contrast between stressed and unstressed syllables is less in CE than in other English dialects, something which it would be useful to test with acoustic measurements. In addition, Santa Ana's CE speakers had a much lower degree of vowel reduction in unstressed syllables than speakers of other dialects have, which I found in my sample as well, particularly in the high vowels. It is not clear whether this is a cause or an effect of the degree of syllable-timing. The lack of glides with certain vowels might also affect the nature of perceived stresses, since there often seems to be compensatory lengthening of these vowels, so that the syllable sounds longer. Whether or not Chicano English is actually syllable-timed, if we think of these two patterns as opposite ends of a continuum, CE is closer to the syllable-timed pole than most other dialects of English.

Intonation

In view of the intermediate position of Chicano English, falling between Anglo English and Mexican Spanish in a number of attributes, it is reasonable to consider whether its intonation patterns may also be intermediate in this way. There are preliminary indications that this is so. Metcalf, in an early study, describes a pattern of intonation in CE which to speakers of other dialects sounds 'wishy-washy and a little crazy... as if [the speaker] is asking a question when he should be making a statement, expressing doubt when he should be certain' (1974:55). This effect may be produced by what Matluck (1952, 1965) and others (see Kvavik 1974; Kvavik and Olsen 1974 for references) have referred to as a 'circumflex' intonation pattern in Mexican Spanish. This pattern involves a rise and sustain or a rise and fall at the end of the spoken phrase. In Mexican Spanish there is a substantially greater range of pitch change and an overall higher pitch within the utterance than would be expected in Peninsular Spanish, and a characteristic rise–fall pattern whose fall does not have the abrupt downslope found at the ends of the usual American English 2–3–1 declarative contour. Like other Spanish intonation contours, this one also often begins with a high pitch and falls to a low, level span until the final rise-fall. To use a familiar but impressionistic four-level notation, with 1 the lowest level, these circumflex patterns may be:

(3–2...-)4–3
(3–2...-)3–2

Sometimes there is no final downturn, yielding a pattern such as:

(3–2...-)3–3
(3–2...-)4–4

Such intonations, used in English or Spanish, are sometimes heard in conversation or in the media as deliberate caricatures of Mexican speech patterns.[6]

In most dialects of American English, such patterns in terminal contours are rare. Something similar is used occasionally as a way to suggest a doubting or inconclusive attitude toward what is being said, as in 'He's a good student ' with a 2–3–3 pattern. The next word expected after the pause would be 'but'; the strength of this expectation supports the impression that it is not a standard final intonation contour in most American dialects. In Mexican Spanish, apart from any regional identification they may impart, such contours appear to be merely declarative. The use of this pattern specifically in the Spanish spoken in Los Angeles and the potential misunderstandings that can occur are illustrated by an anecdote from my fieldwork. I was talking to one of the young speakers, Ricky, in Spanish and asked him what he would like for his future children to have. He answered *Que tengan todo lo que ne- necesiten ellos?* ('That they have everything that they need?,' with the question mark as a vague indicator of a rising intonation pattern). I interpreted his utterance as a request for clarification and responded by re-phrasing the question. Later, listening to the tape, I realized he had been giving me a direct answer, but I had missed it because of the intonation contour.

Matluck's very important discussion of intonation patterns in the Valley of Mexico (1952) makes two crucial points. The first is the identification of the distinctive contour. Matluck was the first to describe it as 'circumflex,' a term that has been quoted in a number of more recent sources:

> La cadencia enunciativa en el habla popular del Valle es muy diferente de la castellana, y en su forma circunfleja está lo característico de la entonación peculiar de la altiplanicie mexicana. De la antepenúltima sílaba a la penúltima hay un ascenso de unos tres semitonos, y de allí a la última un descenso de seis semitonos más o menos; tanto la última como la penúltima sílaba son largas. (Matluck 1952:119)

> [The cadence of enunciation in the popular speech of the Valley is very different from the Castilian one, and what is characteristic of the intonation peculiar to the Mexican plateau is its circumflex form. From the antepenultimate syllable to the penult there is a rise of about three semitones, and from there to the final a fall of six semitones more or less. Both the penult and the final syllables are lengthened.]

He also notes that the lengthening of stressed vowels at the start and the end of a phrase is a feature of lower class usage in that region. These stretchings at start and finish are presumably both due to the corresponding pitch peaks. To anyone who has heard this intonation, his description is unmistakable:

> Las sílabas acentuadas en el habla popular del Valle tienden a alargarse mucho más que entre la clase culta y en el castellano general; en cambio, las inacentuadas se abrevian. La impresión total es de alargamiento silábico al principio y especialmente al final de la frase, y de acortamiento en el centro; por ejemplo: *no seas malo* > *nooo sias maalooo; tengo que hacerlo pronto* > *teengo quiacerlo proontoo*. (Matluck 1952:119)

> [Accented syllables in vernacular speech in the Valley tend to be much longer than those of the educated class and in Castilian generally; on the other hand, unaccented syllables are shortened. The overall impression is of syllabic lengthening at the beginning and especially at the end of the sentence, and of shortening in the

middle. For example, *Don't be bad > Doont be baaad; I have to do it soon > III have to do it sooon.*]

Perhaps the most significant point is that Matluck attributes this pattern to the Nahuatl substratum, supporting this by citing Alcocer:

> La distintiva línea musical en el desarrollo del grupo fónico es, probablemente, el rasgo más saliente que la lengua náhuatl ha dejado en el español del Valle y de la altiplanicie: una especie de canto con su curiosa cadencia final, muy parecido al movimiento melódico del náhuatl mismo.   (Matluck 1952:119)

> [The distinctive musical line in the unfolding of the phonetic group is probably the most striking trace that the Nahuatl language has left in the Spanish of the Valley and the plateau: a kind of song with its curious final cadence, very similar to the melodic movement of Nahuatl itself.]

Besides Matluck, who apparently began his research on this in the 1940s, Wallis (1951), Delattre et al. (1962), Kvavik (1974) and Kvavik and Olsen (1974) all describe very similar patterns in their different notations, sometimes using Matluck's handy 'circumflex' term for the pattern. It should be noted that Uto-Aztecan languages were and are widespread in northern and central Mexico, including Sonora, where this distinctive intonation pattern is also found. If this pattern is indeed borrowed from Nahuatl and its close relatives, it should be possible to find more evidence of it in other parts of the country as well.

However that may be, it is clear that speakers of Chicano English and, still more so, of non-native English, both use these intonation patterns at least some of the time. Penfield and Ornstein-Galicia (1985:48–51) describe something of this type in Chicano English (as sentence final 'rise–fall glides'). However, their discussion does not refer to the papers on Mexican intonation cited above, and does not separate these phenomena from the now widespread 'uptalk' intonation patterns thought to have originated in California (in CAE), and known to be very widely distributed now throughout the United States and beyond. In uptalk, what sounds like a rising question intonation is used repeatedly in place of a falling declarative contour (Gorman 1998). This appears to be what Penfield and Ornstein-Galicia call 'rising glides maintained at the end of a neutral, declarative sentence' (1985:49).

The Chicano circumflex intonation does not sound quite like uptalk, though; the Chicano pattern, like the Mexican one, begins with a raised pitch, whereas the nonemphatic American English contours, uptalk or not, begin with mid-pitch. Older speakers, both native speakers of CE and non-native English speakers, show this particular Mexican influence more often and more clearly in their speech than do younger ones, where the circumflex intonation is present, but within a more compressed pitch range. In some of the younger speakers, both types of contours are found: (a) the circumflex intonation, and (b) the intonation patterns associated with the California Anglo dialect. The prosodic patterns of the matrix California dialects have not been documented sufficiently to provide a basis for a comparison at this time, but some CE speakers, particularly women, clearly incorporate them into their speech. One of my speakers, Erica, even superimposed these California intonations onto her Spanish (which is moderately fluent) in a way that I, despite my alleged linguistic objectivity, found very amusing. As in the case of stress patterns, then, CE displays some intonations which seem to fall between Anglo English and Mexican Spanish norms, and draws upon two sets of possible contours.

Syllable patterns

Syllabification, the segmenting of speech into successive syllables, is not completely dictated by the sequence of speech sounds themselves making up the stream of speech. It can pattern differently for the same types of segments across different languages or dialects. In American English, Spanish and many other languages, syllable boundaries are usually placed somewhere *within* intervocalic consonant clusters. In English and at least some other Germanic languages, such boundaries are often placed within a single intervocalic consonant, which is not true of Spanish. Such 'ambisyllabic' consonants have been recognized since the beginnings of instrumental phonetic studies of American speech. They are one aspect of a tendency toward more frequent 'closed' syllables (those with a final consonant) in Germanic languages, as against more frequent 'open' syllables (those with a final vowel) in the Romance languages. Chicano English appears to be more like Spanish in its pattern of syllabification. However, this conclusion can only be tentative, pending further research on broader samples.

There is another tendency which converges with this shifting of syllable onsets. In ordinary speech, as the rate of speech increases, consonant clusters tend to be reduced, that is, simplified by the loss of one or more components, as in this Anglo English example, showing only three of the possible realizations:

	'What did he say to her?'
Slowly, carefully:	[wətdɪdhiˈsɛjtɨhə]
Casually:	[wəɾɪɾiˈseɾɨwə]
Quickly, casually:	[wəɾiˈseɾɨwə]

In the slow, careful version, all of the apical stops, single or clustered, are present; in the other version, clusters are reduced, and all remaining single apical stops are replaced by voiced flaps. The [h] segments are dropped. In more extreme examples, such as the last version, whole syllables may be lost, especially from the portion preceding the primary stress at the intonation peak, which in this reading coincides with 'say'. The first two syllables, unambiguously closed in the slow version, are now separated by ambisyllabic flaps, and the next two are as well, in both of the faster versions. These examples illustrate the effect of cluster reduction. Independently of any shifting in the pattern of syllable onsets, it leads to more frequent open syllables by reducing the number and complexity of consonant clusters. In both the Anglo English and the Chicano English data, similar patterns of reductions are found. In the Chicano data, however, the reduction patterns of rapid speech interact with a tendency toward placing syllable boundaries in positions which result in even more frequent open syllables. This pattern is also fed by the frequency of deletion of a single final consonant at the word level in CE, which was discussed earlier.

There seem to be three converging tendencies, then, with increasing prevalence as the rate of speech increases:

• consonant clusters are reduced, often to a single consonant;
• some single consonants or whole syllables are omitted;
• some syllable onsets are placed before rather than within intervocalic consonants.

The first two patterns are found in Anglo dialects as well as in CE, although the second is more frequent in CE, especially in the case of single final consonants. The result of these tendencies is to raise the proportion of open syllables in casual speech. This relatively high proportion of open syllables may in turn be one aspect of the 'Spanishness' of CE as perceived by observers who speak other English dialects. The following are some examples of reductions combined with onset shifts to increase the number of open syllables over a comparable Anglo English version of the same string:

[ʔæ'nɛne]
And then they

['duinə 'pʰɪkəps | dɛjpʰʊ'rɛnəðə 'bɪg'tʰɪkɪt̚]
Doing the pickups they put on to the big ticket

The first example is reduced completely to CV syllables. In the second, interestingly, the consonants that are lost, the [ð] in *the* and the [t] in *to*, are initial. Although this process of initial consonant loss occurs in rapid speech for other dialects as well, it is somewhat more frequent in CE.

Creaky voice

A final suprasegmental feature that is very characteristic of CE speakers in the Los Angeles community is creaky voice. This feature seems clearly to be an example of something that comes out of contact with the local Anglo dialect, where creaky voice is extremely prominent. (Even though I have mainly been discussing features that are not shared by Anglos, I include this one because it belongs with the other suprasegmentals.) Helena, a young Anglo speaker that I interviewed, seems to end almost every sentence with a stretch of extreme creaky voice. I hear this also among my Anglo students. The CE speakers use this feature very frequently as well. Though I found it among male and female speakers, it seems to be more common for women, both among Anglo and Latina speakers. Interestingly, Fernanda, one of the older speakers in the sample (she is 53), uses creaky voice frequently, which suggests that it is not necessarily a recent development in Chicano English. The following is a transcription of a short narrative from Veronica, 17; for simplicity, the sections that had creaky voice have been indicated with italics:

Cause another time *um*, my same friend, my best friend? [cf-mhm] Um *she*- she told me to take her mom's *car* to take her shopping, this is a long time ago, like last year, to take her to go get some shoes. *And*- and- I took her and that was the first time I ever drove alone. I didn't have my permit *or anything*. (laughs) And we were driving and then I almost crashed, and then I *was like, real scared*. I bumped a parked *car*. Like, but I was pulling out of *a parking space*, that's why. [cf-that's usually the hardest part] Cause, cause I had never reversed, in my life!

This excerpt provides a good indication of the high frequency of creaky voice among some CE speakers.

Although Laver states that 'used throughout an utterance, creaky voice signals bored resignation, in the paralinguistic conventions of English' (1980:126), in CE and probably also in California Anglo English, its meaning seems more complicated. For example, in Veronica's story, the very last thing indicated by *I was like, real scared* would be boredom.

Clicks

There is a last feature I wish to mention here, which I have noticed but not yet analyzed in detail. Many of my CE speakers, particularly the male gang members, used a click (alveolar or palato-alveolar – a kind of scolding noise) as a discourse marker. This noise was inserted repeatedly into pauses between phrases, and my impression was that it marked a kind of generally disapproving stance toward the topic being covered. I do not know if there is any research on this feature in other communities. In most English-speaking cultures, a click of this type can be used to signify disapproval, but my sense is that in CE it is used both with a wider scope of possible contexts, and with a much higher frequency. Below is a transcript of a narrative told to me by Avery, 16, with the clicks marked with the IPA symbol for a palato-alveolar click [ǂ], which is what it most sounded like to me. I've provided the entire narrative to show the frequency with which the clicks occur (and left out my backchannels while he was telling it).

I have a couple of girl- like a couple of girls that I know? I'm like, and- I'll call one of my girlfr- or like [ǂ] not my girlfriend, she's my ex-girlfriend. [ǂ] I was like, um, 'What're you doing?' And she's like, 'Nothing.' I'm like, 'Where you been at?' She's like, 'I have a bread in the oven!' That was Thanksgiving Day! And she says I have a bread in the oven! She was trying to tell me she was pregnant. And I was like, 'Whaaat?' I was like, 'OK, go t- go take the bread out the oven, huh, before it burns!' And she starts laughing at me. I was like, I said 'Go take the bread out the oven cuz it's gonna burn, huh. And it's Thanksgiving Day.' [ǂ] And she started laughing at me! I'm like, 'What? Did I say something stupid?' She's like, 'Nah! It's just that um, I have a bread in the oven.' I was like, 'Go take it out!' She's like, 'I can't!' I was like [ǂ], 'Man, fool, you could take out the bread out the oven!' And she's like, 'You don't get it, huh?' I was like, 'Yeah, you got a bread in the oven. It's Thanksgiving. You're cooking some

bread.' And she was like, 'Nah, not that!' And I was like, 'What is it
then?' [ǂ] And she's like, 'Hold on!' So I'm thinking she went to go
take out the bread out the oven, cause it was Thanksgiving Day. And
she comes back, and I was like, 'Did you take it out?' And she starts
laughing again at me, and she calls her friend, on three-way, and
she's like, 'This fool [ǂ] this fool wants me to go take out the bread
in the oven.' And they both start laughing at me. And then I was
like, 'I don't know.' And I was like, and then we got together [ǂ] like,
to kick back? And I was like, [ǂ] 'Tell me what's going on!', so she
told all my friends, and they were laughing at me. [ǂ] And I still
didn't get it! I was like, she's got the bread in the oven. It was
Thanksgiving Day. I thought she was making bread. And she's like,
'I'm pregnant.' And I was like, 'Whaaaat? [ǂ] Aw, you should've told
me that before, man.' And she's like, 'But, you know ...' And I was
talking to her on the phone, [ǂ] she's like, 'It didn't meant to happen.' I was like, you know, if you know what you're doing, then, you
know, you're doing- you know what you're doing, so you know
what's going to happen. You know? And if you don't know what
you're doing, you know, the girl n- like some guys get the girls drunk
and- and high, you know, [ǂ] and take advantage of them, and, you
know, the girls don't know what's going on. But most of the time,
girls know what's going on.

There are twelve clicks in the span of this one narrative. For many of
them, the analysis that they indicate disapproval seems accurate,
although the second one in, for instance, seems ambiguous to me. Also
it is interesting that he inserts a click into quoted speech from another
speaker.

3.5   Comparison with the English of non-native speakers

Because native and non-native speakers have not always been clearly
distinguished in the literature, I will give an explicit description of how
CE differs from the English of non-native speakers (NNE or non-native
English). This is not meant to be a comprehensive account of the
phonology of non-native English speakers (NNS) who have Spanish as
their first language, but simply a list of notable features that CE does not
share, or that are more frequent in the speech of people who do not
speak English natively. I have used the English of two speakers who
grew up in Mexico, Rosana, age 56, and Ruben, age 32, as a non-native
speaker comparison group.

Most of the characteristic phonetic features of CE mentioned above are found also among the non-native speakers. This is not surprising, since as we have known all along, CE is a contact dialect, bearing the imprimatur of Spanish throughout the sound system. There are some features which are characteristic of CE and not of NNE, including the centralized [ʉ] for [ə] or [ʊ], and the glottalized realization of final stops. The features associated with California Anglo English, such as creaky voice and the variables that will be discussed in the section below, also tend not to be used by Rosana and Ruben. Interestingly, there are a few features that NNE has that appear also among the older generation of CE speakers, but not among the younger ones. However, most significant in light of the myths and misperceptions about CE are the many features shared by NNE that never occur in Chicano English. These fall into a number of different categories.

Phonemic differences between CE and NNE

There are certain phonemic contrasts in CE that the non-native speakers as a group often do not have in their variety of English. These include the following:

[ɪ] and [i]

While CE speakers often have tense [i] in the *-ing* morpheme, it is extremely rare in other places. The non-native speakers have a much higher rate of this feature, producing a majority of phonological [ɪ] tokens as [i]. In addition, none of my native speakers ever substituted [ɪ] for [i]. The phonological contrast between the high front vowels is clearly in effect in CE, despite the phonetic variation in *-ing*. The NNS on the other hand produce examples such as:

these realized as [dɪz]

All of this suggests that there is not a clear contrast for them between [ɪ] and [i].

[æ] and [ɛ]

Though as will be discussed below, CE speakers occasionally have a raised [æ] variant paralleling the California Anglo dialect, they nonetheless maintain a contrast between [æ] and [ɛ] (see the vowel chart for Amanda, Figure 3.2, to confirm this visually). On the other hand, the NNS seem to use [æ] and [ɛ] interchangeably for phonemic [æ], as in these examples:

dad realized as [dɛd]
handle realized as [hɛndəl]
habit realized as [hǽbɪt]

As the last example shows, some of the NNS also have nasalization, not just on [æ], but on many vowels.

[tʃ] and [ʃ]

All of the native Chicano English speakers in my sample had a clear contrast between [tʃ] and [ʃ]. On the other hand, the NNS use these somewhat interchangeably as in the following examples:

she realized as [tʃi]
shorthand realized as [tʃɔɹhɛ̃nd]
hitchhike realized as [hɪʃhaik]
chairs realized as [ʃɛɹs]

I thought there was a slight preference for [tʃ] initially, but as the last example shows, it is not consistent. The substitution of [tʃ] for [ʃ], is one of the features that I noticed very occasionally among the older CE speakers as well. The vast majority of the time, they produced the standard variant for each of these phonemes, but on rare occasions a word like *she* was produced with [tʃ] or a somewhat ambiguous intermediate form that was hard to classify as one or the other. In contrast, Wald (1984), who is one of the few to clearly distinguish non-native from native speakers in his research, found an interchange of [tʃ] and [ʃ] among native speakers of CE in East Los Angeles, particularly among bilinguals. Interestingly, he notes that because it is so heavily stigmatized, and because it is less common among monolinguals, it is 'not a *stable* dialect feature [of CE] which [will] be transmitted to future generations' (Wald 1984:23). My data suggest that his conclusion is correct, and that this feature has been lost in CE.

[ə] and [ɑ]

Again, in CE, [ə]and [ɑ] are distinct phonemes. In NNE, however, there is a tendency to substitute [a] for [ə], in both stressed and unstressed syllables, as the following examples show:

lucky realized as [laki],
husband realized as [hasbɛnd],
abuse realized as [abjus]

This substitution is not categorical, since the same speakers did have a schwa in other examples, for example

something realized as [səmtiŋ]

The reverse substitution was also sometimes found; some tokens of [ɑ] are realized as [ə], as in:

calmed realized as [kəm]

Another phone that is occasionally substituted for [ɑ] is [o], as in:

saw realized as [so][7]

None of these substitutions occurred in CE.

Phones not found in CE

There is at least one sound found in the inventory of NNE that does not occur in CE. It is the voiceless velar fricative [x]. The CE speakers do not produce this sound, but the NNS substitute it variably for [h], as in:

home realized as [xom]
he realized as [xi]

Differences in processes

There are also phonetic processes that differ between the two groups. CE follows the normal flapping rules of many English dialects, such as California Anglo English, where an intersyllabic /t/ or /d/ becomes an alveolar flap [ɾ], regularly when the following syllable is unstressed, and occasionally before a stressed syllable across a syllable boundary. The NNS follow this rule only variably, and sometimes do not have a flap, as in:

personality realized as [pʰɚsənǽlɪti]

In contrast, a process that occurs in NNE but not in CE is the insertion of epenthetic e- before a consonant cluster beginning with /s/, as in:

spent realized as [əspɛnt]

This is a stereotypical feature of non-native English speakers whose first language is Spanish. It was actually relatively rare among the non-native speakers in my sample, but in CE it was completely absent. One other feature that occurs only among the non-native speakers is the devoicing of final /d/ as in

   ahead realized as [əhɛt]

NNE has more devoicing generally. Interestingly, the older CE speakers have occasional instances of devoicing that are not heard among the younger speakers, such as:

   college realized as [kalɨtʃ]

Variable processes that are more frequent in NNE than in CE

Variable processes that occur in both CE and NNE, but that are more frequent in NNE, are interesting because they may indicate features that came into CE from Spanish. One process that is more frequent in NNE is the substitution of stops for interdental fricatives. In particular, the NNE had a much higher frequency of substitution than the CE speakers when the interdental is voiceless, as in:

   something realized as [səmtiŋ]
   enthusiasm realized as [ɛntusijæsəm]

Another process that is more frequent in NNE is deletion of a (single) final consonant, as in these examples:

   would run realized as [wu ran]
   lock herself realized as [la xəsɛlf]

Although I did not discuss it above, another process which has been associated with CE in the literature (for instance, in García 1984) is the devoicing of final /z/. I decided not to include it in my characterization of CE because, as García notes, it is a process that occurs in other dialects of English as well, and it is very difficult to say whether it is notably more frequent in CE without a quantitative study. However, among the NNS, this process approaches 100 percent; examples include:

years realized as [jɪrs]
ideas realized as [ajdias]

If there were a strong enough quantitative difference to consider this process a feature of CE, that result would probably be related to its frequency in NNE.

Finally, the stress shift patterns described earlier are much more frequent in NNE. Examples at the word level from the NNS included producing the words *terrified* and *realized* with stress on the last syllable. There are also many examples of placement of stress across the sentence or phrase that do not correspond to the typical pattern for Anglo dialects. Rosana produced the following three utterances:

I was not all these things.

They asked me if I wanted to come and work for him.

Children are that way.

The stress in each case is placed on the penultimate word/syllable. In no case did the context indicate a contrastive meaning; for each of these sentences, the meaning is the one indicated by reading the sentence with a neutral stress pattern. For me, that would mean stressing the last word in the first and third sentences, and *work* in the second. This pattern is interesting to me for several reasons. First of all, since a majority of Spanish words have penultimate stress,[8] this creates a de facto situation for penultimate sentence stress to be the typical pattern. Secondly, these examples seem quite parallel to the ones from Avery earlier which I will give again:

Some girls don't think what they're gonna go through.

...but it ain't alright for me to talk to my homegirls?

In the first, the main stress is placed on the penultimate syllable (or word). In the second, it is the penultimate word. It may be that a predominantly phonological pattern from NNE, shifting stress to the penultimate syllable, has been extended by the young CE generation to include shifting stress to the penultimate word, since these two categories would so often overlap.

3.6   Comparison with older studies

As was mentioned earlier, the studies of the early and mid 1980s do not always make clear whether the features they list for 'Chicano English' are used by native or non-native speakers of English. Peñalosa (1980:119–21) lists a number of phonological traits that are said to be characteristic of CE (and are similar to those listed in other works of the same time period). Of these, the ones that appear among the native speakers in my sample are: differences in intonational patterns, differences in stress patterns, deletion of final stops (not necessarily in a cluster), devoicing of final /z/, and stops substituted for interdental fricatives. For the rest of the features he lists, some of them occurred among the non-native speakers in my sample, but none were used by native CE speakers. These features included: softening of voiced stops intervocalically, merger of /tʃ/ and /ʃ/, merger of /ɪ/ and /i/, merger of /b/ and /v/, use of [x] for /h/, use of [dʒ] for /j/, merger of /æ/ and /ɑ/ and merger of /ɛ/ and /ej/. I have already mentioned that the interchange of /tʃ/ and /ʃ/, found by Wald (1984), was not present among my CE speakers. García (1984) also discusses the substitution of [æ] for /ɛ/ before /l/, and describes it as 'a recognizably Chicano trait' (1984:88). Nonetheless, it was not present in any of the speakers, older or younger, in my sample.

There are several possibilities for the discrepancy between the features I have identified as CE, based on my sample from 1994 and the older studies. One is that CE has changed such that features which used to be characteristic of it no longer are found. However, if this were the case, one would expect that some of my older speakers, who would have been in their 20s and 30s at the time these studies were done, would show these features. Another possibility is that native speakers and non-native speakers were not clearly distinguished from each other in compiling the lists (although Wald (1984) is exceptional in this respect). For this reason, I have devoted a fair amount of time to making that distinction in this chapter.

3.7   The influence of African-American English

Language contact as part of the context of CE in Los Angeles involves not only the contact between English and Spanish, but also contact between CE and other local dialects. The speakers of Chicano English in my sample sometimes showed evidence of contact with African-American English (AAE), despite the fact that a majority of the Latino young adults claimed to have little contact with individual African-Americans. The clearest example that appears to indicate unequivocally the influence of AAE is a grammatical one: the use of invariant *be*, which was fairly frequent among the Latino speakers, and is difficult to attribute to any other source. As was seen in the discussion of networks at the school, a few speakers did have African-American friends, and these speakers tended to use more of the grammatical and phonological features associated with AAE.

Of the phonological traits discussed above, a number are common to AAE, particularly those that involve consonants. Among these are the substitution of stops for [θ] and [ð], increased consonant cluster reduction, including reduction of initial clusters, and loss of final consonants not in a cluster. Interestingly, some dialects of AAE have differences in stress patterns for particular words, such as *police* and *Detroit*, which in this dialect receive stress on the first syllable. To some extent this might parallel CE differences in lexical stress.

What is very difficult to determine is whether any of these features are a result of contact with AAE in CE, or whether they developed independently. Many of these patterns could also have a source other than AAE, such as the influence of Spanish, which, for instance, seems to me to be the most probable source in the case of the stress patterns of CE. Wolfram (1974) found that among teenagers in New York City, both African-American and Puerto Rican-American teenagers deleted final consonants not in a cluster. Those of Puerto Rican ethnicity had more frequent deletion than the African-Americans, which Wolfram attributes partly to the influence of Puerto Rican Spanish. However, among the Puerto Rican teens, those with extensive black contacts had even *more* deletion than those with fewer black contacts (Wolfram 1974:129). This suggests that the presence of certain features in AAE might reinforce those patterns in CE, even if they do not originate in contact with AAE. It is also not known whether CE might in turn be influencing the phonology or prosody of local dialects of AAE in some way.

3.8   The influence on Chicano English phonology of California Anglo English

It is a particularly interesting question, from the point of view of sociolinguistic theory, to consider whether or not CE shows any features characteristic of the English spoken by the local Anglo community. There is unfortunately very limited research on Anglo speakers in California. Hinton et al. 1987, though, conducted an interesting diachronic study of possible sound changes in Northern California. They compared a 1986 sample of 22 young native Californian speakers with dialect materials from early in the century and from the 1950s. They looked at three sets of vowel variants: fronting of /o/ and /u/, lowering of /ɪ/ and /ɛ/, and lowering and backing of /æ/. The study found that all of these vowels had shifted in California since the early dialect data were collected. In addition, /æ/-raising, which they had not originally planned to study, emerged as a significant variable (see also Moonwomon 1991). Veatch (1991) confirms the strong presence of /u/-fronting for Anglos in Southern California.

One of the questions that initially motivated my research in this community was determining whether the features of CAE play any role in the Chicano English of Los Angeles. In one of the older studies, Peñalosa (1980) makes the following comment about the influence of regional dialects:

> Another interesting point concerns the model of standard English toward which Chicanos strive when they seek to throw off Chicano linguistic influences. There is evidence that they strive toward national norms, that is, network English, rather than toward a regional norm such as Texas English in its Southern or Midland varieties.   (1980:28)

Setting aside for the moment the fact that there seems to be a patronizing and negative tone involved in the reference to 'throwing off' the Chicano linguistic influences, the view represented here is one that is quite common in the literature, although the 'evidence' referred to is not actually provided in the book. In a later study, Veatch addresses this issue in the Southern California dialect area specifically. He claims that /æ/-raising is not a feature of CE, and suggests that 'Chicanos are not participating in the ongoing phonetic changes in the Anglo communities' (1991:245). However, the fact that he looked at only a single Chicano subject (a 30 year old working-class male) limits the strength of his claim.

Often, members of minority ethnic groups are treated as if they were part of a unified whole, in terms of culture, values and, most relevant here, speech patterns. In fact, a tremendous variation among individuals exists within any community; some of the differences within the group of Mexican-Americans in Los Angeles have already been discussed. Researchers may sometimes be influenced by a sense of the strong ethnic identity of Latinos, leading them to conclude that Latinos would wish to maintain their linguistic system as separate from that of majority Anglo speakers. Whether or not this view of Latino culture is accurate, the actual nature of the linguistic system is a separate matter which must be researched scientifically.

My own recordings of Anglo speakers in Los Angeles provide evidence of the variables mentioned in Hinton et al. (1987), with /u/-fronting being particularly salient. When I began listening to the tapes, it seemed to me that I could hear /u/-fronting and other variables among the Latino speakers as well. I used charts of vowels from several speakers to confirm my impression. When I was first investigating which areas of the vowel space were the sites of interesting variation in Chicano English, I had selected a subset of 15 speakers, including Spanish dominant speakers, bilinguals and both Anglo and Latino monolingual English speakers, and analyzed the following English vowels in their speech:[9]

/i/ as in *heat, meet*
/ɪ/ as in *bit, sit*
/ɛ/ as in *head, said*
/æ/ as in *hat, man*
/ɑ/ as in *hot, caught* (in most California Anglo dialects)
/o/ as in *hope, soap*
/ʊ/ as in *good, book*
/u/ as in *hoot, suit*

I have identified two of the back vowel phonemes as /u/ and /o/, though in fact these are both diphthongs (/uw/ and /ow/) in the California Anglo dialect, because they are so often realized without the glide in Chicano English.

The tapes from which these measurements come were made on a Sony TCM-5000 recorder with an external lavaliere microphone. The segments were digitized, cut and analyzed using the Computerized Speech Resource Environment software produced by Avaaz, Inc. As much as possible, I extracted the tokens of each vowel from passages of speech that occurred well into the interview, preferably during narrative passages, in order to access the most vernacular speech style. I used occurrences of the vowels that received primary or secondary stress, excluding any reduced or extremely rapid tokens in order to get a clear formant structure. I took measurements of the first and second formant frequencies (F1 and F2) for each vowel by using a small averaging window (approximately 15 ms) which I located in the nucleus of the vowel, avoiding any strictly transitional effects of the surrounding environments. From these measurements, vowel charts were produced showing the location of the individual vowel tokens within each speaker's overall vowel space, based on F1 and F2. The vowels on the charts were

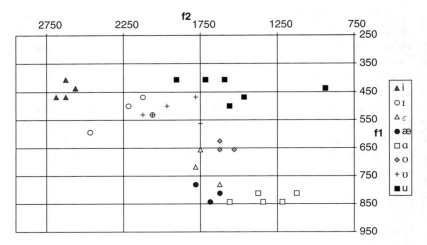

Figure 3.1   Helena: English vowel space

labeled with the IPA symbol for the phoneme that normally occurs in that lexical item in Inland Northern American English.

A clear representative speaker of what I have been referring to as California Anglo English is Helena, whose vowel space is shown in Figure 3.1. Helena is a 17 year old student at Westside Park, who lives in the same area as the Latino speakers, and comes from a similar background to many of them. Rather than having the trapezoidal space usually associated with the American English vowel system (Kent and Read 1992:24), Helena's vowels are organized into a parallelogram, with /u/ noticeably fronted; in addition, many tokens of /æ/ are backed almost into contact with /ɑ/.

Figure 3.2 shows the vowel space for Amanda, a 17 year old Latina speaker. Amanda's vowels occupy the same type of parallelogram formant space that distinguishes Helena. Both Amanda and Helena show several tokens of /u/ that appear to be much farther front than the location of the back of their vowel spaces (as marked by /ɑ/). In fact, for both these speakers many tokens of /u/ are at about the same F2 frequency as tokens of /æ/.

Even this one chart confirms that at least some of the Latino speakers appear to be taking part in sound changes that are observable in the California Anglo community. A number of other speakers patterned with Amanda in showing evidence of /u/-fronting and

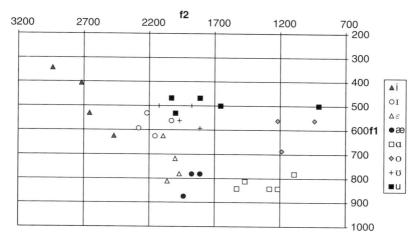

Figure 3.2 Amanda: English vowel space

possibly /æ/-backing. Though she does not appear to have /æ/-raising, others in the preliminary subset of speakers whose vowels I charted do clearly show this feature as well.[10] As will be discussed in Chapter 5, it is a somewhat striking result, with serious significance for sociolinguistic theory, to find that members of minority ethnic groups, in this case CE speakers, can and do participate in many of the same sound changes characteristic of the majority community in their geographic area. Two possible objections to this claim are: (a) that these Latino speakers actually speak California Anglo English rather than Chicano English, or (b) that the generalization holds only for a few speakers who are completely integrated into the Anglo community, and therefore are not really representative of the Latino community as a whole.

The first objection is fairly easy to disprove. All the speakers in my sample show features characteristic of Chicano English. Sylvia, for example, is a speaker who fronts /u/ very heavily, and is in my subjective opinion one of the more standard sounding speakers. Even listening to a random short section of her speech, however, I immediately noticed features characteristic of Chicano English (as discussed above), for example the substitution of stops for initial interdental fricatives in *they* [deɪ] and *there* [dɛɹ] or the use of a tense vowel in the morphological ending *-ing* in *embarrassing* [ɪmbɛɹəsin]. The sociolinguistic variables from California Anglo English are interspersed with these other variables, which the young adults in my sample use in constructing their identity as Latinos and Latinas.

Concerning the second possible objection, assimilation, there is some relevant prior research. Henderson (1995) looked at the distribution of the Philadelphia short *a* pattern among African-American speakers. The study found that middle-class African-Americans, who are ostensibly integrated into the white community in every respect, nonetheless do not show the characteristic Philadelphia *a* pattern. This result casts some initial doubt on the likelihood of integration as an explanation for /u/-fronting in Chicano English. Furthermore, the backgrounds of the speakers do not support the claim. Some of the speakers who front /u/ the most live in the Projects. This low income housing area is occupied almost completely by Latino families, and the speakers who live there would tend to have less rather than more contact with members of the Anglo community. In sum, the results of this preliminary analysis confirm that minority speakers do sometimes participate in sound changes characteristic of the majority community in their geographic area. More discussion of this issue, as well as a quantitative sociolinguistic study of several California sound changes that occur in CE, will be presented in Chapter 5.

4
Syntax and Semantics of Chicano English

This chapter provides a survey of the syntactic and semantic features of Chicano English as found in the community of speakers I studied as well as in other studies of the language of Mexican-Americans. It will focus on features which are not common to all dialects of English, though they may be shared by other non-standard dialects or they may be specifically characteristic of Chicano English. The question of contact with other dialects is an interesting one. As was shown in Chapter 3, Chicano English phonology shows possible evidence of contact with (a) the local California Anglo dialect (CAE); (b) African-American English (AAE); and (c) Spanish. We might expect influences from any of these in the areas of syntax and semantics as well. Though in some cases I have attributed the features to contact with AAE or Spanish, or to some other source, it should be noted that for many of them, multiple explanations are possible, and there might even be a convergence effect of more than one source.

Of course, not all of these features are used by all speakers of Chicano English. Many of them show some correlation with social features such as ethnicity, age or gender. As would be expected, non-standard features are most characteristic of the working-class variety of Chicano English, although some, like negative concord, occur frequently among middle-class speakers also. Any of these variables might be appropriate for a detailed sociolinguistic analysis. I present only a qualitative description of most of them here, but there is a larger-scale quantitative analysis of one of them, negative concord, in Chapter 6.

Part I: Syntactic features of Chicano English

4.1   Features characteristic of many non-standard dialects

To begin with, Chicano English exhibits certain non-standard syntactic features that are common to many non-standard varieties of English, including the local working-class varieties spoken by Anglos (and working-class Californians of other ethnicities). Like non-standard speakers from many diverse communities, Chicano English speakers may regularize agreement patterns, especially where the history of the English language has left irregular morphological patterns and forms. Like many other dialects, Chicano English shows variable lack of agreement in **3rd person singular** forms, as well as some alternation of **was/were**, shown in the following examples:

> *Everybody knew the Cowboys **was** gonna win again.* (Tony, 15)
>
> *Otherwise, she **don't** know Brenda.* (Rita, 17)
>
> ~~subjunctive~~ *(If) somebody else just **come** and take your life, you know.* (Avery, 16)
>
> *He **don't** want me to end up like my sister.* (Erica, 17)

Related to this feature are **regularization of the past tense** and other uses of **non-standard verb forms**. There was a very frequent use of **ain't**, which is included here also. These instances seemed to me to be quite typical of those found in other non-standard dialects of English:

> *It **ain't** okay, but...* (Jesus, 16)
>
> *My name **ain't** exciting either.* (Erica, 17)
>
> *It **spinned**.* (David, 17)
>
> *I haven't **wrote** in a long time.* (Amanda, 17)
>
> *Those were the um- most people that I **hanged** around with.* (Marina, 17)
>
> *I had like, three weeks that I had **came** out the hospital before I got shot.* (Avery, 16)

Chicano English also exhibits some **non-standard forms in the pronoun system**. I noticed particularly many non-standard reflexive forms, and reflexives are also the source of much variation in other dialects, such as AAE. In addition, I noticed several instances of speakers using a resumptive pronoun in a relative clause. Examples of non-standard pronoun use include the following:

*[They] have to start supporting **theirselves** at early ages.* (James, 18)

*Your mom and your dad will always think, 'he's a guy, he could take care of **hisself**'.* (Avery, 16)

*The guy that um, **that they knew he was doing it**.* (Avery, 16)

There is no particular reason to believe that any of the forms discussed so far come specifically from contact with other dialects (spoken by Anglos or African-Americans, for example) which also use them. They might have evolved from such contact, or from non-native varieties of English spoken by Spanish-dominant speakers. However, because they generally represent regularizations of some type, they also might have evolved independently.

4.2   Features characteristic of African-American English

There are also syntactic elements used by some speakers of Chicano English that are found mainly in AAE[1] and are not common in non-standard dialects spoken by Anglos or other groups. In contrast with the features listed above, some of the AAE-related features occurred only among the most 'vernacular' speakers. So little has been written about the history and evolution of Chicano English that it is difficult to know what role AAE may have played in the development of this dialect. Certainly, the amount of contact with African-American speakers varies from community to community, as well as among individuals, in Los Angeles. We would expect that the amount of contact might have linguistic effects. Wolfram (1974), for example, found that Puerto Rican speakers in New York who had many African-American contacts used habitual *be*, or had surface realizations of /θ/ as [f] (cf. also Zentella 1997). It is also clear that the influence of AAE, or at least the overlap between AAE and CE is much greater in the area of syntax than in the area of phonology.

A majority of the young speakers I interviewed claimed to have little contact with African-Americans. At the time of my fieldwork, tensions between Latino and African-American gangs were very high, and had spilled over into the general population to some degree. There were occasional speakers, such as Avery, who did have African-American friends in their networks, and this did seem to correlate, as one would expect, with a greater use of AAE features. Because these individuals were uncommon, I did not attempt to make a formal analysis of African-American contacts as an influence on linguistic patterns. Nonetheless, contact of particular speakers with AAE is not necessary in order for it to be the source for the features in this section. AAE may have influenced earlier stages of Chicano English; though I have not looked in detail at the social history of African-American and Latino contacts, it would be interesting to try to correlate this context with linguistic patterns for Los Angeles and other areas.

Many of the young speakers in the sample used **habitual *be***, one of the most notable features of AAE. I did not notice anything about the use of this form by Latino speakers that differed from what is known about patterns of use for this feature in AAE. Clearly, its distribution is related to social factors; for example, it was much more common among males than females. The following are some examples:

*The news **be** showing it too much.* (Jamie, 17)

*Me and my mom **be** praying in Spanish.* (Jorge, 18)

*My homeboys **be** jacking them.* (Chuck, 17)

Much less common than habitual *be*, but also occurring from time to time was the use of ***it*** (for *there*) as an empty subject pronoun:

***It's** four of us, there's two of them.* (Avery, 16)

*I'll try to do my part, and he'll do his part but, you know, **it's** like nothing I could do a hundred percent by myself.* (Ramon, 18)

Finally, the use of the perfective *had* in places where a simple past form would be found in standard varieties of English, especially as part of a narrative, is characteristic of some CE speakers.

*The cops **had** went to my house...* (Jorge, 18)

*Before we **had** fought, she had came up to see me and I told her I didn't say it.* (Veronica, 17)

In the last example, it is not clear whether the second *had* is of the same type, but in each case, *had* was used where in my dialect I would have expected a simple past, just as occurs in some varieties of AAE, particularly among pre-adolescent speakers (see Rickford and Théberge-Rafal 1996).

4.3 Features of ambiguous origin

I have included in this section features whose source is not immediately evident, and which might, in fact, have multiple sources. Perhaps this is most evident with **negative concord**, which is quite frequent in Chicano English. This syntactic feature may come from contact with AAE (in which case it actually belongs in the previous section) or other local non-standard dialects. However, since I did not find examples of some of the patterns that separate AAE negative concord from patterns of negative concord in other dialects, I did not group it with other features that more clearly represent the influence of AAE. Another possibility is that negative concord in Chicano English represents the influence of Spanish. Some evidence supporting this explanation is discussed in Chapter 6, but it is not conclusive. One does find this feature also among the non-native speakers whose first language is Spanish, as in this example from Rosana:

> I **didn't** have **no** self confidence. (Rosana, 56)

Finally, there is the possibility mentioned earlier that a convergence of different sources contributed to the presence of this feature in Chicano English, and this question may be a difficult one to resolve. For now, I will simply give a few illustrative examples:

> Things **ain't** gonna **never** change in L.A. **no** more. (Avery, 16)
>
> I **don't** think that **nobody** really knows anything. (Chuck, 17)
>
> **None** of the girls **don't** like her. (Amanda, 17)

Chapter 6 will present more detail on the different patterns of negative concord that I found among the Latino speakers, and provide a socio-linguistic analysis of how the variable correlates with social factors in the community.

Another feature that seems ambiguous to me is **subject-auxiliary inversion in embedded questions**. Here is an example from Wald (1984:25):

> ... then they asked them **where did they live**. (A.R., 12)

The context for this form was fairly infrequent, but there were a few examples of this among the CE speakers in my sample:

She was telling my aunt to tell them, you know, what, I mean, **what's the reason**? (David, 17)

And he told them **who was it**. (=*who it was*). (Avery, 16)

I don't know **what color are we**, *but it doesn't matter.* (Marina, 17)

I don't know **what's the deal with that**. (Christian, 18)

Note that in the first example, the second *tell* actually means 'ask' (see below).

This subject-auxiliary inversion pattern is found in AAE and other non-standard dialects (Wald 1984, Martin and Wolfram 1998). However, as Wald argues, there is also evidence to support its origins in contact with Spanish, since in embedded wh- questions in Spanish, the subject and verb or auxiliary would normally be inverted. For instance, in Spanish the second example (Avery's sentence) would require that the (empty) pronoun be dropped from the relative clause:

*Y   les   dijo   **quien   era***

and them (DATIVE) told who was (3RD SING)

In the third example, the pronoun would be optional, but if it occurred, it would be inverted with the verb:

*Yo no   sé   **de qué color somos (nosotros)**, pero da   igual.*

I   NEG know of what color are   (we),   but gives the-same (idiomatic)

Marina is a very fluent bilingual, which might add some support to this theory. On the other hand, this variable also occurs in other non-standard dialects, including AAE, so one of these might be a possible source, or the sources might converge to reinforce this feature in CE.

4.4   Features particular to Chicano English

Unlike the features discussed earlier, those in this section do not seem to have any clear parallels with other non-standard dialects. They fall into two basic categories: **modals** and **prepositions**. The modals are one of the few areas of Chicano English syntax where there has been some previous research; Wald (1984, 1993, 1996), has a series of articles on this topic also based on fieldwork conducted among Mexican-Americans in Los Angeles. In addition to those discussed by Wald, I have found other areas of interest among the modals as used by the CE speakers in the community that is the focus of this book.

Use of modals

To begin with, Wald describes the English modal system as being 'notorious for its historical restlessness' (1996:519), quite apart from contact with other languages, which I think provides an important context for looking at variation in modals. He discusses the use of **would** in *if*- clauses among his east LA speakers. In particular he focuses on an interaction of *would* with stative verbs in the present, which is usually disfavored in other dialects, as in the following example (Wald 1996:520):

> If **he'd be** here right now, he'd make me laugh. (F.R., 42)

Although I did not come across any examples of this type, it is a fairly rare construction, so its absence might be a result of the infrequency of the context. Wald also suggests that there might be a quantitative difference between CE and other dialects in the co-occurrence of *would* with *if*- clauses, a pattern which seems to be more frequent in CE. Although I have not formally assessed frequency, I found many examples of this combination among my speakers, as in the following:

> If I **woulda** been a gangster, I woulda been throwing signs up. (Reina, 17)

> If Thurman Thomas **wouldn't've** dropped those fumbles, then the Bills woulda won. (Avery, 16)

In Spanish, the same verb form (the pluperfect subjunctive) could be used for both clauses (Butt and Benjamin 1988:294). The Spanish translation would be:

Si	*Thurman*	*Thomas*	*no*	*hubiera*	*perdido*	*la*	*pelota,*	*los*
if	Thurman	Thomas	NEG	would-have	lost	the	ball,	the
Bills	*hubieran*		*ganado.*					
Bills	would-have		won					

The Spanish construction, then, might reinforce the frequency of this pattern in CE.

An interesting use of modals that I heard among many of my speakers (but have not seen mentioned in the literature) was the extension of the modal **could** to environments where the basic meaning was 'competence'; in this situation, standard varieties of English would generally use *can*. For example, most speakers of other English dialects would not be able to substitute *could* for *can* in the sentence *She can speak Swahili*, unless a different meaning was intended (something that involved a future scenario, not just present competence). But for most Chicano English speakers, *She could speak Swahili* used simply as a way of listing someone's talents is completely acceptable. Other examples from my group of speakers include:

> *He **could** talk, like, smart, y'know... he's like a straight-A student.* (David, 17)

> *I learned that people that are left handed **could** draw better than people who are right handed.* (James, 18)

> *Nobody believes that you **could** fix anything.* (Christian, 18)

This pattern was very widespread, more so than some of the other non-standard features.

As far as I know, this feature has not been documented for AAE. It also does not seem to have any relationship to Spanish syntactic patterns, unlike the use of *would*, since Spanish uses different tenses for the 'can' meaning and the 'could' meaning, paralleling the standard English usage. For ability, one would use the present tense *puede*, and for a hypothetical future event one would use the future conditional *podría*. It is not possible to use *podría* to indicate ability. It is also not a pattern that is found locally among the Anglos I interviewed. An informal poll of my students who are speakers of California Anglo English shows that most of them find such a usage ungrammatical, although it would not surprise me if this were to change in the future.

Use of prepositions

Of all the features that have been discussed in this section, the one that seems most clearly tied to Spanish and unlikely to come from any other dialect is the non-standard use of prepositions. Many speakers substituted alternate prepositions for those that would be expected in other varieties of English. Following are some examples of this phenomenon:

> ***For** my mom can understand. **For** she won't feel guilty.* (Jorge, 18)

> *We're really supposed to get out of here **on** June.* (Christian, 18)

*We all make mistakes **along** life.* (Hernan, 47)

*So they just pulled **on** the side of him, and they opened the door.* (Avery, 16)

*He was **in** a beer run.* (Rita, 17)

*How is it **over there**?* (=*in Philadelphia*) (Erica, 17)

*Some gangsters from Santa Monica stopped us, and they **got off** the car.* (Reina, 17)

For most of these, the tie to Spanish is clear. For example, when Christian says *on June* for *in June*, it reflects the fact that Spanish uses a single pronoun, *en*, for both *in* and *on* (which also applies to Rita's example). Similarly, Jorge's use of *for* to mean *so that* is probably triggered by the construction *para que* in Spanish, which means 'so that,' but would literally be translated as 'for that.' Most of the substitutions tended to vary somewhat by individual. The exception is *over there*, which was used by almost everyone. This may in fact be a different type of construction altogether, although it does parallel the Spanish term *allá* ('there, a long distance away'), as a deictic term for a place that is farther than *allí* (unmarked 'there').[2] However the phenomenon of preposition substitution, even if the specifics varied by individual, was common enough among different speakers to be counted as a 'feature' of Chicano English.

The fact that this pattern indicates the influence of Spanish is confirmed by the many examples of this type that I heard from the non-native speakers in the community, as in this comment from Rosana:

*Must have been **on** the fifth grade or so.* (Rosana, 56)

Also notable is the fact that the young speakers who produced the examples cited above are all bilingual, though Jorge is one of the least fluent Spanish speakers in the sample. It is possible that monolinguals in the community also have these usages and I just didn't happen to hear any, since they were quite infrequent even among the speakers who produced the above examples. But it may be that an alternative use of prepositions is one of the few features that in some sense distinguishes the bilinguals in the community from the monolinguals.[3]

This use of prepositions in a non-standard manner is quantitatively much less frequent among native speakers of CE than among non-native English learners. Yet it is just the type of feature that leads people to conclude that Chicano English is typical of people who 'haven't learned English yet.' What is striking to me is how *few* examples that clearly indicate Spanish influence there are among these features. Unlike the phonology of Chicano English, where Spanish influence was shown to be fairly prominent, in the area of syntax, the features that characterize Chicano English tend to be shared with (and possibly borrowed from) other dialects, or independent developments not attributable to Spanish.

Part II: Semantic/lexical features of Chicano English

In this section I will present some lexical items and discourse markers that occur in the Chicano English of the speakers I interviewed. I will also discuss some instances where the semantics of particular words differs from their use in other dialects of English. As with the other sections of this chapter, I do not claim this to be an exhaustive list. It is a sampling of items that I heard frequently, across speakers, and that are not common across other dialects of English, although again they may be shared with some other non-standard dialects. Since the speakers I interviewed were mostly quite young, and since slang is particularly characteristic of adolescents, it might be argued that the lexical items are more characteristic of teenagers than of Chicano English speakers. Nonetheless, many of them are not used by Anglo or African-American speakers of the same age, and undeniably these terms are part of the construction of identity that is so salient in this age group, in this case construction of a Latino or Latina identity. I include the terms with the same caveats given earlier, namely that not all speakers of Chicano English use them.

On the other hand, I have not included here the long list of terms associated with gang membership that I heard in the interviews. A number of these are covered in Chapter 2, within the discussion of gang culture. However, these terms are more clearly characteristic of a limited sub-group, and do not seem to have a wide enough applicability to be considered features of Chicano English in any broader sense.

4.5   General lexical items

In this section are a handful of lexical items that I heard across several speakers and that caught my attention as differing from other dialects of English with which I'm familiar.[4] For most of these lexical items, many of which would fall into the category of slang, the translation is fairly straightforward, so I will present them in list form with the word, its definition and some examples:

1. *fool*, meaning approximately the same thing as 'guy' (although in the last example, Avery is actually talking to a girl); not necessarily pejorative.

   Examples:

   *That's discouraging too, to some other **fool** that wants to do the same thing that I want to do.* (Chuck, 17)

   *I'm gonna go shoot at those **fools**, they dropped me!* (Avery, 16)

   *Man, **fool**, you could take out the bread out the oven!* (Avery, 16)

2. *kick it*, meaning 'to hang around', but also more generally 'to wait for a while'.

   Examples:

   *Nah, just **kick it**, do it tonight.* (Avery, 16)

   *If I get stopped [by police], I'll be **kickin' it** on the corner for an hour.* (Jamie, 17)

3. *talk to*, meaning 'to date'.

   Examples:

   *We started talking and then I didn't **talk to** him no more.* (Reina, 17)

   *I **talk to** his sister.* (Sancho, 19)

4. *clown*, meaning 'to tease'.

   Example:

   *They **clown me** for shit like that.* (Chuck, 17)

5. *from somewhere*, meaning 'in a gang'.

   Examples:

   *And I told him I **wasn't from anywhere**.* (Reina, 17)

   *I'm **not from nowhere**.* (Chuck, 17)

6. *American*, meaning 'European-American or white'.

    Examples:

    *It wasn't the **American** lady, it was the other one.* (Magda, 19)

    *Are you **American**?* [to me]. (Marina, 17)

7. *some*, meaning 'this' in its colloquial use as an indefinite determiner.

    Examples:

    *I was running towards the back to open **some** little gate.* (Avery, 16)

    *I'm seeing **some** girl; she's white, also.* (Salvador, 18)

8. *tell*, meaning 'ask'.

    Examples:

    *If I tell her to jump up, she'll **tell** me how high.* (Avery, 16)

    *She was telling my aunt to **tell** them, you know, what, I mean, what's the reason?* (David, 17)

    *It depends on what you **tell** me.* (In response to 'Can you answer questions in Spanish?') (Chuck, 17)

9. *barely*, meaning 'just recently'.

    Examples:

    *He just **barely** got a job you know back with his father.* (Chuck, 17)

    *I just **barely** checked in.* (He has been there only 3 weeks)   (Jesus, 16)

    *They **barely** graduated from high school.* (Hernan, 47)

Interestingly, the majority of these terms do not have any particular relationship to the semantics of Spanish, as far as I can tell. The first four seem to be the usual type of slang found, particularly among young people, in all communities. The expression *to be from somewhere* is a euphemism of sorts, a vague generalization used to stand in for the more direct *gang member*. Though I have generally not listed gang-related vocabulary, this term is used by many people in the community to refer to gang members, and is at a more general, less specialized level than the actual gang terms. This and the expression *not a gang member but he knows them*, which is discussed in Chapter 2, seem to be related in terms of their vaguely euphemistic qualities. The use of *American* for white is one of the few terms that might in fact be related to Spanish, since Mexican nationals tend to use the word *Americanos to* mean white people (and seldom for African-Americans or Latinos born in the USA). On the other hand the use of *some* where other dialects (in an informal style) would use *this* does not appear to have any source in Spanish, where the two words have quite different translations. Again this seems like a fairly natural semantic extension that does not require a complicated explanation, and it may be that this usage can be found in the Anglo population also, although I did not recognize it, and to me as a native Californian, these sentences sound odd.

The only other terms on this list where I can see a possible connection to Spanish are the use of *tell* for *ask* and the specialized use of *barely* to mean 'just recently'. Wald (1984) noted the use of *tell* for *ask* among his east LA Chicano speakers. In a later article (Wald 1996) he explains this as coming from the Spanish verb *decir*, which according to him can mean 'say,' 'tell' or 'ask.' My own intuitions as a speaker of Spanish (confirmed by the Langenscheidt New Standard Spanish Dictionary 1988) are that *decir* cannot, in fact, mean 'ask,' only 'say' or 'tell.' My hypothesis about the origins of this feature is that in Spanish, it is perfectly acceptable to say *Me dijo que si quería comer* (literally 'He said/told me if I wanted to eat'). I think it is acceptable (informally) in some dialects of English to say *He said did I want to eat*, but *He told me did I want to eat* is more marginal, for me at least. Since the Spanish verb *decir* is ambiguous between 'say' and 'tell,' it may be that in translating sentences with embedded questions, non-native speakers sometimes pick the less acceptable alternative in English, with *tell*, and that this is how the use of *tell* to mean *ask* came about, first with embedded questions, and later in other contexts.

The other term that might have a source in Spanish is the extension of *barely* to mean 'just recently'. García first documented this use in 1984, for speakers from east LA.[5] There is some overlap here with the use of *barely* in other dialects. For example, in many dialects (including my own) one can say:

Don't leave, you barely got here!

or

He barely started working here, so how could he know that?

However, completely ungrammatical in my dialect is the example from Chuck (in example 9 above), or the following, said to me by a Latino technician who came to service our home treadmill:

These were expensive when they barely came out.

The 'overlapping' cases cited above, which are grammatical in both dialects and mean something along the lines of 'only recently,' suggest that the semantics of this form might have been extended quite naturally, a fairly unremarkable language change, without there needing to be any influence from Spanish. However, it is also true that the Spanish adverbial form *apenas* can mean (a) that something almost did not happen but then it did (the main use of *barely* in many English dialects), or (b) that something happened recently (as in the overlapping cases, and also the examples that extend this usage in Chicano English). So while Spanish influence need not be the explanation here, it is one possibility.

There were also two items which were quite infrequent, but which showed unequivocally the effect of contact with Spanish. The first is the use of the term *brothers* to mean 'brothers and sisters' or 'siblings,' as in:

*My **brothers** don't want to I- don't want me to leave because they love the baby.*   (Rita, 17; she has one sister and two brothers, who all help her with the baby)

*To my **brothers** I usually talk English.*   (Marta, 16; she has four sisters and one brother)

This is a direct translation from the Spanish kinship term *hermanos* (grammatically the male plural, like *brothers*) which can refer either to a group of male siblings or a group of brothers and sisters.

I also heard a Spanish (more specifically, Mexican Spanish) discourse marker, *ey*, used occasionally in English, generally by men, as in:

*If a girl's pretty you know and she feels the same for me, **ey**, I got it right there.*   (Avery, 16)

As with most discourse markers, it is difficult to give an exact translation for this term, but I might render it as *yeah*, more or less. When talking with speakers in Spanish, they would often backchannel with this term if I said something they agreed with. I would distinguish this from a type of codeswitching, since Avery, for example, did not insert any other Spanish words into his English conversation, and did not use codeswitching as a style of discourse when talking with me.

It should be noted that there were also, of course, examples of terms in the Spanish dialect of my speakers which showed the influence of English. There is a separate body of research on the Spanish spoken in the USA (cf., for example, Silva-Corvalán 1994), and on integrated borrowings into Spanish of words from English. My focus here is on Chicano English, so I will not go into detail on this topic. But I do want to mention a couple of examples that caught my attention. First of all, a number of speakers used the term *hablando con* ('talking to') to mean 'dating' when speaking Spanish, a clear translation of this expression and its particular meaning in English, discussed earlier. Also, Erica repeatedly ended her sentences in Spanish with *o lo que sea*, the literal translation of 'or whatever.' This is a common formula for ending sentences in many dialects of English, especially among younger speakers, and not peculiar to Chicano English. But its Spanish translation is not generally used in this way by monolingual Spanish speakers.

4.6   Use of *like*, *be like*, and *be all*

Just as Chicano English phonology includes elements borrowed from the matrix dialect, California Anglo English, there are also discourse markers and other semantic constructions that appear to come from contact with this dialect. I discuss *like*, *be like*, and *be all* as features of Chicano English because although these items, which originated in California, have now spread across the country and even overseas (Macaulay 2001), their presence in Chicano English is not a given. It would not be surprising if Latino speakers, particularly those who do not want to be seen as assimilating to the dominant culture, specifically rejected these features, to the point where they would be found only among the most assimilated members of the community, in the middle class, and so on. While there may well be some quantitative correlation between the frequency of the discourse marker *like* and social factors (such as middle-class status), all of these forms were found across the entire group of speakers.

Perhaps no feature is so stereotypically associated with the speech of young adults, particularly Californians, as the discourse marker *like* (cf. Fought forthcoming). It is interesting that *like* turns up with very high frequency among Chicano English speakers, given that it is both stigmatized and associated with the Anglo community. A small number of characteristic examples are given below:

*He could talk, **like**, smart, y'know, **like**, he's **like** a straight-A student.* (David, 17)

*They go by us, and there were **like** two of em.* (Avery, 16)

*I don't know, it's **like**, the whole, the whole **like**, idea for everybody around here is that **like** you know, if you go fuck around and read and education and this and that it's **like**, it's just, you're not supposed to do it, it's **like**, you know.* (Chuck, 17)

Related, but different in function, is the use of *be like* as a quotative. Again, most of the speakers used this form, and for many of them it appeared to be the primary way of introducing quoted speech. A few examples are:

***She's like**, 'No, you leave the house when you get married.'* (Marta, 16)

*I **was like**, 'Don't worry about it man.'* (Avery, 16)

The other somewhat marked quotative that the Chicano English speakers used was *be all.* It had been suggested to me informally by a colleague that Latino speakers used *be like*, but only Anglo speakers would use *be all*. However, I did not find this to be the case. Although *be all* was much less frequent than *be like* for introducing speech, a number of speakers used it, as in these examples:

***He's all**, you know, what's your name?* (Christian, 18)

***He's all**, 'I'm working for you. Everything I have is for you.'* (Erica, 17)

*I **was all**, 'No, I'm not giving you the keys to my car.'* (David, 17)

*I **was all**, 'Am I going to be all right?'* (Chuck, 17)

The speakers from whom these examples come cover a wide spectrum in social categories. Some are from working-class or low income backgrounds (Marta, Christian), some are gang members (Erica, Avery), and both male and female speakers are represented.

In general, I think the degree to which the dialects associated with minority ethnic groups are permeable to contact with Anglo varieties has been underestimated. As will be discussed more in Chapter 5, there has been a tendency in the field of sociolinguistics to view ethnic minority communities as resisting local sound changes and other features of Anglo dialects. The vowel charts in Chapter 3 demonstrated that the variety of Chicano English being discussed here is a *California* variety, one that shows evidence of California sound changes occurring in other local groups. Similarly, the use of discourse markers and quotatives associated with California also reinforces this picture of Chicano English in Los Angeles as a *Californian* dialect of English.

As was true also of the syntactic elements discussed earlier, very few of the lexical items or expressions presented here reflect unequivocally the influence of Spanish. I am putting some emphasis on the lack of Spanish sources for many Chicano English patterns because of the myth I discussed in the Introduction, that this dialect is simply English influenced by the mistakes of speakers whose first language is Spanish. Not only is this not true for individuals; it is not true of the dialect as a whole. Undeniably in its phonology, and occasionally in other components of the grammar, Chicano English does contain influence from Spanish. It is a dialect born in a bilingual community and retains the evidence of that contact. However, it is unquestionably an autonomous dialect now, separate from Spanish, and as such shows the kinds of spontaneous developments and language changes that affect all living dialects.

Part III: The older generation of speakers

As with phonology, there are areas of the syntax and semantics of CE that are slightly different for the older generation of speakers. Some of the older speakers exhibit features indicative of transfer from Spanish that one rarely finds among the younger generation; often, these transfers are somewhat surprising because they occur in speakers who may sound very standard otherwise and have fewer phonological or syntactic markers of CE than others. A good example is Fernanda, age 53, whose dialect is very close to the local Anglo standard. Unlike some of the other speakers, I cannot imagine anyone mistaking her for a non-native speaker of English. I classify her as a CE speaker because she does have some features consistent with CE phonology, such as some unreduced high vowels (she often says [bikəz] for *because*) and, variably, lack of offglides with /ij/, but (at least in the interview) she does not use negative concord, non-standard verb forms and so forth. She does use a tremendous amount of creaky voice, which is a feature that apparently entered CE from contact with the Anglo community (see Chapter 3).

Despite the overall standardness of her dialect, Fernanda has certain very marked constructions that represent borrowings from Spanish. For example, she says:

*My father was always very strict in **the way how** his girls were dressed.*

The boldfaced portion, which sounds odd in English, is a direct translation of the Spanish construction *la manera como*, which would be used in this context. She used this expression several times. Later, she commented about her husband:

*He **picks up** weight.*

I realized from the context (his hobbies) that this meant her husband worked out with weights at the gym, in other words, that he *lifts* weight. In Spanish, there is a single word *levantar*, which can mean 'lift' or 'pick up,' and in this context, Fernanda inserted the wrong one of the two for standard English. Again, while Fernanda is bilingual, there is no justification for classifying her as Spanish dominant. She was born in the USA, and her English is completely fluent and close to a standard variety.

Joaquín, age 45, exhibits many more features of CE than Fernanda, but is also a middle-class speaker, completely fluent (perhaps dominant) in English. He used some similar constructions, such as the following:

*The mothers would **take out** the sticker.*

The intended meaning here is that they would *take off* the sticker. It seems to be a hallmark of CE in the older speakers that some of these direct translations come through in an idiosyncratic way. There was almost no overlap between the non-standard grammatical constructions that occurred across the different older speakers. Though they were infrequent overall, these constructions were particularly noticeable in the context of their otherwise fairly standard varieties. For the younger speakers, there was a core group of features reflecting Spanish influence (non-standard prepositions, *barely*, *brothers*) that were used across many speakers. For the older speakers, their 'translations' were more idiosyncratic. Of course the highest number of these translation type mistakes occurred among the non-native speakers. I have not attempted to summarize the syntactic deviations of non-native English speakers specifically here, because there are too many of them and they vary too much from speaker to speaker for such an analysis to contribute anything of substance to the understanding of CE. Nonetheless, the origin of some of the CE syntactic and semantic features in non-native English is evident.

5
Sociolinguistics of Chicano English I: Phonetic Variation

5.1 Introduction

In Chapter 3, I presented an overview of the Chicano English (CE) phonological system. A preliminary comparison of the vowel systems of a California Anglo English (CAE) speaker and a Chicano English speaker, revealed evidence of /u/-fronting, a sound change taking place in the local Anglo community of Southern California. In this chapter, I will explore the distribution of this sociolinguistic variable in more detail, as well as looking at two other local variables, /æ/-backing and /æ/-raising.

The bulk of general sociolinguistic research on sound change in the United States has focused on majority communities, often on speakers of Anglo ethnicity in large urban settings. The studies that have been done in minority ethnic communities (for example, in African-American communities) have often focused on linguistic elements that are distinctive of the speech of the ethnic group in question; some examples include grammatical constructions such as habitual *be* or copula deletion in African-American English, or codeswitching in bilingual Latino communities. There are almost no studies done in ethnic minority communities with a general focus on sound change (see Fought 2002).

The discovery that there is /u/-fronting, a variable clearly associated with sound change in the Anglo community, among Chicano English speakers is a significant finding in terms of sociolinguistic theory. Sociolinguistic studies focusing on Anglos (but incorporating more than one ethnic group) have often reported that minority ethnic groups do not participate in the local sound changes affecting Anglo speakers (Labov 1966; Labov and Harris 1986; Bailey and Maynor 1987). Even though sound change within ethnic minority communities has rarely been studied, sociolinguists have tended to generalize from a relatively small group of studies such as those mentioned above to conclude that speakers in these communities *never* participate in the sound changes found among local Anglos. For example, Labov (2001) makes the following claim:

> But for those children who are integral members of a sub-community that American society defines as 'non-white' – Black, Hispanic, or native American – the result is quite different. No matter how frequently they are exposed to the local vernacular, the new patterns of regional sound change do not surface in their speech. On the deeper levels of syntax and semantics, the African American community is carried ever further away on a separate current of grammatical change, and a very sizeable fraction of the Hispanic speakers move with them.   (2001:506)

The field of sociolinguistics is a relatively young one, and it is worth emphasizing the danger inherent in generalizing about 'non-white' (a term I find unscientific when used in this manner) ethnic groups, until more information is collected.[1] We know almost nothing about the English of Native American groups, for example, although Wolfram and Dannenberg's (1999) study of the Lumbee raises intriguing possibilities. The studies that Labov cites to support his claims were all conducted in African-American communities. Nowhere in the discussion does he cite a single reference on Hispanics/Latinos or Native Americans to support these sweeping generalizations. Because this is my area of specialty, I keep a very close eye on articles relating to the language of Latinos, and I know of none that might back up the conclusion about grammatical change found in the last sentence of the citation.

I have heard the opinion that members of ethnic minority communities don't participate in Anglo sound changes expressed informally to me by numerous colleagues, and repeated in the sociolinguistic literature. In fact, this idea seems to have become a part of the sociolinguistic canon, as its appearance in Labov (2001) suggests, even though it involves a generalization from a handful of studies across the tremendous variety of ethnic minorities that one finds in the USA. Why should we expect results from Labov and Harris' (1986) study of African-Americans in Philadelphia to apply, for example, to a Latino community in a rural area of the Southwest? This is particularly questionable when one considers that there *are* studies which show members of minority communities participating in sound changes characteristic of local Anglo speakers. One such study is Poplack (1978), very relevant here because it also focused on a bilingual Latino community, Puerto Rican Americans in Philadelphia. Fought (1997), which presents a preliminary study of one of the variables discussed in this chapter, is another example. The Wolfram and Dannenberg (1999) study of the Lumbee shows that they have certain phonological variables typical of the local Anglo community, including the fronting of [ow].

In the case of the Chicano English community in Los Angeles, I did, as discussed in Chapter 3, find evidence of local sound changes. At first I was somewhat surprised to find /u/-fronting among young Latino speakers, since I, like many others, had assimilated the generalization mentioned above. However, in listening to my tapes of certain speakers, I realized that I could clearly hear elements typical of the Southern California Anglo dialect. Some of the girls had stretches of the interview in which one might say that they sounded like 'Valley Girls,'[2] while clearly exhibiting features characteristic of Chicano English at the same time. When one thinks about how identity is constructed and practiced, socially and linguistically, this pattern makes perfect sense. The identities of these young speakers are complex and constituted from many elements, so it is not at all surprising that in speaking they would draw on varied sets of linguistic norms. In this chapter I will explore the patterns associated with some phonetic variables in Chicano English that are also found among Southern California Anglos.

An important issue to consider is whether the social factors as traditionally used and defined in studies of majority sound change (such as age, sex and social class) are sufficient for an explanation of sociolinguistic variation in this community. As discussed in Chapter 2, a number of non-traditional social categories, including some related to the sub-culture of gang membership, were relevant to the speakers in this community. All these factors, as well as the salient variable of whether or not the speakers are bilingual, will be taken into account in the analysis of the sociolinguistic variables.

5.2   Measuring /u/-fronting

The vowel periphery

Those vowels that are at the extremes of the vowel space have an important role in sound change and particularly in chain shifts (Labov 1994:32). Several of the major sound changes that appear to be in progress in California involve peripheral vowels, including the fronting of /u/, and the backing and lowering of /æ/ (Hinton et al. 1987). In addition, the pattern of /æ/-raising mentioned earlier appears to be significant in the Chicano English community. Therefore, I decided to begin my phonological analysis with four peripheral vowels in English: /i/, /u/, /æ/ and /ɑ/. This group includes the vowels that have been discussed in terms of possible sound changes and sociolinguistic variation. In addition, I have included /i/, which is fairly stable and subject to a minimum of variation in English (Kent and Read 1992:91) and so might be useful in normalizing data from different speakers. It will also be helpful to include a mean value for /ɑ/ as part of the normalization (see the discussion below). I measured and graphed eight to eleven tokens of each vowel initially, using the methods described in Chapter 3, and later added approximately four to eight tokens for /æ/ and /u/, the vowels most likely to show sociolinguistic variation.

Evidence of /u/-fronting in Chicano English

As was discussed earlier, some Chicano English speakers produce fronted /u/ tokens, while others do not. Of course, the decision as to whether a particular token of /u/ is fronted can be ambiguous. To begin with, there is a transitional effect of coronals that causes /u/ after a coronal to begin with a slightly higher F2 (that is, more fronted) than after other types of segments (Kent and Read 1992:117) However, the degree of fronting in California is well beyond the level of phonetic influence from a preceding segment, with the formants taken from the nuclei of some /u/ tokens even straying into the area of /i/. Often, there was an initial fronting effect of a coronal but the vowel quickly stabilized at a lower F2, and I took measurements from the lower, stable part of the nucleus. Setting aside the spectrographic measurements, it was also possible to hear a fronting effect in the tokens with relatively high F2s, but I used my own auditory judgments only to check and confirm the more precise measurements of the spectrogram. Rather than labeling any particular token as fronted, I decided to distribute them on a vowel chart for each speaker, based on the spectrographic measurements, and allow the arrangement of /u/ tokens relative to the speaker's other vowels to guide the analysis.

While I will not present the details here, a study of the phonetic contexts for /u/-fronting clearly showed the preceding environment to be the most important conditioning element. Though there were occasional tokens of fronted /u/ in other contexts, the great majority occurred after coronals, particularly after alveolar stops, palatal fricatives and affricates. Generally, the most frequent environment for the phoneme /u/ in English is after an alveolar stop, due to common lexical items like *do, too, two*, etc. Having determined that alveolar stops provided the most favorable environment for fronting (other than the relatively infrequent palatal fricatives and affricates), I added more tokens of this type for each speaker to increase the data set.[3]

A comparison of two individual speakers can be used to illustrate the extremes of variation in the location of /u/ on the F2 axis. Ramon (Figure 5.1) shows a high level of /u/-fronting, while Avery (Figure 5.2) shows no significant fronting at all. Both have the same number of /u/ tokens after alveolar stops, the most favored environment for fronting. But while some of Ramon's tokens are so far front as to overlap with his /i/ space, all of Avery's tokens remain well back, none of them overlapping with /æ/ in F2 space, and further back on average than /ɑ/. Even from a quick visual analysis it is evident that the F2 of /u/ can vary significantly among the speakers in this community, suggesting that a quantitative sociolinguistic analysis of this variable is worth doing.

Normalization and statistical assessment of variation in /u/-fronting

In order to compare the degree of /u/-fronting across speakers, it is necessary to normalize the raw data in such a way that differences due

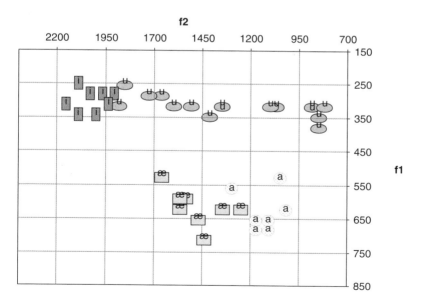

Figure 5.1 Ramon: English vowels

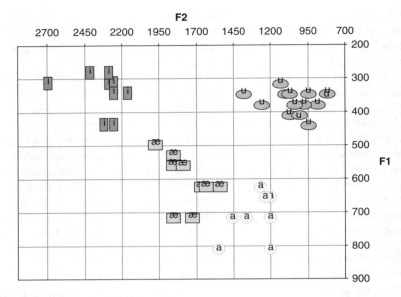

Figure 5.2   Avery: English vowels

to physiological variatíon, particularly vocal tract size, are minimized or eliminated. The largest effect of vocal tract size can be seen when speakers are sorted by sex. For instance, the women in my study had a mean F2 frequency of 2601 Hz for /i/, with a standard deviation of 216 Hz. The mean /i/ F2 for the men was 2157 Hz with a standard deviation of 154. In order to look at /u/-fronting, the data must be organized in such a way that /u/ tokens are judged for frontness in relation to the speaker's own vowel space, and that comparisons across speakers are based on such relationships rather than on absolute frequencies.

As mentioned earlier, the high front vowel /i/ is subject to less social variation across speakers than some of the other vowels, so we might expect differences in the location of /i/ to correspond to physiological differences. I confirmed that this was true for my particular group of speakers by separating them according to gender. This narrowed the variation in /i/ dramatically. (The standard deviation of F2 for the sample, for example, was reduced by about 50 percent for both the women and the men, when they were separated.) In addition, most speakers had /i/'s that were relatively tightly clustered in comparison with their other vowels. To some degree the same was true of /ɑ/, which also emerged as a fairly stable vowel in Chicano English, certainly showing much less variation across speakers than /u/ or /æ/. The /u/-fronting variable involves both closeness to /i/ and frontness relative to /ɑ/. These measures can be used together for greater accuracy in the normalization, and proportions (rather than differences) are the appropriate measure where the goal is normalization for speakers whose vocal tract size varies. Only the F2 of the vowels was analyzed, since the F1 varied within a much narrower range and did not appear to affect fronting in any significant way. For each speaker, the mean F2 values for /i/ and /ɑ/ vowels were calculated: ī and ā. Then the F2 for each token of /u/ for that speaker was divided by the mean value for /i/, yielding a set of ratios û representing the closeness of each /u/ token to the /i/ space proportionally within that speaker's vowel system:

$$\hat{u} = u / \bar{\imath}$$

where u = {set of /u/ F2 values for this speaker} and ī = the mean F2 value of /i/ for this speaker.

The higher the value, the greater the proximity of that token to the mean /i/. In the same fashion, the F2 value for each token of /u/ for that speaker was divided by the mean F2 value of /ɑ/, yielding a set of ratios ù representing the position (that is, frontness) of each /u/ token relative to the /ɑ/ space within that speaker's vowel system:

$$\grave{u} = u / \bar{a}$$

where u = {set of /u/ F2 values for this speaker} and ā = the mean F2 value of /ɑ/ for this speaker.

A value greater than one would indicate that a particular token was farther front than the mean /ɑ/. A value less than one would indicate that the token fell behind the mean of the /ɑ/ space. These sets of values represent the frontness of the /u/ tokens normalized for the size of the particular speaker's vowel space, and also preserve the variance among tokens which can later be analyzed separately. Using the two sets of values together increases the reliability of the normalization, since two different dimensions of the speaker's vowel space are being taken into account.

I decided to focus only on the most favorable contexts for fronting: preceding alveolar stops, palatal fricatives or affricates, since /u/-fronting was relatively uncommon in other environments, and in any case, the favoring environments were also the most frequent by far, as discussed earlier. I took the mean of the set of normalized values for each speaker in just these contexts, one mean for u–i closeness, and one for u–ɑ position. Figure 5.3 presents these values graphed against each other for 34 of the speakers in the study. It is clear from looking at the chart that there is a correlation between the two fronting measures, which is confirmed statistically: the Pearson correlation coefficient is .78, p < .001. There is also significant variation in the use of this variable across speakers in the community. I have included two Anglo speakers on the chart (Helena and Richard, in italics) to serve as reference points for /u/-fronting in the majority community, although their values were of course not included in the statistical analysis. The speakers who appear in the upper right quadrant of the graph are those who front /u/ the most. Those in the lower left quadrant front the least. The distribution generally coincides well with my own auditory evaluation of which speakers seemed to front /u/.

5.3   Social categories, identity and /u/-fronting in Chicano English

Figure 5.4 shows the same /u/-fronting chart as Figure 5.3, with the speakers labeled for social class. (The method for assigning social class was discussed in Chapter 2.) The chart shows a correlation between /u/-fronting and social class, with a tendency for the middle-class speakers

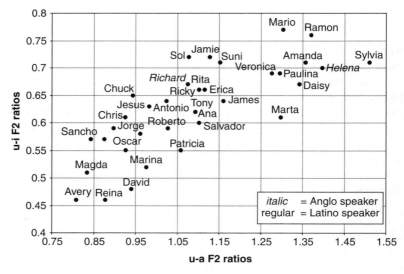

Figure 5.3   Degree of /u/-fronting for all speakers

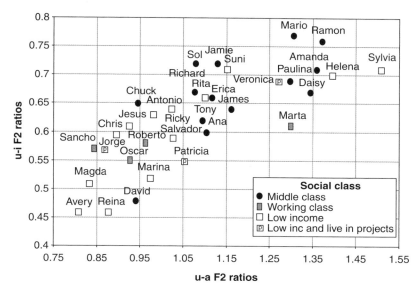

Figure 5.4   Degree of /u/-fronting by social class

to fall at the higher-fronting end, and the working-class and low income speakers to fall at the opposite end of the chart. A *t*-test of the means for middle-class versus working-class and low income speakers meets the .05 significance level for both /u/-fronting measures, suggesting that the difference is significant, if just barely. But a look at Figure 5.4 reveals that some speakers strongly contradict this pattern. Why, for example, are Sylvia and Veronica heavy /u/-fronters, given that they fall at the lowest part of the socioeconomic scale? What are middle-class speakers like David and Chuck doing in the group that fronts the least?

Looking at the social factor of gang status explains some of this variation with respect to the correlation of the variable with social class. As was discussed in Chapter 2, for the young adults in this study, gang membership is a salient social category, both for individuals who are gang members or otherwise affiliated with the gang, and for those who choose very definitely not to be involved with gangs in any way. Figure 5.5 shows the relationship of gang status to /u/-fronting. The pattern is in some ways reminiscent of that which was seen for social class. Gang members and those affiliated with the gang are found in the lowest part of the chart, while the highest /u/-fronting values occur mainly in people who have no gang affiliation (including the taggers); this difference is significant at the .001 level (in *t*-tests of both the u–i and u–ɑ measures). Once again, however, there are some individuals who seem to be exceptions. Amanda, a Culver City gang member, has very high /u/-fronting, while Roberto, who has no connection to the gang, shows very low values.

There are four speakers whose status with respect to gang membership is not completely clear. Rita and Marina are *moms* who are still technic-ally gang members, but who participate less in gang activities since the births of their children. James was a CC gang member until his family moved to a different area of Los Angeles for 2 years after James finished junior high. On his return, he had lost touch with his friends and, as he put it, 'wasn't into that [gang activities] anymore.' Mario represents the exceptional case of an individual who decided to leave against the will of the gang. This was a frightening process during which he was unable to return to his house for some time and felt constantly in fear for his life, but he did finally succeed in getting out, and now works as a paralegal.

These four speakers are spread across the range of values for /u/-fronting, which makes sense given their different histories. Mario, who would be expected to have the strongest affective dissociation from the gang, does the most fronting. James, who left the gang in a much more passive fashion, is the next highest fronter. When I spoke with him, his affective distance from the gang was less pronounced than that of Mario. Nonetheless, both Mario and James clearly indicated that they did not consider themselves gang members. In a dichotomous system of classification, they both belong with the non-gang group.

The role of gang affiliation in the identities of the two women is more difficult to evaluate. Rita's fronting level is similar to that of James, while Marina's is somewhat lower. Both Rita and Marina specifically mentioned to me in their interviews that their lives had changed since having a baby. Rita expressed it in terms of not going out as much as she used to. Marina said that she didn't want her kids to behave the way she had, missing school, etc. But neither of them experienced a clear break with the gang; their dissociation is a slower process begun over the last few years (Marina's baby is 2, and Rita's is 7 months). For now, I will consider them both gang-affiliated.

One possible difference between these two women is their degree of identification with the group of *moms*. Marina told me she had 'no friends,' and when I asked specifically if she had friends among the *moms*, she said, 'Yes, but it's like "hi" and "bye".' Rita appears to be more closely identified with this group, as can be seen from the following exchange:

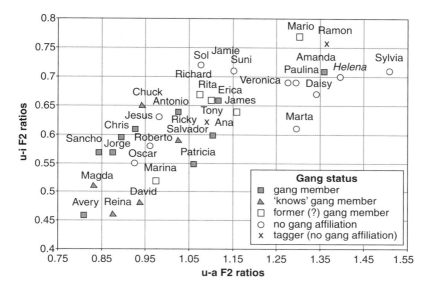

Figure 5.5   Degree of /u/-fronting by gang status

CF: Are most of your friends Mexican too?

Rita: Yeah. There's only – there's only one black girl that takes her kid, and … and one, um, Belize? The rest are Mexican.

Even though I asked generally about friendships and not specifically about the *moms*, Rita answers with reference to this group. At first it seems possible from the wording of the example that Rita knows just 'the black girl' from the moms, and the others from other contexts. But I happened to know that the girl from Belize is also one of the moms. Rita's identity as a mom may influence the strength of her gang affiliation.

In sum, Figure 5.5 shows a strong relationship between gang status and /u/-fronting, with gang-affiliated people fronting less than other speakers. But the exceptions noted above (for example, Amanda) remain.

5.4   Interacting social factors and the role of gender

The pattern of /u/-fronting among Chicano English speakers with respect to social factors so far has shown two correlations, one moderate and one quite strong, but neither of these factors has been able to explain the distribution of /u/-fronting without there being clear exceptions. Furthermore, the anomalous individuals were different for each social factor, in contrast with what one would expect if certain speakers were exceptional in some way, for example with respect to the normalization. Several studies of sound change, such as Eckert (1989) and Labov (1990), have stressed the importance of looking for interactions among variables. From the perspective of language and identity, this is also an important concept. If we view speakers as constructing their identities in a complex and layered fashion, rather than focusing on isolated elements such as social class, we obtain a more realistic picture of how linguistic variation functions in the performance of identity. It is crucial to explore the use of /u/-fronting as it relates to the construction of complex identities involving combinations of various social factors.

One of these factors will be gender, which, though it has not yet been discussed here, might be expected to play an important role, particularly given the nuances of gender identity in the Chicano community that were discussed in Chapter 2. I began by charting /u/-fronting by women and men separately. Figure 5.6 shows the degree of /u/-fronting for women, labeled to show both their gang status and their social class. Figure 5.7 shows the same factors for /u/-fronting by the men. On both charts, the speakers who *know* gang members are labeled gang-affiliated, and taggers, as discussed in Chapter 2, are included with the non-gang group. Working-class and low income speakers were combined in the working-class category, since this distinction had no statistical significance.[4]

As can be seen in Figure 5.6, for women non-gang affiliation is the strongest social variable affecting fronting. Those women who have no involvement with the gang at all appear in the upper right quadrant of the chart; a possible exception is Sol, who has a very high ratio for only one of the measures, but can clearly be heard to front /u/. Interestingly, Sylvia shows an even higher degree of fronting than Helena, the Anglo speaker. Many of these women were from lower socioeconomic groups, a factor which in Figure 5.4 appeared to have a negative effect on fronting generally. Veronica, for instance, lives in the Projects, but the rejection of the gang as an element in her identity overrides social class in her linguistic behavior. For the women as a group, social class was not a significant determiner of /u/-fronting (it did not reach the .05 level), while gang status showed a highly significant correlation at $p < .007$.

Social class status does play a secondary role among the women, however. Appearing at the top of the chart along with the non-gang-affiliated women are Erica and Amanda, both gang members. What sets them apart from the other gang-affiliated women is social class; both these speakers are from middle-class backgrounds. Gang members with

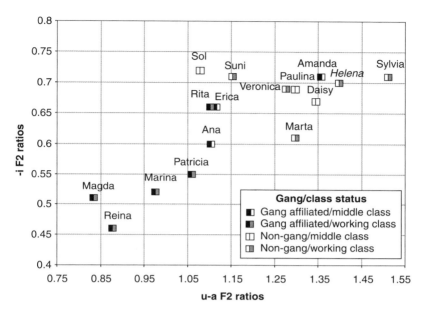

Figure 5.6 /u/-fronting for women by class and gang status

lower socioeconomic status fall at the bottom of the chart. Those with middle-class status fall higher on the chart. Though the numbers are small, the difference is significant at the .05 level. It is possible for middle-class gang members to front as much as or more than some non-gang-affiliated women (explaining the behavior of Amanda, who looked anomalous in Figure 5.5). It should also be noted that women like Magda and Reina, who are gang-affiliated but not themselves in a gang, clearly pattern with the women who are gang members. Looking at combinations of social factors in the construction of identities yields correlations with the linguistic variable that are highly statistically significant, and the speakers who seemed anomalous before can now be seen to fit the pattern.

Figure 5.7, showing the male speakers, looks somewhat different from Figure 5.6, particularly as regards the group of highest fronters. The women at the top of the chart in Figure 5.6, for example, were mixed with respect to social class. But the top six men in terms of /u/-fronting are all from the middle-class group. The social class factor shows a significant (p < .05) correlation with the linguistic variable for

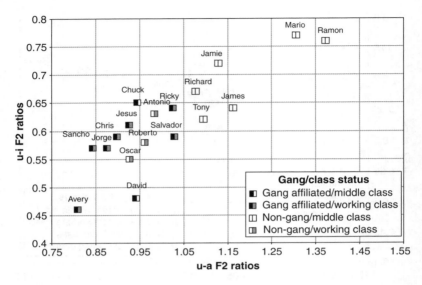

Figure 5.7   /u/-fronting for men by class and gang status

men as a group but not for women as a group. Also, the effect of gang affiliation is much stronger for men. Some gang-affiliated women had relatively high /u/-fronting if they were middle class. However, none of the male gang members appears in the top part of Figure 5.7 (comparable to Amanda in Figure 5.6); this could be attributed to the fact that there are no middle-class male gang members in the sample. However, there are two gang-*affiliated* speakers who belong to the middle-class group, David and Chuck. These two speakers pattern with the gang members, in the lower part of the chart. Among the men who have no connection to the gang, those who are also middle class do significant /u/-fronting, but those in the working-class group, like Roberto, fall at the middle or low end of the /u/-fronting scale. Again, speakers who at first seemed anomalous (like David, who is middle class but doesn't front /u/) now clearly fit a pattern that makes sense relative to social identities in the community.

In summary, if the CE speakers constructed their identities to include two or more categories from column A in the list below (for example, a female middle class gang member), then they had higher amounts of /u/-fronting. If their identities involved two or more categories from column B (for example, a male working-class non-gang member), then they had lower amounts of /u/-fronting.

A	B
female	male
middle class	working class/low income
non-gang member (or tagger)	gang member (or affiliated)

Some reasons why the categories might group together in this way, relating to social structure and the construction of identity among adolescents, will be discussed later in the chapter. The statistical significance of this interaction between the three variables of sex, social class and gang status will also be confirmed through a multivariate analysis of the data.

One intriguing result of this research is the finding that /u/-fronting, a sound change in progress in California, shows a pattern of social distribution in the Latino community that does not fit the traditional 'curvilinear pattern.' In the studies of what is usually termed 'untargeted' sound change done on majority communities, the interior social classes are expected to lead the change, as summarized in Labov (1994):

> The pattern now seems clear, at least for cities in the United States. In the course of change from below, the most advanced vowel systems are found among younger speakers: young adults and youth in late adolescence. Furthermore, these innovators are found among 'interior groups' – that is, groups centrally located in the class hierarchy. ... In terms of social class labels, this means the upper working class and lower middle class.   (1994:156)

In an earlier section Labov notes that 'the occupational groups with highest and lowest social status disfavor the changes in progress' (Labov 1994:62). However, in the Chicano English speaking community of Los Angeles we find that the group with the highest /u/-fronting includes women from both middle-class backgrounds and very low socioeconomic backgrounds. In general, for both men and women, gang status has a greater effect than social class on the variable.

There are several possible reasons why this pattern might be found in the Latino community, and I will discuss some of them here. One possibility might be that the class representations made for these women are inaccurate; in other words, is it possible that the 'low income' women are actually from a higher social class? The answer is clearly no, despite the difficulty in applying traditional social indices to this community. Veronica lives in the Projects, which means that by definition her one-parent family is from the lowest end of the socioeconomic scale, yet she fronts /u/ clearly and frequently.

Another possibility would be that this is not a classic *change from below*, but rather more like a *change from above*, or *targeted change*, such as the pronunciation of post-vocalic /r/ in New York City. Labov describes these as representing 'borrowings from other speech communities that have higher prestige in the view of the dominant class' (Labov 1994:78), which could in theory apply in this case, since the variable comes from the Anglo community. On the other hand, these changes are often associated with public awareness and almost always with use in careful speech, neither of which is true of /u/-fronting in Chicano English. Also, if this were, in fact, a case of targeted change, we would expect to find the highest social classes leading, with a gradual decline in use of the variable as we went down the social scale. Again, this is not the pattern in the data from the CE speakers. While some middle-class speakers show high degrees of /u/-fronting, others are at the low end of the /u/-fronting scale. The case of the women from the Projects who show heavy /u/-fronting would also remain unexplained.

The best explanation for this pattern, and the only one of the three presented here that fits the data, stems from the fact that gang status has such a high level of importance among this young adult segment of the Latino community, both for those associated with the gangs and for those who have clearly chosen other paths. Rather than playing a strong independent role, social class in this community interacts with gang status and other factors in a complex pattern, as discussed above. The possibility that sound change in minority groups may not show a curvilinear pattern with respect to social class is worth further investigation with a larger sample and in other communities. However, the availability of an alternative explanation based on community-specific factors which fits the data closely, along with the high level of significance revealed by the statistical model, suggests that these results are not simply an artifact of sample size. As further general sociolinguistic studies of minority communities are conducted, more data will become available to allow linguists to test the universality of the conclusions that have previously been drawn from studies limited to majority ethnic communities.

5.5   Phonetic variables beyond /u/: /æ/-backing and /æ/-raising

The results presented here have shown that it is possible to learn a great deal about sociolinguistic variation in a community by looking at a single variable. However, Eckert (1987), Labov (1994) and many others suggest that a more complete view of language use in the community can be obtained by looking at several variables in combination. A preliminary phonological analysis of the Chicano English speakers' vowels revealed evidence of two other variables besides /u/-fronting that represent sound changes in progress in the California Anglo English: backed /æ/, and raised /æ/. In this section, the distribution of these additional variables in the Chicano English community will be added to the analysis, with the goal of understanding more about the social factors that correlate with linguistic variation. For instance, gang affiliation or non-affiliation proved to be crucial in understanding the distribution of /u/-fronting. It is worth investigating whether gang status is also significantly correlated with one or both of the /æ/ variables. In addition, the interaction of gang status and social class patterned differently for men and women. If this is also true of the /æ/ variables, there will be more data available for forming hypotheses about why the gender patterns are distributed as they are.

Determining which tokens were raised or backed

I have treated /æ/-raising and /æ/-backing as two separate variables because there is no strict inverse relationship between them; in other words, some speakers do a relatively high amount of both, and while all speakers have at least occasional raising, some speakers never back. Additionally, some tokens appear to be subject to both backing and raising. For the /u/-fronting variable, measuring the F2 of tokens occurring after a coronal (the most favoring environment) was sufficient for attaining a reliable measure of how much fronting a particular speaker did. With the two /æ/ variables, on the other hand, I quickly discovered that no combination of measurements could accurately predict which tokens sounded fronted or backed. For instance, tokens of /æ/ that sounded clearly backed to myself and other phonetically trained listeners could involve lowering of F2 and either raising or lowering of F1, or they could involve only lowering of F1. I therefore decided to use judgments of the tokens by myself and another linguist to rate individual tokens for raising or backing, with measurements on the vowel space charts used occasionally to help resolve ambiguities. A preliminary sample showed that there was good agreement between judges on the ratings.[5]

Phonetic conditioning of the /æ/ variables

The /æ/ variables also involved a more complex pattern of phonetic conditioning than /u/-fronting, and because the tokens were taken from natural speech, individual speakers differed in the exact contexts for /æ/ that were sampled. I examined the effects of preceding and following consonants on the frequency of occurrence of raised and backed tokens.[6] I found a tendency of /æ/ to raise before nasals, which is a common pattern, although backing can occur in this context as well. There also seemed to be a positive effect of a preceding liquid on backing.

In light of these various contextual influences, rather than taking the straight percentages of raising and backing for each speaker, I submitted the tokens to a loglinear analysis using the VARBRUL program (the version adapted for the IBM-PC by Susan Pintzuk). The dependent variable was either /æ/-raising or /æ/-backing, and the independent variables included the preceding context the following context and the speaker. The analysis took into account the various contextual effects, and then assigned a weight to each individual speaker. This weight was used as the raising or backing value for each speaker in the statistical analysis. Note that some speakers did not have any backed tokens at all.

5.6   Quantitative analysis of the three linguistic variables

I used generalized linear models (GLM) to analyze correlations between each of these three linguistic variables (the dependent variables) and the social characteristics of the Latino speakers. The independent variables included sex, social class, gang status and language competence. Again, speakers were classified into two social class groups, middle class and working class. For gang status, speakers were classified as either affiliated with the gang in some way or not affiliated in any way (gang or non-gang). Those speakers who *know* gang members were grouped with the gang for the reasons discussed above. The language competence sub-groups included Spanish-dominant speakers, who immigrated from Mexico between the ages of 9 and 13 (and are fluent in English), other bilingual speakers and English monolinguals.

A generalized linear model of /u/-fronting

The first dependent variable analyzed was /u/-fronting (using the /u/ to /ɑ/ mean F2 ratio). Since some analysis of /u/-fronting has already been done, this variable can be used to some extent to gauge the reliability of the method. Table 5.1 shows a GLM analysis with /u/-fronting as the dependent variable and the four independent variables discussed above, including several possible interactions. It shows two significant main effects[7] and one significant interaction. Both gang affiliation and sex are correlated with /u/-fronting, as is the sex/gang/class interaction. Figures

Table 5.1 GLM of /u/-fronting (Analysis of Variance)

Source	Sum-of-squares	DF	Mean-square	*F*-ratio	P
Class	0.030	1	0.030	2.312	0.143
Gang	0.254	1	0.254	19.775	**0.0001**
Sex	0.196	1	0.196	15.275	**0.001**
Language	0.023	2	0.023	0.905	0.419
Gang*class	0.006	1	0.006	0.444	0.512
Sex*class	0.002	1	0.002	0.135	0.717
Sex*gang	0.000	1	0.000	0.011	0.917
Sex*gang*class	0.114	1	0.114	8.831	**0.007**
Error	0.283	22	0.013		

Dep Var: UAF2RATIO; *N*: 32; Multiple *R*: 0.859; Squared multiple *R*: 0.739

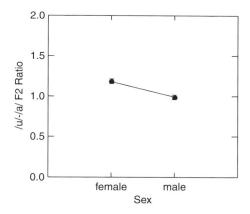

Figure 5.8 /u/-fronting by sex (GLM)

5.8 and 5.9 show the two main effects: non-gang speakers front more than gang-affiliated speakers, and women front more than men.

Even though in Table 5.1 social class alone was not significant, in a model that excluded the non-significant variables (Table 5.2), it did reach the 0.05 level of significance, with middle-class speakers fronting /u/ more (see Figure 5.10). Class also plays an important role in the *interaction* of the social variables, as had already been suggested in the earlier analysis; the four charts in Figure 5.11 show the interaction of sex, gang status and social class. Women front more than men, but this effect is much more pronounced among two sub-groups of speakers: the non-gang working class speakers, and the middle class gang-affiliated

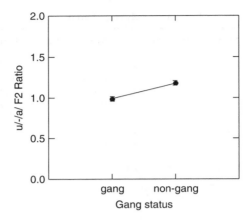

Figure 5.9   /u/-fronting by gang status (GLM)

Table 5.2   GLM of /u/-fronting with significant variables only (Analysis of Variance)

Source	Sum-of-squares	DF	Mean-square	*F*-ratio	P
Class	0.066	1	0.066	5.787	**0.023**
Gang	0.273	1	0.273	23.836	**0.000**
Sex	0.264	1	0.264	23.010	**0.000**
Sex*gang*class	0.147	1	0.147	12.874	**0.001**
Error	0.309	27	0.011		

Dep Var: UAF2RATIO; *N*: 32; Multiple *R*: 0.845; Squared multiple *R*: 0.714

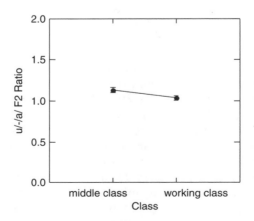

Figure 5.10   /u/-fronting by social class (GLM)

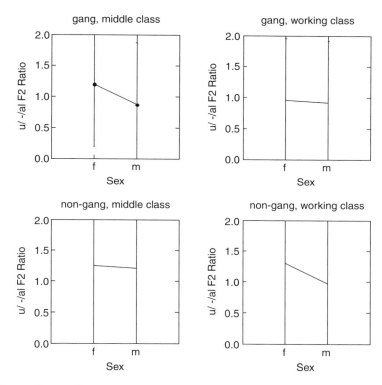

Figure 5.11 The interaction of social factors in /u/-fronting

speakers. I will discuss some possible explanations for this below. This analysis confirms the effects that were found earlier, including the ambiguous role of social class, suggesting that the GLM model has accurately represented the variation.

A generalized linear model of /æ/-backing

The next dependent variable I looked at was /æ/-backing, which I suspect is a somewhat newer variable in the community than /u/-fronting. Table 5.3 shows a GLM model for /æ/-backing with the same independent variables used above. Again, gang membership and sex are both significant as main effects, but the interaction with social class does not occur. Figures 5.12 and 5.13 show the same distribution as was found with the /u/ variable, with women backing more than men, and non-gang speakers backing more than gang speakers. These results seem to indicate

Table 5.3   GLM of /æ/-backing (Analysis of Variation)

Source	Sum-of-squares	DF	Mean-square	*F*-ratio	P
CLASS	0.015	1	0.015	0.352	0.559
GANG	0.200	1	0.200	4.592	**0.043**
SEX	0.752	1	0.752	17.274	**0.0001**
LANGUAGE	0.072	2	0.036	0.826	0.451
GANG*CLASS	0.004	1	0.004	0.100	0.755
SEX*GANG	0.015	1	0.015	0.356	0.557
SEX*CLASS	0.013	1	0.013	0.297	0.591
SEX*GANG*CLASS	0.000	1	0.000	0.002	0.964
Error	0.957	22	0.044		

Dep Var: BACKVARB; *N*: 32; Multiple *R*: 0.770; Squared multiple *R*: 0.592

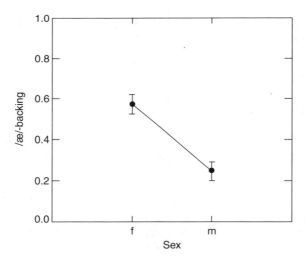

Figure 5.12   /æ/-backing by sex (GLM)

that women and non-gang members are more likely to use variants from the majority community as part of their linguistic expression of identity, although it will be seen that /æ/-raising does not follow the same pattern.

A generalized linear model of /æ/-raising

Interestingly, the last variable, /æ/-raising, shows the opposite pattern from the other two. Table 5.4 shows the results of the GLM estimate for

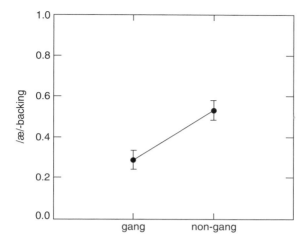

Figure 5.13   /æ/-backing by gang status (GLM)

Table 5.4   GLM of /æ/-raising (Analysis of Variance)

Source	Sum-of-squares	DF	Mean-square	*F*-ratio	P
Class	0.015	1	0.015	0.842	0.369
Gang	0.043	1	0.043	2.390	0.136
Sex	0.183	1	0.183	10.088	**0.004**
Language	0.022	2	0.011	0.594	0.561
Gang*class	0.001	1	0.001	0.038	0.848
Sex*gang	0.005	1	0.005	0.302	0.588
Sex*class	0.013	1	0.013	0.723	0.404
Sex*gang*class	0.046	1	0.046	2.518	0.127
Error	0.399	22	0.018		

Dep Var: RAISEDVARB; *N*: 32; Multiple *R*: 0.680; Squared multiple *R*: 0.462

/æ/-raising. There is a clear main effect of sex and, as with /æ/-backing, class is not significant. Gang status also does not appear significant in this run. In a model with fewer factors (not included in these tables), however, the probability of error associated with the gang variable came out to 0.081, so there is at least a suggestive tendency with respect to this factor (gang members raise more).

The same is true of the gang/sex/class interaction, which in Table 5.5 is associated with a 0.076 probability of error. Figures 5.14 and 5.15

134   *Chicano English in Context*

Table 5.5 GLM of /æ/-raising with significant variables, plus gang status (Analysis of Variance)

Source	Sum-of-squares	DF	Mean-square	F-ratio	P
GANG	0.029	1	0.029	1.792	0.191
SEX	0.251	1	0.251	15.649	**0.0001**
SEX*GANG*CLASS	0.055	1	0.055	3.404	**0.076**
Error	0.449	28	0.016		

Dep Var: RAISEDVARB; *N*: 32; Multiple *R*: 0.629; Squared multiple *R*: 0.395

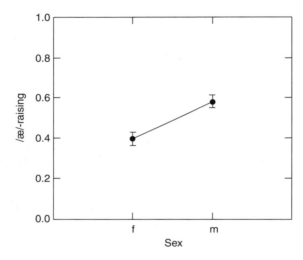

Figure 5.14   /æ/-raising by sex (GLM)

show the relationship of /æ/-raising to sex and gang status. The pattern is the opposite of that which was found for the other two variables: men raise /æ/ more than women, and gang members tend to raise more than non-gang members. Although the effect of gang status is not statistically significant, and no real conclusions can be drawn from it, I include it because the direction of the difference parallels that of the gender difference (which *is* statistically significant). In both cases, the variable is favored more by exactly those groups that disfavored the other two phonetic variables that have been discussed. If this is a more recent variable in terms of sound change than /u/-fronting, these other tendencies may come to be significant when the variable has progressed further in the community.

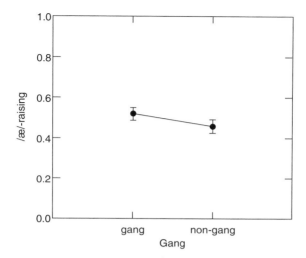

Figure 5.15 /æ/-raising by gang status (GLM); not satistically significant

Figure 5.16 shows the interaction of sex with gang status and social class, as it affects /æ/-raising. Though this tendency does not quite reach the 0.05 significance level, I present it because it shows a striking parallel with Figure 5.11. Again the largest gender differences in use are found among middle-class gang or working-class non-gang speakers. There is also a lead by men in the working-class gang group though it is less prominent. But there is very little sex difference for this variable in the non-gang middle-class group.

While all three of these variables presumably come from the Anglo community, their distribution in the Latino community differs by variable. This can be seen from Table 5.6, which shows the strong Pearson correlations among the three variables across the list of values by speaker. The /æ/-backing and /u/-fronting values for individuals are positively correlated with each other, and the /æ/-raising values are negatively correlated with both. I will discuss some possible reasons for this below.

5.7   Implications of the sociolinguistic patterns

The limits of social class as a predictor

Interestingly, the class variable was not independently significant for two of the three variables, and only significant for /u/ in the second run,

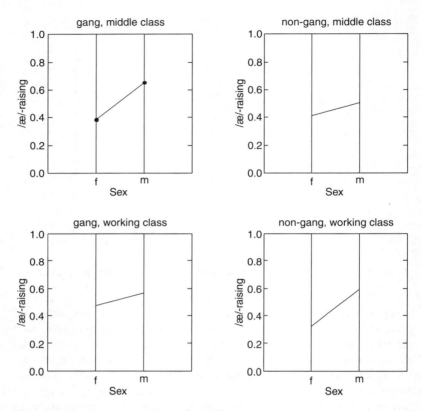

Figure 5.16   The interaction of social factors in /æ/-raising

Table 5.6   Pearson correlations of values by speaker for three variables

Variables	Coefficient	Significance
/æ/-raising to /æ/-backing	−0.5379506	p < .005
/æ/-backing to /u/-fronting	0.50308958	p < .005
/æ/-raising to /u/-fronting	−0.47300993	p < .005

unlike gang status and sex. With respect to the GLM model, it might be argued that the lack of significance for social class is an artifact of my having collapsed the class distinctions into two large categories. However, I estimated models for all the variables in which more class distinctions were preserved (anywhere from 3 to 5) and the significance of class decreased rather than increased. Furthermore, in looking at individual speakers it becomes clear that there is a basis for the model's rejection of class as having a main effect, even in the first run of /u/. Sylvia, for example, is among the top five speakers in both /u/-fronting and /æ/-backing; however, she is from the *lowest* socioeconomic group in the sample. Among Latino young adults, social class simply does not have a strong *independent* effect on linguistic variation when compared with other factors such as sex and gang status. Again, this means that the curvilinear pattern said to be typical of Anglo sound changes is not in effect.

The comparability of bilinguals and monolinguals

One of the goals of studying sound change in this community is to determine what effect the fact that it is a bilingual community might have on this linguistic process. One plausible answer is none, given that bilinguals did not differ from monolinguals in their use of any of these variables (see Tables 5.1, 5.3 and 5.4). In fact, in listening to the English of these speakers, I have as yet been unable to identify any phonological or phonetic element that distinguishes the two groups; informal evidence for this conclusion is provided by my experiment with playing tapes of bilinguals and monolinguals to students, described in the Introduction.

One interesting side note to consider is that all three variables can be found to some degree among fluent second language speakers of English whose first language is Spanish. Although there were no statistically significant effects of language competence on any of the variables, it is possible that the presence of these two variants in the community, among non-native speakers, might have facilitated their adoption as sociolinguistic variables from the majority community. In other words, the effects of the community being a bilingual one might be found not at the individual level, but as influencing CE in a more general way.

The role of gender in the interaction of social factors

The most visually striking pattern among these variables is the interaction of gender with gang status and social class illustrated in Figures 5.11 and 5.16. These two variables were measured in completely different ways: the /u/-fronting values represent the means of various acoustic measurements of F2 in Hertz, while the /æ/-raising values come from categorical judgments by linguists, adjusted for phonetic conditioning by the Varbrul program. The two variables also represent opposing patterns in the community: the speakers who front /u/ the most are those who raise /æ/ the least. Yet in both cases, the gender effect is particularly strong among the groups of middle-class gang-affiliated speakers and working-class non-gang speakers. Why?

I believe that this pattern reflects the intersection of conflicting social norms in the construction of identity among young Latinos and Latinas, particularly in the construction of gender identity. Represented in this community are both social affiliations that stress 'toughness' (for example 'gang member') and social affiliations that might be called 'conservative' (for example 'middle class'). This type of pattern was also found by Eckert in her (1987) study of adolescents in the Detroit area, focusing on the categories of *jocks* and *burnouts*.[8] She notes that social pressures related to gender can conflict with the expectations associated with other social categories relevant to the identities of adolescents:

> Girls are still expected to be 'good' in other ways – to be friendly and docile ... Boys, on the other hand, are expected to be physically powerful and able to defend themselves ... Just as the jock boys are caught between conservative corporate social norms and 'tough' gender norms, burnout girls are caught between 'tough' urban norms and conservative gender norms.   (1987:106–8)

The existence of a 'toughness' value associated with certain linguistic elements was also found in Labov (1972b). Orientations to these norms are reflected in speakers' kinetic behavior, clothes and so on, as well as in their language.

An explanation that takes into account these types of norms and social pressures fits the structure of the Latino young adult community very well. The gang members represent the ultimate end of the toughness scale: people whose lives depend on others perceiving them as tough and who are involved in violent acts of many types. Similarly, the working class has a traditional association with toughness, as Eckert notes, and the middle class with conforming to social norms for what constitutes 'good' behavior. Middle-class speakers in the Latino community are also associated (often negatively) with assimilation, which besides conforming to dress styles and so on could include 'sounding white.' The dichotomy of gender norms, as cited above, is maximally true of the Latino community: girls are expected to be feminine and submissive, boys are supposed to be tough.[9]

It is not surprising, then, that the greatest amount of linguistic differentiation by sex occurs when other factors that play a role in the speaker's construction of his or her identity, such as social class, represent opposing values of 'tough' vs. 'conservative' (as seen in Figures 5.11 and 5.16). In the case of gang members who are also middle-class, and non-gang members who are also working-class, the construction of identity is likely to involve opposing pressures both to be 'tough' and to conform to conservative norms. Speakers whose identities are complex in this way seem to use the sociolinguistic variables more strongly to express their gender roles. If women front /u/ more than men generally, then working-class non-gang women and men exaggerate this difference by using even more and even less of the variable respectively.

The homogeneous groups, in other words, the 'tough' working-class gang members or the middle-class, non-gang speakers (who are the *least* 'tough', and represent the highest degree of conservativeness) tend to show less gender variation. As Figure 5.11 shows clearly, the largest gender differences are in the two heterogeneous groups, middle-class gang members and working-class non-gang members, with women using significantly more of the prestige variable (fronted /u/). This explains why female gang members might front /u/ if they were from the middle class. It also makes sense, given the strong influence of gang membership in the community, that even women from the lowest socioeconomic backgrounds use language norms associated with the middle-class group to mark their non-gang status. On the other hand, it may be more difficult for Latino men to express their disassociation from the gang linguistically, even among men who have made a clear choice not to be gang members. When these men are also middle class, the combination of their class status and non-gang membership is enough to override the pressure to sound tough. However, when non-gang men are from the working class, another group associated with toughness, the effect on their speech patterns is greater, and results in less /u/-fronting.

I have not yet discussed why in this Latino community one of the variables (/æ/-raising) is correlated negatively with the other two, a situation which does not occur among Anglo speakers in the same area. With the strong presence of these complex, sometimes conflicting norms as part of the identity construction of young Latino and Latina adults, linguistic variables are needed to express the social oppositions. In other words, it is insufficient for one group to favor all the changes in progress and the socially opposite group to disfavor them. Each group needs its own linguistic symbols (see Eckert 1991 for more discussion of this). Though I cannot say at this point why raising of /æ/ rather than another variable seems to represent the toughness norm, I am not surprised that the three variables are divided in a way that mirrors the opposing social norms of the community.

6
Sociolinguistics of Chicano English II: Syntactic Variation

6.1   Syntactic variation: negative concord

In general, a greater percentage of sociolinguistic studies looking at language variation and change have focused on phonetic rather than syntactic variables. Some of the more interesting recent studies (for instance, Rickford and McNair-Knox 1994) have looked at both types of variables at once. Comparing the patterns of different types of socio-linguistic variables within the same community can provide a more complete picture of how speakers use linguistic variables in construct-ing their identities and can illuminate the complex nuances of social structure. Having looked in detail at several phonetic variables among young Latino adults in the last chapter, I will now focus on a syntactic variable in the same community: negative concord.

Negative concord (also known as multiple negation) has played a cen-tral role in the history of sociolinguistics and in the descriptivist/pre-scriptivist battle in general. Most of us who teach linguistics have had the experience of presenting an analysis of negative concord in our introductory classes, walking students through the canonical proof in which we point out that negative concord is the standard structure in Spanish, Russian and so on, and that it was the rule in earlier stages of our own English. Additionally, there is a principle that I refer to as the Mick Jagger Comprehension Corollary: when Mick Jagger sings 'I can't get no satisfaction' it does *not* produce a sudden confusion in 'standard'-speaking listeners whereby they have to wonder if maybe since there are two negatives Mick is saying that he *can* get satisfaction after all.

This feature represents one of the great shibboleths of English, prob-ably due to its presence in so many non-standard dialects (spoken by Anglos, or African-Americans or Latinos), as well as its great appeal to

140

language mavens as an example of 'faulty logic,' and even perhaps its occurrence during the acquisition process of English-speaking children. Eckert calls it 'arguably the most common stigmatized variable in the English language' (2000:216). Noland (1991) points out the persistence of negative concord throughout the history of English, and adds:

> We can lament a powerful, ancient, and legitimate formation that prescriptive pressures have virtually forced to disappear from the poor, depleted standard.   (1991:177)

For whatever reason, this form, alive and well in dialects other than the standard, evokes some unusually strong reactions, pro and con.

Negative concord is a central feature of Labov's seminal book *Language in the Inner City* (1972a). Several other pioneering studies of non-standard dialects included it as well (Labov 1966; Shuy, Wolfram and Riley 1967; Wolfram 1969, 1974). Nonetheless, not much research has been done on negative concord since the early studies. Weldon (1994) presents a comprehensive and quantitatively impressive study of AAE (African-American English) negation in general, but she treats negative concord only in relation to other factors, and hers is not a sociolinguistic study per se. Schneider (1989), on Earlier Black English, looks at negative concord in a fair amount of detail, but again, this is not a study that involves correlation with social factors. Wolfram (1974) is one of the few to actually look at negative concord in a Latino community, Puerto Rican English speakers in New York City. The early studies of Chicano English (for example, Ornstein-Galicia 1984; Penfield and Ornstein-Galicia 1985) mention that negative concord occurs in this dialect, but provide no actual data on the details of its occurrence.

This chapter presents a qualitative and quantitative study of negative concord among Chicano English speakers. The data are taken from the same sociolinguistic interviews of young Latino adults that were used in the study of sociophonetic variables (Chapter 5). Some tokens of possible negative concord that were collected originally, were excluded from the analysis. These included: (a) negations with *barely* (which were excluded because of the special semantics of this word among Chicano English speakers; see Chapter 4), and also those with *hardly* which are similar, and (b) sentences with a negative subject, where negative concord would have to be on the auxiliary, as in *Nobody told him/Nobody didn't tell him*, which will be discussed below. In the end, the sample that was analyzed included a total of 323 negations from 28 speakers.

Overall, 41 percent of the tokens for the whole group of Chicano English speakers showed negative concord. The figure rises to 49 percent if we exclude those speakers who categorically did not use negative concord. This figure is lower than Labov (1972a) reports for AAE, where a number of his speakers showed categorical negative concord. Wolfram's (1974) study of Puerto Rican English, a dialect that is generally assumed to have something in common with Chicano English found 87.4 percent negative concord overall, much higher than for my Chicano English speakers, although this could be due to the characteristics of the two samples as much as to differences between the dialects.

6.2   Qualitative differences among dialects

Chicano English negative concord follows the same basic syntactic rules as in AAE. More than two negations are perfectly permissible, as in

Things ain't gonna never change in LA no more.   (Avery, 16)

Like AAE, Chicano English does permit a negative to be transferred to a lower clause, as in a famous example from Labov (1972a), *It ain't no cat can't get in no coop.* An example from my data would be:

I don't think there's nothing I could change out there.   (Amanda, 17)

In this case Amanda means that she doesn't think she can change anything, so unlike in most non-standard Anglo dialects, a negated verb in the lower clause is not understood as introducing a separate negation. This type of construction is quite infrequent. I had twelve total environments of this type produced by speakers who had some negative concord, and three of those had negation in the lower clause. The other two examples are:

I don't think that nobody really knows anything.   (Chuck, 17)

I don't need girls wi-, you know, that have no man in the pen.   (Avery, 16)

These examples also came from three different speakers. Despite its infrequency, we do find instances of this type of negative concord, with a single semantic negation intended, so I would conclude that the form is present in Chicano English. This contrasts with Wolfram's (1974) study of PRE speakers, among whom he found no instances of negative transfer to a lower clause.

One of the other constructions that separates AAE negative concord from Anglo non-standard dialects is negative inversion, as in *Didn't nobody play in the sandbox*. I did not find negative inversion among the Chicano English speakers, which constitutes a difference from AAE. Negative concord on the auxiliary with a negative subject, for example, *Nobody wasn't after him* (also found in AAE), was very rare among Chicano speakers. I had only a single example:

None of the girls don't like her.   (Amanda, 17)   [handwritten: not found in Sp]

As mentioned above, these rare constructions were excluded from the analysis. Wolfram (1974) similarly found no examples of negative inversion among his Puerto Rican English speakers. He had only two occurrences of the negative transfer to the auxiliary type in his entire corpus, and he concludes that, again, this is not a feature of negative concord in Puerto Rican English.

6.3   Quantitative differences

I prepared the data for analysis by the VARBRUL program (see Chapter 5). The dependent variable was whether the negation was single or multiple. I did not code more than two negations separately, since these cases made up a very small fraction of the total. In terms of the independent variables, I coded for internal (syntactic) and external (social) factors.

Syntactic coding

The syntactic categories used to code for different types of negative concord, with an example of each, are listed in Table 6.1. Generally speaking, I have followed the counting method used in Wolfram (1969).

For category 4, a negative auxiliary with the environment for negative concord being a determiner, I have counted both *a* and *any* as non-applications for the tabulation. This was a matter of some controversy in the early studies. Labov (1972a) adopts an analysis in which *no* (as in *He has no friends*) comes from underlying 'NEG + *any*' rather than from NEG + the determiner *a*, and he excludes negative sentences with *a* from the pool of possible negative concord contexts. But there are numerous examples that raise questions about this approach (in which negative sentences with *a* are routinely excluded from the count of non-realized occurrences). Just to take one case, we have the example from Fasold (1975; cited in Wardhaugh 1986:328) of the following sentence:

Table 6.1   Syntactic categories used to code negative concord

Category	Example
(1) neg subj + pron, adv, or det	*Nobody said nothing/anything.*
(2) neg aux + pronoun	*I can't say nothing/anything.*
(3) neg aux + adv	*I won't do it no more/any more.*
(4) neg aux + determiner	*They didn't have a/any/no car.*
(5) neg outside clause	*She's not dead or nothing/anything.*
(6) neg transferred to lower clause	*I don't think he did nothing/anything.*
(7) neg adv + other neg (incl. *not*)	*I never dated nobody/anybody black.*
	... ticket for not having no/any/ø headlights.

This ø not no spoon [note: eye dialect has been removed]

It comes from a video of a classroom interaction, and was produced in a repetition task where the teacher was prompting the child with *This is not **a** spoon*. Considering that repetition tasks are often used by sociolinguists in determining underlying structures, I think the relation between *a* and *no* shown here is relevant, and should be taken into account in identifying environments for negative concord.

Wolfram (1969:160–1) gives an alternative analysis, in which tokens of *a* that are generic are counted as potential occurrences, while tokens of *a* that have specific referents are excluded. Labov (1972a) notes that if one includes *a* it changes the percentages radically, however we now have statistical models for variation that were not available at the time of the early studies which can be used to test whether a particular type of context has a disfavoring effect and to separate it out from other effects. With respect to my own data, I have used Wolfram's (1969) method, counting instances of NEG + *a* + generic noun as potential environments for negative concord, and left it to the statistical model to reveal the effect of this context on the variable.

Table 6.2 lists the percentages of negative concord for the various syntactic environments, as well as the results from a step-up/step-down Varbrul analysis in which the syntactic environment factor group was selected as significant (which it always was). Where the number of tokens was small, I have provided this information in the first column. The most favorable environments are a negated auxiliary with an adverb (category 3), for example, *She didn't go there no more*, or with a pronoun (category 2), for example, *He didn't do nothing*.

An environment that disfavors somewhat is the negation being transferred to a lower clause. Wolfram (1969), on AAE, also found transfer to lower clause very infrequent, and Wolfram (1974) found none for Puerto Rican speakers. Also disfavoring were negations with determiners, in which I included the generic 'a' and so on. (Wolfram (1969) found this to disfavor negative concord for AAE.) The most strongly disfavoring environments are examples of negation outside the clause, such as *either* or *or anything* (which all of the older studies also found to be disfavoring) and the first negation being in the subject or on an adverb rather than on the auxiliary. Note that these last two categories involve a relatively small number of total tokens. In general, my findings on these constraints agree with those of previous studies, and suggest that CE negative concord is very much like negative concord in other dialects.

Coding for social factors

As the second type of independent variable, I have coded for the same social categories used in the analysis of sociophonetic variables in Chapter 5. These include sex, social class and gang status, which had independent and interacting effects on the phonetic variables, and bilingualism versus monolingualism, which did not have any effect on those variables, but which I suspected might be relevant for negative concord. The factor groups and their values are:[1]

Table 6.2 Negative concord by syntactic category (in order of weight)

	% Neg conc	**Factor weight**
neg aux + adv	74	.79
neg aux + pron	64	.67
neg in lower clause (*n* = 12)	25	.43
neg aux + det	37	.34
neg adv + other (incl. *not*) (*n* = 13)	23	.21
neg subj + pro, adv or det (*n* = 9)	22	.16
neg in outside clause	15	.14
Total: N = 272	49	

Sex: female
              male

Social class: middle class
              working class
              low income

Gang status: gang member
              gang affiliated
              non-gang member
              tagger

Bilingualism: monolingual
              bilingual

The details of how I determined social class, the various gang statuses and so on, can be found in Chapter 2. I decided to use a very simple binary system of coding bilingualism to begin with, leaving open the possibility of more elaborate coding later; I classified all the speakers who could carry on a conversation with me fairly easily in Spanish as bilinguals, and those who could not as monolinguals.[2]

Background to the sociolinguistic analysis

The sociolinguistic analysis of the phonetic variables in Chapter 5 revealed that the local variables associated with the California Anglo community, such as /u/-fronting and æ/-backing were also present among Chicano English speakers. Which speakers used these variables the most was determined by an interaction of sex, gang status and social class, according to the generalized linear model I applied. I have suggested that these category groupings represent the influence of 'conservative' vs. 'tough' norms. In essence, if people were affiliated with two or more conservative categories (see Table 6.3), for example, a female middle class gang member, then they had higher amounts of /u/-fronting. If they were affiliated with two or more tough categories, for example, a male working class non-gang member, then they had lower amounts of /u/-fronting. I wanted to see how negative concord (a syntactic sociolinguistic variable) might be similar to or different from the phonetic variables that were previously analyzed.

6.4   Results and comparison with phonetic variables

Table 6.4 shows the results of a step-up/step-down VARBRUL analysis of negative concord, with syntactic context as a linguistic factor group and

Table 6.3   'Conservative' and 'tough' categories

('Conservative' norms)	('Tough' norms)
Female	Male
Middle class	Working class/low income
Non-gang member (or tagger)	Gang member (or affiliated)

Table 6.4   VARBRUL analysis of factors that affect negative concord

	Factor weight	% Neg conc
Gang status (range = 0.74)		
tagger	0.94	69
gang member	0.65	56
gang affiliated	0.47	41
non-gang member	0.20	19
Syntactic type (range = 0.66)		
neg aux + adv	0.80	74
neg aux + pron	0.65	64
neg in lower clause	0.42	25
neg aux + det	0.35	37
neg adv + other	0.21	23
neg subj + pro, adv or det	0.15	22
neg in outside clause	0.14	15
Social class (range = 0.40)		
middle class	0.33	29
working class	0.36	26
low income	0.73	60
Bilingualism (range = 0.19)		
monolingual:	0.38	37
bilingual:	0.57	44

Total: N = 323
(factor group not selected = sex)
Significance threshold = $p < 0.05$ Input: 0.37   49

sex, social class, gang status and bilingualism as the social factor groups. The number in the first column indicates the order of selection of the factor groups. The only factor group not selected as significant was, interestingly, sex. Gang status was the first factor selected by the model. Since this was one of the most significant influences on the phonological variables also, this result is not surprising, although I will comment below on some of the ways in which gang status patterned slightly differently in comparison with the phonetic variables. The second factor group selected was the syntactic environment, which was discussed in detail earlier.[3]

The third factor group to be selected as significant by the analysis was social class. The low income speakers used much more negative concord than the middle-class speakers (unsurprisingly, since this is a non-standard variable), with the working-class speakers intermediate, but closer to the middle-class group. In the study of the phonetic variables, the working class and low income speakers had behaved more or less the same, so the pattern for negative concord is slightly different. Also, for the phonetic variables social class interacted with the other factors, but was not always statistically significant on its own. Notice here too, though, that what Preston (1991) calls the 'variation space' is somewhat narrower for social class than for gang status and the syntactic environment. The variation space for the gang status factor group is 0.74, and for syntactic category it is 0.66, whereas for social class it is 0.40.

The last factor group to be selected as significant by the model was bilingualism. Whether someone was monolingual or bilingual was not found to have any effect on the phonetic variables. But with negative concord it did have an effect, specifically, bilingualism favored negative concord. Since it was the last factor group selected, and since the variation space is relatively small (0.19), this factor is not at the same level of importance with respect to negative concord as the others, yet it is still a result worth keeping in mind. Even though the correlation with bilingualism could potentially be an artifact of the sample size or some other factor, there are individuals who seem to confirm its validity, such as Daisy. Daisy is not in any way affiliated with the gangs. She is middle class on the scale presented in Chapter 2, works in a bank, goes to a community college, and her speech sounds fairly 'standard' to me. It is Chicano English in its phonology, but with few non-standard syntactic features. From my impression of her, and note that I interviewed her several times, I was convinced that she would not use negative concord at all. In compiling the data, I was listening to one of her interviews, expecting to collect only examples of standard negation, when to my surprise she used an example of negative concord. She then used three or four more in rapid sequence. I was quite startled, and could not think of a way to explain this result at first. Daisy, though, is also one of the most fluent bilinguals in the sample. This provides suggestive anecdotal support for the monolingual/bilingual effect.

The one factor group that did not come out as significant in the analysis, either on step-up or step-down, was sex. I expected this factor to be quite significant, and assumed that males would use much more negative concord than females. Wolfram (1969), for example, found that among his AAE speakers, males showed 4–27 percent more negative concord than females. But among the CE speakers in this study, if one looks at raw percentages, the women actually had a higher percentage of negative concord than the men. In some of the early runs, once the model took all the other factors into account, women were evaluated as having a lower weight for negative concord (favoring it a little less) than men. It was surprising to me to find that this difference was nonetheless not significant at all. Gender was a highly significant category with respect to the phonetic variables.

One possible hypothesis about this result is that it reflects the confluence of different sources for negative concord in CE. For example, male speakers in this community appear more likely to show the influence of AAE, at least with respect to syntactic features. Although I haven't fully analyzed the data that would support this hypothesis, it was clear from listening to the interviews that the male speakers used, for example, more instances of habitual *be* than the female speakers did. On the other hand, it is possible that female speakers might be more likely to incorporate influences from Spanish. Again, I have not collected quantitative data on this pattern, but I had the sense that overall the female speakers had a more positive attitude toward Spanish than the males, regardless of their level of fluency. Also, the use of the term *brothers* to mean 'brothers and sisters', a feature that was strongly associated with the influence of Spanish, occurred only among women in my sample. It may be that negative concord in CE has roots both in AAE and in Spanish, that male and female CE speakers are both influenced to use negative concord but by different sources, and that these disparate sources cancel out the gender effect that one might otherwise expect.

6.5   Constructing identities: what the use of these variables reveals

It is enlightening to look in greater detail at the gang status factor group. In Chapter 2, I talked about various sub-groupings of gang status

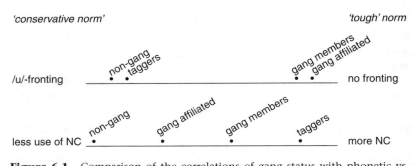

Figure 6.1 Comparison of the correlations of gang status with phonetic vs. syntactic variables

in this community, namely: (a) gang members; (b) people who are affiliated with or 'know' gang members; (c) non-gang members; and (d) taggers (who are also not gang members, but are what one might call a separate anti-social group). Figure 6.1 shows a comparison of the effects of gang status on /u/-fronting, one of the sociophonetic variables, and on negative concord.

For gang members and non-gang members, the pattern is consistent across phonetic and syntactic variables: what the gang members favor, the non-gang speakers reject. Gang members use more negative concord and less /u/-fronting than the non-gang speakers. The variation, as we might expect, comes with what Eckert (1991) might call 'the in-betweens.' Speakers like the taggers and people affiliated with gangs, who fall between the two groups socially, show a different pattern for the two types of linguistic variables. On the less perceptually salient phonetic variables, the taggers and affiliated people 'sound' like the people they spend time with. The people affiliated with the gang sound like gang members, in terms of the phonetic variables I looked at; there is even a suggestion that they may reject /u/-fronting beyond what the gangsters do. The taggers, who are often middle-class and who definitely do not hang out with the gang members, do not pattern with them on the phonetic variable; they have fronted /u/'s, just like non-gang members.

But with the more perceptually salient syntactic variable, the groups appear to be using it to make a kind of statement about their identities. The taggers seem to be trying to talk (syntactically) more 'tough' than even the gangsters, by using even more negative concord. This makes sense in terms of the social structure of the community, because taggers are definitely not perceived as threatening in the way that the gangsters are, although most taggers would like to be perceived this way. The gang-affiliated group seems to be trying to be syntactically *less* like the gangsters, by using less negative concord. This idea is supported by how frequently sisters of gangsters talked about explaining to someone that they are not themselves gang members (although ironically they sometimes do this by saying 'I'm not from nowhere').

6.6   Possible sources for negative concord

One question that hovers over all of this is where negative concord came from in Chicano English. The top contenders seem to be that it came from contact with AAE or other non-standard dialects, or that it reflects some influence of Spanish, or both. And it is possible that it came from neither of these, and simply developed independently. This is an enormous question that my study alone, of course, cannot answer. But the information presented so far seems to be more consistent with the 'origins in Spanish' analysis. To begin with, a number of the typical syntactic patterns that separate negative concord in AAE from negative concord in Anglo dialects are not found in Chicano English. And many of those, such as negative inversion, were not found by Wolfram among Puerto Rican English speakers in New York City either, where there was a great deal of contact with AAE speakers at the time of the study, and probably more contact historically than in the Los Angeles area.

In addition, there is the significance of bilingualism to consider. The fact that being bilingual seems to favor negative concord could be an indication that it reflects some influence of Spanish. Of course there are other possible explanations. One question I considered is whether knowing Spanish simply lessens the stigma associated with using double negatives. Most of these young adults will have been taught that double negatives are wrong, hearing the entire prescriptive catechism that I mentioned at the beginning of this chapter. Maybe speaking Spanish and knowing that two negatives are accepted there makes this lesson less effective for the bilingual speakers, so that they 'correct' it less in somewhat formal situations like linguistic interviews than the monolinguals who do not have a language with standard negative concord in their frame of reference. I have been told of anecdotal evidence that some native Spanish speakers nonetheless exhibit strong negative reactions to negative concord in English (Carmen Silva-Corvalán, personal communication), but this would be an interesting phenomenon to study in a more systematic fashion. In any case, whatever the original source, the use of the form currently might be reinforced by a number of influences.

7
Bilingualism and Spanish Fluency

7.1   Background: degrees of bilingualism in the community

This book is concerned with presenting Chicano English *in context*, and Spanish forms a crucial part of that context for most Latino communities in the USA. Other chapters have shown how Spanish has had an influence on CE generally, in the areas of phonology, syntax and semantics, as well as how individual levels of fluency in Spanish affected a sociolinguistic variable in English (negative concord). But how many individual Latino young adults speak the language of their parents and grandparents? What role does Spanish have in their lives? As was described in Chapter 2, Los Angeles is a place where Spanish thrives, in the media, in business interactions, at schools and in homes. As one of my speakers put it, 'Wherever you go, everybody speaks Spanish in LA.' It is not clear a priori, though, whether the vitality of Spanish in Los Angeles is due only to new immigrants from Mexico and other countries, or if Spanish also has some significance and presence among those born in the USA.

Despite the generally positive attitudes toward Spanish expressed by most speakers in this community (which will be discussed in Chapter 8), the actual usage situation suggests that covert attitudes toward Spanish are considerably more complex. In some ways, the patterns of Spanish usage in Los Angeles reflect the higher prestige of English more clearly than they reflect the association of Spanish with ethnic pride and the belief that speaking Spanish is important. In general, the Latino community being discussed in this book follows the norm that has been found again and again in previous research, namely that by the second generation, speakers tend to be monolingual and do not retain fluency in the heritage language, in this case, Spanish (see, for example, Lipski 1993; Silva-Corvalán 1994). However, there are many factors that influence Spanish acquisition, maintenance and use, and it is revealing to explore these individually, particularly for the first generation of speakers, who have a better chance at preserving their linguistic heritage.

I have a personal interest in this topic, which motivated me to do the research presented here. I am myself a first-generation speaker; my mother is a native of Spain who came here as an adult, and I grew up speaking both English and Spanish from infancy. When I was in my early twenties, I heard, for the first time, my voice speaking Spanish on an answering machine tape. I was distressed to discover that my phonology in Spanish, while certainly very good, was not completely native. I turned to my mother, who was with me at the time, and said, 'Mom! I have an accent in Spanish! Why didn't you ever tell me?' She said, 'Well, it's not a very big accent. Although you do say a few words funny. But I didn't think it was important.' (I will refrain from discussing here how it is possible that my mother could think that I, a linguist, would not find such a tidbit important.) Nonetheless, my experience raises some interesting questions about language acquisition. As I will discuss later, it is often taken for granted that children who begin acquiring a language from a very early age will invariably achieve native fluency. My individual case does not support this claim. One of the questions I will address here is whether this represents an exception to an otherwise strong rule, or whether varying levels of fluency are common among first generation speakers in some bilingual communities who grow up speaking two languages.

The effect of Chicano family structure on language use

In Chapter 2, I presented a qualitative view of the structures and cultural patterns of Mexican-American families in this community. Many of these patterns may have important repercussions for questions of bilingualism and language acquisition. For example, most of these speakers lived at home with their parents, moving out only if they married, and sometimes not even then, continuing to live with their spouse at their parents' home, often in some semi-separate space, such as an 'in-law' house. It was mentioned earlier that if the bilingual children in this community are spending more time at home, both daily and over their lifetimes, their parents and siblings will make a particularly significant contribution to their linguistic environment. In other words, while peer group influence has been shown to outweigh parental influence in some areas of first language acquisition (Payne 1980), we cannot assume that the results of studies done on Anglo speakers apply equally to the culturally different Latino speakers.

The role of parents in bilingual acquisition particularly needs to be examined, especially in this type of traditional family. For example, as regards the acquisition of Spanish, closeness to one's parents could be a contributing factor to the level of fluency attained. It is also possible that the generally stricter rule system for girls might lead to some gender differences in the area of Spanish fluency. In traditional families, the sibling relationship structure around a speaker should also be considered as a possible factor in language development and use. It is worthwhile to examine, for example, whether position in the sibling hierarchy correlates in any way with degree of acquisition of Spanish (see Silva-Corvalán 1994:10), a factor which will be considered later in this chapter. But we must keep in mind from the earlier discussion that not all Latino parents follow a traditional system, and there was a great deal of variety in the construction of the parenting role within the community.

Several speakers mentioned the role of baby-sitters in their early up-bringing, almost always with a specific connection to language use. Chuck, who claimed he had 'forgotten' Spanish, told me that when he was young, he had exclusively Mexican baby-sitters who spoke Spanish with him. Rita and Marta both experienced the opposite situation. Though Rita grew up speaking Spanish with her parents, she had an 'American' (meaning Anglo) baby-sitter, so unlike some of the speakers whose 'first' language is clearly Spanish, she feels she learned both English and Spanish at the same time. Marta also learned Spanish from her parents, but claims that a family friend who took care of her taught her English as a child too, and after this point she began speaking both with her parents. I had not been aware that baby-sitters (other than family members) had a prominent role in the Latino community. Any further investigation of acquisition should certainly take this fact into account.

Finally, it was noted in Chapter 2 that Latino families are larger and encompass a more extended network than most Anglo families. An important factor to consider when looking at language acquisition is the location of the extended network. Some studies (Peñalosa 1980; Lipski 1993; Silva-Corvalán 1994) have suggested that grandparents may play a crucial role in providing linguistic models for a child acquiring Spanish. This role would be particularly significant where the parents of the child were rapidly learning English or were themselves born in the USA. I encountered several possibilities with respect to the grandparents of my informants. One was that the grandparents had also immigrated to LA, and had regular contact with their grandchildren, sometimes living in the same household. Other speakers had grandparents living in Mexico, in which case the family might or might not have regular contact with them. A few of my speakers had grandparents who were themselves US born and spoke mainly English. Finally, in a few cases the grandparents were no longer living.

The case of the grandparents in Mexico is the most complex from a linguistic perspective. On the one hand, if the family did not regularly go to Mexico to visit, the speaker would have less contact with the grandparents than someone whose grandparents were in the USA, so linguistic influence would presumably be less. On the other hand, if the presence of the grandparent (or other family) in Mexico caused the family to visit there often, the speaker would have access not only to the (presumably monolingual) grandparent, but to other monolingual speakers of Spanish: neighborhood children, shopkeepers and so on. Contact with Mexico might thus play a role in the acquisition (and retention) of Spanish by these young adult speakers (but cf. García and Cuevas (1995) for a case where it does not).

The role of monolinguals in the community

Despite my knowledge of the literature on bilingual communities, and my familiarity with this community in particular, I was still surprised by the number of monolingual English-speaking Latinos I encountered. All of the speakers I interviewed whose parents had also been born in the USA were monolingual in English. There is some ambiguity about third-generation speakers in the literature on bilingualism. Appel and Muysken (1987:42) suggest that the typical pattern in immigrant groups is for this generation to be bilingual, though with the majority language dominating. Silva-Corvalán (1994:11), however, claims that the normal pattern is for these speakers to be monolingual, as was found here, or possibly passive bilinguals (see discussion below). I had only a single case of a speaker with one parent born in the USA and the other born in Mexico, Erica Otero, and she is bilingual. However, the fluency question goes beyond a simple generational division, since the children of parents born in Mexico exhibit many degrees of Spanish fluency, as will be discussed later in the chapter.

Because of the many attitudinal factors that can influence self-report of linguistic competence, I tested the receptive and productive competence in Spanish of speakers who claimed to be monolingual. I used very simple tests, but these were sufficient for me to ascertain that in fact the speakers had almost no productive competence in Spanish, and very limited receptive competence. In terms of production for example, Patricia attempted to produce the most elementary Spanish sequence: *¿Cómo estás? Muy bien.* ('How are you? Fine.') She struggled over the words and finally gave up, even though I could recognize what she was trying to say. This sequence had been brought up by her when I asked if she knew any Spanish at all. Similarly, when I asked Chuck his age, he was able to understand the question but not produce the number for the correct response (which was 17).

It has been found that in bilingual communities such as this one, there are often 'passive bilinguals' (Peñalosa 1980:49), individuals who do not speak the heritage language, but who understand it very well. Some of the monolinguals in my study claimed to be in this category, saying that their friends use Spanish around them and that they understand even if they are unable to join the conversation. However, when I tested these speakers, many turned out to have a fairly low level of comprehension, and some could not understand even simple questions at all. Among those who had some comprehension was Tony. When I asked him where his mother was from, though, he answered as if I had asked where she was. Chuck followed most of my questions, but was occasionally confused. Amanda, Patricia and Veronica did not seem to understand any Spanish at all. Only a few of the monolingual speakers, such as Jamie, seemed to fall clearly into the passive bilingual category.

Patricia made a comment that sheds some light on the fact that many of these people claimed to understand Spanish well. She told me that she understands her friends when they speak if they 'mix English and Spanish,' and she mentioned that her grandmother does the same, that is, codeswitches regularly. In this case, the speakers may have a sense of understanding Spanish because massive codeswitching allows them to follow the conversation, even though when I spoke to them in unmixed Spanish, they found it difficult to follow.

Interestingly, many of the monolinguals had been to Mexico, and some made frequent trips. I asked one speaker, James, how he managed to communicate, and he said that in Mexico enough people speak English so that he is able to talk with them. This suggests that the frequency of trips to Mexico, which I had originally suspected might contribute to the level of Spanish fluency achieved, may not be a very useful measure. Some of the monolinguals who had not been to Mexico, like Amanda, nonetheless expressed concern over the fact that if they went they would not be able to talk with anyone.

The monolinguals' attitudes about Spanish and their frequent expression of a desire to know more Spanish will be discussed in the next chapter. Nonetheless, in the community as a whole the value of Spanish is not high enough to prevent generational language loss for children of parents who were born in the USA. It may be that in many cases the process is one of acquisition and loss rather than non-acquisition. Chuck, for instance, claims that he spoke Spanish as a young child, but, 'once I got to school, I had to speak English so I just kind of forgot it.' Several other speakers also mentioned that their Spanish was previously 'better.' Whether this type of self-report is accurate or not, the issue of possible language loss is an interesting one to which I will return later in the chapter.

Passive bilinguals and asymmetrical communication

Closest to the category of passive bilinguals among my speakers are some who were able to interact with me in Spanish only at very limited levels. These include Sylvia, Sol and Magda, who apparently understood everything I asked them perfectly, but who made the types of mistakes when speaking Spanish that would be expected of a beginning or intermediate student in a language class. My request that they use Spanish in the interview brought up a situation that they do not often encounter, in which they were obligated to use Spanish productively. It was clear that while they had some limited productive abilities, having to use Spanish this way was not a situation they often experienced, and they had a great deal of trouble completing even simple sentences.

Part of the explanation may lie in a pattern that has often been observed in bilingual communities (for example, Sanchez 1982), which can be described as *asymmetrical communication*. This is a situation in which the speaker is often addressed in Spanish (or another minority language) by parents or grandparents, but always responds in English. Of course this is only possible in households where the relatives in question understand English. Although Paulina is very fluent in Spanish, she often uses this mode of interaction with her mother, and described it to me clearly:

> That's why I think my Spanish is not the best. Uh, because, people think it's funny, my mother will say something to me in Spanish and I'll answer her in English.

Many of my speakers described this asymmetrical English–Spanish mode of interaction as the usual one for their family. Jamie, for instance, told me that his grandmother addresses him in Spanish and he responds in English, until eventually his grandmother switches to speaking English as well.

This pattern clearly has roots in language attitudes within the community, where English is the language of higher prestige. As will be discussed in the next section, Paulina, for example, went through a phase as a child of expressing her negative feelings about speaking Spanish by answering her mother Ofelia only in English. Ofelia was able to convince Paulina to break that pattern, and she (Paulina) is now a highly fluent speaker of Spanish, as we will see later. In my visits to their home, I noticed instances of Paulina using asymmetrical communication with her mother, but I also observed stretches of conversation where both of them spoke Spanish. This may represent a case of Spanish loss having been averted by an alert parent.

Codeswitching

There are numerous thorough studies of codeswitching (including many in Spanish/English communities, such as those in Duran (1981) or Zentella (1997)) so I have chosen not to spend much time on it in this book, except for an attitudes section in Chapter 8. In general, however, my experience was that codeswitching among the young CE speakers occurred mainly when the dominant language of the discourse at the time was Spanish, and that it was fairly rare in the English portions of the interviews. There were occasional emblematic switches, intended to highlight ethnic identity; such as when several speakers referred to their *nina* ('godmother'), but otherwise little switching to Spanish. This may be related to the fact that a relatively small number of my speakers had native-like competence in Spanish, and that what one might call 'intentional' codeswitching, not related to lexical gaps, does tend to occur most among fluent bilinguals (Valdes 1988).[1] Zentella (1997) found that a relatively small percentage of codeswitches in the Puerto Rican community she studied could be attributed to not knowing a particular lexical item in the other language, despite the assumption by speakers in the community that lack of competence was their main motivation for switching. My sense was that with many of the young speakers I talked to, codeswitching when they spoke Spanish was, in fact, related to a lack of fluency. Sometimes they would say explicitly that they were having difficulty explaining something in Spanish and would have to continue their story in English.

All of this suggests that codeswitching in one direction may have different motivations and meanings from codeswitching in the other, a fact worthy of further study. It is possible, of course, that these speakers codeswitched more from English in other settings. Or it might simply be that this varies from community to community, and other Latino areas would have more mixing as part of the rhythms of everyday speech, particularly if Spanish fluency were a little higher overall than in this community.

An exception to this pattern of not codeswitching when speaking English, though, was the small group of older speakers in the study. For example, Joaquín Guerrero, who is 45 and has lived in Los Angeles all his life, does extensive codeswitching from English, as in the following section:

> But I am the only one that came out *músico*. My- all my brothers were into sports, basketball, baseball, *y todo,* and I couldn't do that. *No me gustaban.* I could, you know, play *y todo, pero a mi me gustaba más la guitarra.*[2]

Unlike the pattern found among the younger speakers, this clearly bears no relation whatsoever to lack of competence. Since the younger speakers were interviewed by me, and the older speakers by someone else, the nature of the interviewers is a possible explanation for this effect. However, my observations of the younger speakers when they were not being interviewed (there was not much codeswitching), and the fact that the more standard-sounding older speakers did not tend to codeswitch much with the other interviewer, suggest to me that there is an actual pattern here. In addition, since the most fluent bilinguals among the younger speakers did not seem to codeswitch nearly as much as the older speakers, I think it is not simply an issue of competence in Spanish. My guess is that codeswitching while speaking English may have a particular political and cultural significance to the older speakers, who grew up amid the charged political climate of the 1960s and 1970s, when civil rights issues for Mexican-Americans and others were a crucial focus. The younger generation does not seem to have these strong associations.

7.2   Patterns of language use among bilingual speakers

General summary of language use among bilinguals

The general language use patterns of the bilingual speakers in the study are shown in Table 7.1. A blank space indicates that there were no data

Table 7.1 Language use among bilingual speakers

Pseudonym	Grandprts	Mom	Dad	Siblings	Friends	Boyfriend/girlfriend
Bilinguals						
Antonio Quintero		S	S	SE	SE	
Salvador Garcia		S	SE		SE	SE
Suni Padilla		S	S	S		
Christian Fernandez		S	S	SE	ES	
Oscar Marino		S	S	S	S	
Paulina Mendez		ES	S		ES	
Roberto Olmedo		S	S	ES		ES
Daisy Olmedo		S	S	ES		x
Ana Flores		S	S	E	E	
Carlos Olmedo		S	S	ES		E
Marina Elenda		S	S	SE	ES	SE
Sancho Campos		S	S	E	E	E
Rita Diego	S	S	S	ES		ES
Avery Valdes	S	SE	SE	ES	SE	ES
Ricky Torres				SE	ES	
Mario Iglesias		ES				
David Herrera	S	S	E	E		
Erica Otero	S	SE	SE	SE	ES	
Marta Ugarte		ES	ES	E	E	
Jesus Ybarra		ES	ES	ES	ES	
Reina Perez	S	S	S			
Sol Esquival	S	E	x			
Sylvia Barcos	S	ES	x	E		
Jorge Gomez		S	x	ES	E	
Ramon Ibanez					E	
Magda Huerto	S (uncles)	ES	ES	E		
Monolinguals						
Chuck Ruiz		E	x	E	E	
Patricia Avila	E	E	x	E	E	E
Tony Lopez	E(S?)	E	E	E	E	
James Santana	E	E	E	E	E	
Jamie Diaz	E(S?)	E	x	E	E	
Veronica Nido	E	E	x	x	E	
Amanda Quinto		E	E	E	E	

S = Spanish; E = English; ES = more English than Spanish; SE = more Spanish than English; x = no interaction; blank = no data

for this interaction, while x's indicate that the interaction is not applicable (for example, the speaker does not know his or her father). In the case of some of my speakers, I was actually able to observe interactions with parents, siblings and so on. However, in those cases where this was not possible I have had to draw the data from self-report, which may be subject to attitudinal biases. In cases where I interviewed a speaker's parents as well, I was able to get information from more than one source about language use in the family. In addition, the principal at Westside Park had given me access to some additional language data unrelated to my interviews, the Bilingual Home Survey (BHS), which was on file for most of the students. The specifics of this form will be described below, but it provided me with another way to check reported use.

Most speakers use Spanish with their parents at least some of the time. For some of the students, when I asked them what language they spoke with their parents, they replied, 'English and Spanish.' I have recorded this as ES on the chart, however in some cases I suspect that what they really were indicating was the asymmetrical mode of communication, in which the parents spoke Spanish to them and they replied in English. Magda, for instance, told me that they speak 'more English than Spanish' at home. Later in the interview she claimed that she only spoke Spanish with her parents, but that they 'understand English.' Magda was not a very competent Spanish speaker. Though she tried her best to speak with me in Spanish, it was immediately clear that she is unaccustomed to exercising any productive ability in Spanish, though her comprehension was clearly very high. All these details suggest to me that Magda probably uses English with her parents when they speak Spanish to her.

With siblings on the other hand, there was a much greater use of English. Even those who said they spoke both languages with their siblings often added that they spoke mostly English. Spanish was often identified as the language that siblings would speak at a family gathering, or if the parents were around (see Rita's story about arguing, below). Otherwise, it seems, the siblings were most likely to speak English to each other. Usually, the same language was reported as the one used with all of the different siblings. One exception was Avery, who speaks Spanish with his baby sister only and English with the older kids.

In the domains of friends and boyfriends/girlfriends, even less Spanish was used. Some speakers, like Marina who will be discussed in the next chapter, specifically said that their friends were embarrassed to speak Spanish, or did not like to. Mario said this about his girlfriend, who is half Anglo and half Latina. Occasionally, a speaker would specifically mention codeswitching as the way they normally communicated with their friends; Avery, for example said he normally 'mixes' when he talks with his friends around the school. Of course, codeswitching is not limited to friends; Marta described this style as the normal one for her family.

Finally, as I expected, monolingual or Spanish-dominant grandparents sometimes provide a context for Spanish use. In some cases, such as Sylvia and Sol, this may be the only person with whom the speaker regularly uses Spanish. Ofelia encouraged her daughter Paulina to speak Spanish by reminding her that it was the only language she could use to talk to her grandma in Mexico. Sol was embarrassed that when she tried to talk to her grandmother, her Spanish was not good enough. These relationships with the extended family may be an important source of motivation for Spanish use.

Language use and the Bilingual Home Survey

The Bilingual Home Survey (BHS) form is sent home with each student who enrolls in the school for the parents to fill out and send back. The form is in English on one side and in Spanish on the other, so that parents who do not themselves speak English can complete it.[3] The BHS asks about four areas of language use: (a) the language the student first learned to speak at home; (b) the language the student now uses most at home; (c) the language the parents use in addressing the student; (d) the language the adults at home use to speak to each other. For each question, the parents can respond with English, Spanish or both languages. The purpose of the survey is to identify students who might have special needs in the area of language. Table 7.2 contains the data from the BHS survey for the bilingual speakers from Westside Park.[4]

Interestingly, the parents reported for all but three of the students that they learned Spanish as their first language, and of these, two (Erica and Rita) were described as having learned both English and Spanish as children. There is a further explanation in each of these two cases. Erica is the only speaker I interviewed who had one parent born in Mexico, and one born in the USA. Rita told me that she had an 'American' baby-sitter as a child who taught her English. The one speaker who supposedly learned only English first is David, the *wanna-be* who, as will be discussed in Chapter 8, refused to speak Spanish with me and seemed very insecure despite his relative fluency. Possibly his family shares the same insecurities about Spanish that David has (or David filled out the form himself) so that this report may be inaccurate, over-reporting use of the prestige language, English. In any case, it seems reasonable to conclude that most children of Mexican-born parents in this community are exposed to Spanish first, in the home.

This information is relevant to the earlier discussion of whether non-native fluency among the speakers is due to language attrition or imperfect acquisition. One reasonable hypothesis regarding speakers

Table 7.2 Language use as reported on the Bilingual Home Survey

Pseudonym	1st language spoken	What child uses at home	What parents use to child	What adults use at home
Salvador Garcia	S	E	S	S
Christian Fernandez	S	S	S	S
Oscar Marino	S	S	S	S
Ana Flores	S	B	S	S
Marina Elenda	S	S	S	S
Sancho Campos	S	E	S	S
Rita Diego	B	B	S	S
Avery Valdes	S	S	S	S
Ricky Torres	S	B	S	S
David Herrera	E	B	S	B
Erica Otero	B	E	B	B
Marta Ugarte	S	E	S	S
Reina Perez	S	B	S	S
Sylvia Barcos	S	E	E	E
Jorge Gomez	S	E	B	B
Ramon Ibanez	S	S	S	S
Magda Huerto	S	B	B	S

S = Spanish; E = English; B = both.

with low fluency levels might be that these speakers did not receive sufficient input in Spanish for acquisition to take place. If a speaker's parents mainly spoke to him or her in English, and the only opportunity for speaking Spanish involved the extended family mentioned earlier, then limited input might well account for low fluency. However, the BHS data (as well as the responses to questions about language use in the interviews) suggest that limited input was not a factor in acquisition for most of these speakers, and that they did in fact use Spanish with their parents as children.[5] While this information does not absolutely rule out imperfect acquisition, a pattern of normal acquisition with subsequent attrition is more consistent with the data.

The second question on the BHS, asking which language the child mainly uses at home, shows much more variation. Some of this variation probably reflects elements of the language use patterns described above. If the child uses Spanish to the parents and English to the siblings, then the report of home use would depend on whether the parents answered with reference to the language the child uses with them or with his or her siblings. Another influencing factor might be asymmetrical communication, a way of interacting that the parents might have had difficulty classifying as either English or Spanish.

The last two questions are about the parents' use rather than the child's. As with the first question, the response to the question about what language the parent speaks to the child is almost always Spanish. The only parents who claim to speak English or both to their children are those of Erica (whose mom is US born), and those of Sylvia, Jorge and Magda. These last three are some of the lowest-fluency Spanish speakers in the study. With respect to the final question, about which language is used among the adults in the household, the response is again almost always Spanish. The exceptions are all among the same speakers that have already been discussed, such as Erica.

Use of different languages for different family members

In discussions of bilingualism, and in particular in treatises on how parents might bring their children up to be bilingual (for example, Saunders 1982), there are often references to *strategies of person* (or 'one person–one language'). The idea is that a child will more easily acquire two languages if he or she speaks them with different people, rather than addressing the same people sometimes in one language and sometimes in the other. Paradis and Lebrun (1984), for example, claim that:

> it appears advisable to keep the two languages as distinct as possible. Mixed bilingualism does not seem to lead to as high a level of verbal competence as a learning situation in which the two languages are separated. (1984:215)

Usually this involves each of the parents speaking a different language with the child, although in principal any two or more family members might be involved. Merino (1983) found some correlation between this style of interaction among family, friends and so on, and the retention of Spanish by elementary school children. Her conclusions are tentative, since her sample did not permit her to separate children who spoke English to most people from those who spoke Spanish to most people, however the effect is statistically significant.

I had only a few speakers who described different language use patterns for each of their parents. David, for instance, reported that he spoke Spanish with his mom and mainly English with his dad, and similarly Salvador claimed to speak both with his dad and only Spanish with his mom. On the other hand, there are a fair number of individuals who speak only Spanish with their parents, and English with siblings, friends or other people. It will be interesting to see if there is an effect on fluency of a segregation of languages by speaker, vs. use of both languages with most speakers; this idea will be explored quantitatively in a later section.

Interactions beyond the family

One factor in the linguistic development of some of these speakers was the presence of many bilingual programs in the early grades throughout Los Angeles area school districts. In Chapter 2, I recounted my attendance at an elementary school holiday assembly, where I observed a significant use of Spanish. Even in schools where there is no bilingual program per se, Spanish is often taught as a subject nonetheless, beginning in the earliest grades. There was a high level of awareness of this trend among my speakers, including among speakers who had not participated in such programs. Magda, for example, excused her low fluency in Spanish saying, 'You know how when you go in elementary they teach you Spanish? I never had that.' Reina, who writes to her Mexican grandmother in Spanish, says she was taught to read and write Spanish in elementary school. She pointed out with amusement that, as a consequence, she knows more Spanish than her older brother who was actually born in Mexico (though he came over as an infant). The possible use of Spanish in elementary school is very significant, especially in light of the fact that elementary school appears to be the locus for language loss (Merino 1983).

The speakers who had jobs also mentioned the use of Spanish in the workplace; this is a feature of work for Paulina, for instance, who is an editor at a newspaper. She told me that any time someone who didn't speak English well would call on the phone, it would be passed to her, even though it sometimes turned out that the person spoke a language other than Spanish. Marina, whose part-time job is working in the Westside Park office, told me that she usually calls parents at home and talks to them in English, but if they don't understand, she switches to Spanish. Erica, the daughter of restaurant owners, is someone that I was able to observe in her actual workplace. Many of the clientele are older Spanish monolinguals, and it was clear that Erica was accustomed to interacting mostly in Spanish at her job. The need to use Spanish at the workplace may be another factor in acquisition and maintenance.

7.3 Rita and Avery: two individual cases

In order to give a more complete picture of the use of Spanish in the community, I will present the cases of two individuals, Rita and Avery,

in more detail. These cases can bring to light possible factors in acquisition that might be overlooked because they do not apply to all speakers.
In addition, they can provide a more specific answer to the questions
raised earlier about the role of Spanish in the lives of Latino young
adults.

Rita

Rita is 17 years old and lives with her family in the Projects. She is the
oldest of four children; the others are a sister, 14, and two brothers, 11
and 8. Her parents were both born in Mexico, where Rita still has family (including two grandparents), though she was born in the USA. She
says she visits often and would not mind living in Mexico, in part
because it is much safer than Los Angeles. Rita also has a baby, who was
7 months old at the time of the interview. She said she would like to
move out and live with her boyfriend, but was unsure whether this
would ever happen. The boyfriend, Juan, also attends Westside Park,
although I was not able to interview him. Rita is a member of the Culver
City gang, but apparently her involvement has decreased sharply since
she became a parent; as she puts it, 'Now, I'm more responsible.'

In terms of Spanish fluency, Rita scores fairly highly, and is judged to
sound like Spanish monolinguals about 50 percent of the time (see section 7.4, below). However, Rita herself is aware of flaws in her own
Spanish. She told me that she 'used to know perfect Spanish' but now
sometimes gets 'confused' when speaking it. As mentioned earlier, she
claims to have had an Anglo baby-sitter, so presumably Spanish was not
her only language at any point, unlike the speakers who first learned
English when they entered school.

In the course of her interview, Rita brought up several interesting
points about her language use. Generally she uses Spanish with her parents and grandparents, and both English and Spanish with her siblings.
When I asked in more detail about language use with her brothers and
sister, she told me that 'mostly we're fighting...we always argue in
English.' I then asked if she could ever remember arguing with them in
Spanish; Rita thought about this and said, 'Only when my mom's
around...that's kind of weird, huh?' This type of detail is fascinating
from the point of view of audience design, and also indicates the complex family situations that must be taken into account in researching
language acquisition and use.

Rita told me that she and her boyfriend Juan speak more English to
each other than Spanish, but that they do also speak Spanish sometimes. Like her, his parents are from Mexico, but he was born here. She

mentioned that one of the situations in which they always use Spanish is when either of their mothers is present; it was not clear whether this did not apply to the fathers or whether they were simply not around them as often. When I asked about terms of endearment or lovers' talk, Rita laughed and told me that for this she and Juan invariably used English.

Rita speaks both Spanish and English to her baby. She is confident that the child will learn English in school, and is committed to teaching her Spanish at home. When I asked why she felt it was important for her daughter to learn Spanish, however, Rita had a great deal of trouble answering and finally said it was 'hard to explain.'

One final interesting point came up when I was asking Rita about having friends of other races or ethnicities. She told me that in general most of her friends were Mexican, but that she had previously had an African-American boyfriend. Though his race per se was not a problem for her, she said 'It was harder for me because I couldn't talk Spanish to him or anything…That's the only thing I didn't like about it.' I hadn't asked her anything about language use at that point, and was frankly surprised to hear her comment, since she had admitted that with her current boyfriend she mostly speaks English anyway. Later in the interview, however, Rita brought up a fact that confirms this point about the importance of Spanish to her, mentioning that with her former boyfriend, she had sometimes found herself speaking to him in Spanish 'by accident.' Overall, Spanish does seem to have an important role in Rita's life.

Avery

In many ways, Avery's background is similar to that of Rita. He also lives in a low-income area (though not the Projects), is a gang member, was born in the USA, and has two Mexican parents. His grandmother lives in Mexico, and Avery has been there several times to visit. Like Rita, he is the oldest child, 16, with a sister who is 15, a brother who is 9 years old, and a baby sister who was 21 months old at the time of the interview. Avery said he often is responsible for taking care of the baby, and he is one of many speakers who felt they should set a good example for their brothers and sisters.

Avery's fluency is at a level similar to Rita's, at least in phonological terms (see below). It was difficult for me to evaluate his level of grammatical accuracy, because he did not speak much Spanish during the interview. He expressed no qualms about my asking him questions in Spanish when I broached the subject, however after several brief (and perfectly grammatical) turns in Spanish, he began to answer me in English. Even though I continued in Spanish, I was unable to coax him into switching back. Avery claimed that with his parents, he normally speaks Spanish, sometimes English. Based on this and on his strategy with me in the interview, I suspect that Avery may be one of the speakers who uses the asymmetrical mode with his parents, addressing them in English even though they speak to him in Spanish. On the other hand, his BHS indicates that he speaks mainly Spanish at home.

Avery provided a fascinating insight into language attitudes about Spanish and small children. When I asked him what language he spoke with his brothers and sisters, Avery said he spoke English with the older ones and Spanish with the toddler. I then asked him why he spoke Spanish instead of English with the toddler, and he replied:

> Cause she don't understand, she's small. Well, sometimes I tell her to 'come here,' she understands that, but– you gotta keep– you know, you gotta keep going constant so they could understand you. I don't feel like repeating the same thing every day.

The implication seems to be that children don't understand English until they are older, and have been specifically taught, whereas they just naturally understand Spanish! This is a fairly logical inference given the nature of the community, in which the children of immigrants learn Spanish in their infancy from parents and add English later, sometimes after starting school.

Outside of his own family, Avery is 'talking to'[6] a girl who speaks Spanish and has two children, ages 8 and 5, for whom Avery shows a great deal of affection. He told me that the children know Spanish, and that the 5-year-old sang the children's song 'Three Little Monkeys' for Avery, first in English and then a version in Spanish. He hopes to have kids of his own someday, and like Rita, he feels that teaching them Spanish is important. In contrast, he does not feel that it is important for children to have a sense of their ethnic heritage or to 'feel Mexican.' As part of this discussion about his possible future children, Avery mentioned that in general the girls he dates almost always speak Spanish. When I asked if this meant that he spoke Spanish with them, he replied that he never talks to them in Spanish on the phone, but sometimes does in person. It is not clear what motivates this taboo about the use of Spanish on the telephone, but it suggests an intriguing area for further study.

Unlike many of the speakers I interviewed who claimed to speak only English with their friends, Avery immediately said that he spoke both English and Spanish with his. He clarified this further by saying 'I mix, like.' I had not asked any questions about codeswitching in the interview yet, but had noticed it occasionally around the school. Avery's opinion of this way of speaking was positive. It may be the case that some of the speakers who said they spoke English with their friends actually codeswitch but do not see this as 'speaking Spanish.' In any case, it is clear that, as with Rita, Avery uses a certain amount of Spanish and has some definite attitudes and ideas about its role in his life.

7.4   Experimental evidence for factors that affect Spanish fluency

The acquisition of Spanish in the home

As I began interviewing young Latino adults in Spanish, one of the first things that came to my attention was that their levels of fluency varied greatly. There was a strong generational effect, with those whose parents were born in the USA being uniformly monolingual English speakers. However, among those whose parents were born and raised in Mexico, the levels of Spanish fluency varied from those who spoke the language effortlessly, and, in my first estimation at least, in a native-like manner, to those with some receptive competence but who could barely construct a sentence in Spanish. In fact, I found a great deal of accompanying linguistic insecurity about Spanish competence, as the following comments from two of the speakers indicate:

> I try to [speak Spanish] but my Spanish is so broken up it's pathetic.
> (Sol, 18)

> I feel weird, I feel like I'm gonna say something wrong and they're gonna laugh or something.   (Marta, 16, about speaking Spanish with friends)

Attitudes toward Spanish will be discussed more in Chapter 8.

It is often taken for granted in discussing bilingual communities that all children who grow up in bilingual homes will achieve native-like fluency. Appel and Muysken (1987), for example, conclude that 'not only do very young children acquire a second language rapidly, they also seem to be able to acquire two languages simultaneously without special difficulties' (1987:95). With respect to phonology specifically,

Strozer (1994) in her review of the field of acquisition, says, 'Generally, an accent-free pronunciation is said to be "virtually certain if acquisition begins before age 6"' (1994:160). Many of the speakers in this sample, however, despite acquiring Spanish from infancy, do have difficulty speaking it, and are not native-like at all. For them, these generalizations about bilingual communities do not hold, just as they do not for me and my own level of Spanish fluency, as I discussed earlier.

The learning of Spanish by these US born Latino young adults suggests aspects of both first (L1) and second (L2) language acquisition. On the one hand, most of them began learning Spanish from birth, in a naturalistic setting, as in first language acquisition. However, all of them speak English natively, and for most of them it is their stronger language. Many of these speakers show elements of transfer from English in their Spanish, including the types of mistakes that would never be made by a native speaker. At least superficially then, the language role of Spanish among speakers born in the USA is more reminiscent of second language acquisition. A similar conclusion is reached by Schlyter, who looked at Swedish–French bilingual children. She found that

> the stronger language in a bilingual child is exactly like a normal first language in monolingual children, whereas the weaker language in these respects has similarities with a second language.   (Schlyter 1993:305)

Before looking at the actual levels of acquisition among these speakers, it may be enlightening to explore the various theories that have been put forth to explain second language acquisition and to consider how they might apply to this community.

The question of acquisition versus loss

One factor to consider is that these young Latinos and Latinas may reflect, not imperfect acquisition, but rather a possibly native level of acquisition with subsequent attrition, as was discussed earlier. Several speakers specifically mentioned that they used to know more Spanish, such as Rita or Chuck (who is now monolingual). The questionnaires collected by the school on language use also indicate that most of these speakers learned Spanish first in their homes as children, though their fluency levels now vary, suggesting that attrition may have taken place. Recently, there has been more research on first language attrition, although the emphasis has most often been either on aphasics, or on aspects of morphological and syntactic loss. Seliger and Vago (1991) provide the most complete collection of articles on attrition to date, yet even they comment that '[p]honological/phonetic investigations of L1 attrition are scarce, beyond impressionistic observations' (1991:9). However, such studies are crucial, particularly since there is increasing evidence to suggest that successful acquisition of an L2 favors or may even imply a corresponding loss in the L1 (cf. Major 1993).

There is a further piece of evidence relevant to the question of imperfect acquisition versus language loss, found in Merino's (1983) study of bilingual acquisition. This study was planned as an exploration of bilingual language development among groups of children in the kindergarten to 4th grade age groups, intended to show how different structures are acquired simultaneously in two languages, English and Spanish. To the surprise of the researcher, however, it was found that while language development in English proceeded as expected, increasing in the higher grades, Spanish productive ability actually deteriorated. The children in the 4th grade group showed a significant attrition in their Spanish production to a point where their scores were similar to those of the kindergarteners. The study was done in two parts, including a longitudinal study in addition to the cross-sectional one, and both parts confirmed the results concerning Spanish loss. Interestingly, attrition took place only in productive abilities and there was no corresponding loss in comprehension, which remained at a constant level.

The children selected as subjects for Merino's study were all considered to be balanced bilinguals when they had entered the school at age 5, by which is meant that they 'could speak and understand English and Spanish with equal or near-equal proficiency' (Merino 1983:281). Since some development in Spanish was seen between kindergarten and grade one, however, we cannot say that these children had a complete command of Spanish when they entered school. Additionally, the study focused exclusively on grammatical forms and did not include any assessment of phonological skills. In looking at the acquisition of phonology then, this study cannot be directly applied. The implications of these findings are nonetheless very striking in that they clearly reveal a pattern of development with subsequent attrition in early childhood. This strongly contradicts the extension of the CPH discussed above: children acquiring a language before a certain age have no guarantee of reaching native-speaker levels of competence, since language attrition may affect them before their language development is complete.

Second language acquisition and the Critical Period

Perhaps no other issue in the field of second language acquisition (SLA) has received so much attention as the alleged existence of a 'critical period' or 'sensitive period,' after which it is impossible to acquire a second language natively. The general premise of the Critical Period Hypothesis (CPH) is that at a certain age (originally thought to be around the onset of puberty) a child loses the ability to acquire native-like fluency in a second language, particularly as regards the phonology of the L2. In other words, a child immigrating to the USA before the critical age will learn English and be indistinguishable from a person born here, whereas after that age, he or she may retain a slight accent, generally stronger as the age at immigration goes up. The phenomenon is usually attributed to some type of maturational constraint, biological or cognitive, and has sometimes been linked with cerebral lateralization. This aspect of the theory is usually associated with Lenneberg (1967; but cf. also Asher and Garcia 1969/1982, Scovel 1969, and Oyama 1976/1982). The research that has been done does provide evidence for age of acquisition as a strong factor in the achievement of native-like fluency, especially in the area of phonology (see Long 1993).[7] It has also been suggested that it is a 'sensitive' period, optimal for learning, rather than a 'critical' period which is involved.

In addition, there have been some alternative proposals (other than biological ones) for why children are more successful than older learners in the acquisition of phonology. Schumann's acculturation model relates language acquisition at any age to the learner's motivations and attitudes toward the community that speaks the second language. Schumann (1978) suggests that children assimilate more easily overall to a new community in terms of their affective states, making their acquisition more rapid and complete. This idea is consistent with numerous studies of language maintenance, shift, and loss (Lambert and Freed 1982, Dorian 1981, Stevens 1986, Stanford, Lin, and Hogan 1982) in which affective factors were found to play an important role. Major (1993) presents evidence that acculturation is particularly crucial in L1 attrition. Flege (1981) proposes another explanation. He suggests that it is not the lack of phonetic learning ability that causes adults to have an accent, but rather their more stable phonological representations for the sounds of their native language. In other words, adults are more likely to identify a sound in the L2 with a similar but not phonetically identical phoneme in the L1, a process that Flege calls *equivalence classification*. Since Flege's initial proposal, there have been numerous studies which seem to provide evidence for this claim about accentedness, such as Flege and Hillenbrand (1984).

In all of these studies the focus has been on the inability to acquire native-like phonology after a certain age. Yet it has sometimes been assumed that native-like pronunciation is guaranteed with sufficient exposure *before* a certain age. For instance McLaughlin claims that 'children who experience balanced exposure to two languages develop both languages as do monolingual speakers of either language' (1981:23). Similarly, Saunders remarks:

> Phonological transference is what is perceptible in a person's speech as a foreign accent.... This type of problem is usually confined to persons who have become bilingual after the age of about 12. Children who acquire a language before this age usually do so with no or very few traces of a foreign accent.   (1982:188)

The question of whether a foreign accent necessarily constitutes a 'problem' is debatable. More importantly, however, Saunders sets a fairly specific and late date for acquisition of accent-free pronunciation. As will be seen below, even if the existence of a 'critical' or 'sensitive' period is accepted, there is evidence to suggest that the early studies may have set the age limit too high, in other words, that acquisition must begin even earlier than anticipated in order to produce native-like phonology.[8]

Goals of the experiment

I have already discussed the fact that young CE speakers in Los Angeles showed a wide range of variation in their phonological acquisition of Spanish. In examining the actual levels of fluency achieved by bilingual speakers in the community, my goal will be to see how the various theories of language acquisition and language loss might or might not apply. This analysis should provide more evidence for or against the extension of the Critical Period Hypothesis, since these speakers generally began their acquisition of Spanish as infants. It should also help to assess the merits and drawbacks of the many theories proposed to account for differences in the acquisition of phonology by children and adults. Finally, the results of this study should extend our knowledge of the extra-linguistic factors associated with language attrition, building on the work of studies such as Merino (1983).

My goal in designing an experimental evaluation of Spanish phonology (or 'accent') among the CE speakers was to determine how their Spanish sounded to others in the community, specifically by having a group of raters evaluate a small segment of each person's speech. In particular, I wanted to know the following:

- Are there any US born speakers in the sample who sound as native as the older adults born and raised in Mexico? Alternatively, can people in the community consistently distinguish foreign born and US born Spanish speakers?
- Do bilingual young adults who are relatively recent immigrants from Mexico show any influence of English on their Spanish or are they rated exactly like older, strongly Spanish-dominant speakers who immigrated as adults?
- What is the range of phonological nativeness represented by the US born bilingual young adults, and can these levels of fluency be correlated with any extra-linguistic variables?

Design of the experiment

Many studies have shown good correlations between the assessments of speakers' phonology made by a linguist based on quantitative data, and the ratings those same speakers received by linguistically naive judges (Ryan, Carranza and Moffie 1977; Brennan and Brennan 1981). A particularly interesting series of studies was done by Sankoff and Thibault (Thibault and Sankoff 1993; Sankoff and Thibault 1994) on French–English bilingualism in Montreal. In Sankoff and Thibault (1994), the researchers elicited raters' evaluations of fluency by asking about the degree of influence of the other language on the person's speech. I have incorporated this and several other elements from their study into the design of my own experiment.

The area of language judgments is a somewhat treacherous one for the design of social science experiments, in the sense that people's attitudes and ideas about language can so easily color their supposedly linguistic judgments. Therefore, great care must be taken in designing an experiment of this type. Bongaerts, Planken and Schils (1995), for instance, present the results of an experiment designed to test whether 'late' second language learners, who began acquiring a second language after age 12, can sound like native speakers. The form of the experiment is very similar to the one I have used here. The researchers asked native English-speaking judges to rate speech samples from a group of native and non-native speakers in terms of their degree of accentedness, on a scale from 1 ('very strong foreign accent: definitely non-native') to 5 ('no foreign accent at all: definitely native').

Unfortunately, when they examined the ratings given to native English monolingual subjects (the control group), the researchers found that not all of them received a rating of 5. In fact, different speakers from the control group received *all* of the ratings from 1 to 5, across more than one judge; sometimes native English speakers were classified as 'very strong foreign accent: definitely non-native'! The mean rating across four judges for the spontaneous speech samples was only 3.70 for the native speaker group. Bongaerts et al. (1995) ascribe this to the fact that some of these subjects might have had features of regional dialects in their English, despite the researchers' having identified them as speaking 'neutral' British English.

This lack of reliability within the control group invalidates their claims about the second language learners. The researchers were surprised to find that many of the Dutch late learners received higher scores than the native speakers; the learners' mean rating for spontaneous speech was 4.10, higher than that of the native speakers. Bongaerts et al. (1995) interpret this to indicate that it is possible to acquire a native-like pronunciation after the age of 12. However, it is clear that the control group speakers were being rated on some factor other than nativeness of pronunciation since they are all, in point of fact, native speakers.

The obvious candidate is the one mentioned in the study: regional accent. Since all of the learners had been carefully trained in RP (Received Pronunciation), it is not in the least surprising that they were rated more highly than the native speakers. What is impossible to determine is how many actual non-native features the judges might have heard and ignored because of the overall prestige of the dialect the learners spoke, whether natively or not. This study highlights both the difficulty for the experimenter of knowing exactly what it is that raters are judging, and the importance of comparison with a control group.

The data for the experiment I designed consisted of short taped segments of Spanish speech by 28 of my informants, collected onto two audio tapes. Most of the speakers have been mentioned in the chapters on English, except for the four strongly Spanish-dominant older native speakers that I used as controls, and Carlos, whose interview was conducted entirely in Spanish.[9] I used spontaneous speech rather than standardized text because I was planning to have each rater hear approximately 16 speakers, and I felt that hearing the same utterances over and over would tire the raters. Additionally, I felt that spontaneous speech would most closely represent the person's vernacular phonology, rather than the more self-conscious formal style expected in repeating or reading a fixed text. This decision, of course, introduces its own difficulties. The segments from each person's interview were selected so that the content was completely neutral. In addition, since my goal was to determine whether the speaker's *phonology* was similar to that of native speakers, I had to exclude segments where there were grammatical errors in Spanish (not regional non-standard features, but learner errors). I also eliminated segments that included codeswitches into English.

I decided to select segments of 3–5 seconds in length. Sankoff and Thibault (1994) established experimentally that there was a high correlation between ratings on a short segment of speech and on a longer passage by the same person. For a few of the least competent Spanish speakers it was simply not possible to find a segment of this length where their Spanish did not include any grammatical mistakes (Jorge and Sol). Rather than exclude these speakers from the study, I chose to include them as a type of secondary control for the experiment. Their overall fluency level is low enough that there is no possibility they would be mistaken for a native speaker of Spanish in the community. Since I planned to include strongly Spanish-dominant native speakers as the control group, this low-fluency group could serve to anchor the other end of the scale. In a few other cases (Avery, Marta and Reina), there were no grammatical mistakes but the speaker used English fillers (such as *um...*) so frequently that I could not exclude them from the speech sample. These speakers were also included in the analysis, although I kept track of the fact that they had used fillers. Two different tapes were made, each consisting of speech segments from 16 test speakers and one sample speaker, with the sample segment being the same in both cases. Additionally, five of the speakers were used on both tapes to serve as a type of control for the two rater groups.

The twenty raters were all members of the Latino community of Los Angeles, who ranged in age from 16 to 59. They were selected by a native Spanish-speaking research assistant in Los Angeles as people who, in her estimation, spoke Spanish with native fluency, although some of them were born in the USA. All the materials, including the explanation of the experiment, were presented in Spanish. On the cover page of the questionnaire, the raters were asked how old they were, where they were born and what age they were when they came to the USA if they were not born here. They were also asked a question about their English fluency, modeled on Sankoff and Thibault (1994): When was the last time that you had to speak English? (today, this week, several weeks ago, I almost never use English, I never use English).

Respondents were specifically told that they did not need to put their name on the response sheet.

The rating sheet for each speaker consisted of six questions.[10] Two asked the rater to give his or her opinion of the speaker's personality, rating each speaker on friendliness and intelligence. One question asked the rater to select the person's ethnicity, from a list that included Hispanic, Black, White or other race. Another asked where the rater thought the speaker was born, with the following options: in Mexico, in Mexico but has lived in the USA for some time, in some other Latin-American country or in the USA. Of the two questions about language, the first asked simply what language the rater thought was the speaker's 'mother tongue' (*lengua materna*): English, Spanish or another language.

The other language question, on which the results presented here will focus, had a similar form to a question used by Sankoff and Thibault (1994). The raters were asked to select one option to complete the following sentence: *Cuando habla español, el modo de hablar de esta persona suena* —— [When speaking Spanish, the way this person speaks sounds ——]. The options given were: *puro español, español bastante puro, un poco influido por el inglés, bastante influido por el inglés, muy influido por el inglés* [purely Spanish, relatively pure Spanish, a little influenced by English, somewhat influenced by English, very influenced by English].

Administering the experiment

Before the main part of the experiment was carried out, several additional raters were used as pilot subjects, some by myself and some by the research assistant. It was determined that each segment needed to be repeated twice in order for the raters to feel comfortable answering the questions about the speaker. Some raters expressed some hesitation about rating the speaker's intelligence or race, however since these questions are not essential to the evaluation of language, I did not make any changes in their form.

The experiment was administered to the final group of twenty raters (ten for each tape) by the research assistant mentioned above. The raters were thanked for their participation, and told that the study was about 'what you can tell about a person just from hearing their voice.' They were asked to answer the demographic questions about themselves before the rest of the experiment was administered. Then, they were told that they would hear different people speaking briefly, and that after hearing each one they would be asked to answer some questions about the speaker. They were also told that they should answer all the questions even if they were unsure and had to guess. It was explained that the first speaker was just an example for practice. The research assistant then played the sample segment and monitored their responses, asking them if they had any questions, and so on. Then the rest of the experiment was administered, with the research assistant pausing the tape after each speaker's segment had been heard twice so that the responses could be entered.

Results of the ratings for the control group

The results presented here will focus only on the single question about the degree of English influence on the person's Spanish (their accent). As I expected from my subjective evaluation, the speakers were rated over a wide range of categories. I was also not surprised to find that the control subjects did not always receive a rating of '1', even though they immigrated as adults, generally speak little or no English, and speak Spanish without any accent that I could discern. In answering language questions generally, many raters do not like to use the top rank, or feel uncomfortable rating someone's language skills as perfect, since this sort of evaluation is often tied to ideas about 'educated' speech, and so on.

However, the four control speakers (Ofelia, Esperanza, Lola and Mercedes) received a score of either one or two across all twenty raters, except for a single instance where Mercedes was rated '3'. The rater in question gave relatively lower scores overall than some of the other judges. Note that this score represents only one out of 50 total ratings given to control speakers by the judges in both groups. This 98 percent level of consistency is sufficient to justify using these speakers as a control group. In addition, the system I used for evaluating the speakers does not rely on knowing the meaning associated with any individual scores.

Accent ratings for the bilingual speakers

I began by calculating the number of times that a particular speaker was given the same rating as the control group speakers (Ofelia, Lola, Esperanza and Mercedes) by a particular judge. For example, if a judge gave Ofelia, Esperanza and Mercedes all a rating of '1', then I would count any other speaker who received a '1' as being given the same rating as the control speakers. If the rater gave Ofelia and Mercedes a '1' and Esperanza a '2', then I counted as 'the same' any speaker who received a '1' or a '2', without distinguishing among these cases. For the single judge who rated Mercedes as a '3', a rating of '1', '2', or '3' was considered the same as the control group.

The native-rating percentages for each of the bilingual speakers are given in Table 7.3 (excluding the four control speakers). For those speakers who appeared on both tapes, the number is a total percentage over the twenty judges. The other speakers were each rated by ten judges. There are three Spanish-dominant young adults in the group: Antonio and Oscar, who both immigrated to the USA at age 9, and Suni, who came at age 13. These three individuals still speak a variety of CE that retains some non-native features, although their competence in English is quite high. Roberto and Daisy, who came over at ages 5 and 3 respectively, speak Chicano English completely natively, so it would be inappropriate to call them Spanish-dominant, although it is possible that having been born in Mexico might have an impact on their level of Spanish competence. All of the other speakers were born in the USA.

The first question that the study was designed to address is whether any US born speakers in the sample sound as native in Spanish as the older speakers who immigrated from Mexico as adults. At first glance,

Table 7.3 Accent ratings for the bilingual speakers

Pseudonym	Rated as native speaker?
Antonio Quintero	90%
Salvador Garcia	90%
Suni Padilla	90%
Christian Fernandez	80%
Oscar Marino	80%
Paulina Mendez	80%
Roberto Olmedo	70%
Daisy Olmedo	67%
Ana Flores	60%
Carlos Olmedo	50%
Marina Elenda	50%
Rita Diego	50%
Avery Valdes	45%
Ricky Torres	40%
Mario Iglesias	30%
David Herrera	25%
Erica Otero	20%
Marta Ugarte	20%
Jesus Ybarra	15%
Reina Perez	10%
Sol Esquival	10%
Sylvia Barcos	10%
Jorge Gomez	0%
Ramon Ibanez	0%

the fact that no speaker received a score of 100 percent might seem to suggest that the answer is no. However, the expected variance between scores must also be taken into account. As an approximate measure, I took the scores for the three control group speakers who appear on tape B, Ofelia, Esperanza and Mercedes. I arbitrarily elected Ofelia to represent the native standard, and calculated the percentage of the time that Esperanza and Mercedes were rated the same as (or higher than) Ofelia by the ten judges. This figure came out to 80 percent for both of them, which suggests that a rating of 80 percent may be sufficient to classify a speaker as being generally rated the same as the control group. Of course, this test entails a comparison with only one speaker (and one rating), whereas the bilingual subjects are actually being compared with a standard of ratings across several control speakers, so this latter comparison should be even more reliable.

Returning, then, to the original question about whether US born speakers can achieve native-like fluency, the answer is yes. Salvador, Christian and Paulina all received scores of 80 percent or 90 percent, indicating that their Spanish sounds as native as that of the older Mexican control group. My own impression in listening to these individuals was also that they sound perfectly native. The fact that young adult immigrants like Suni and Oscar fell within the same range further confirms this finding. The ratings for Antonio, Suni and Oscar also answer the second question that the study was designed to address, namely whether younger, bilingual immigrants would show some influence of English on their Spanish which the older, mainly monolingual Spanish speakers do not show. The answer seems to be no, at least in terms of judgments by raters from the community. These young adults were scored exactly like the older immigrants.

Interestingly, the two other Mexican-born speakers, Daisy and Roberto, fell just outside the range of the Spanish-dominant speakers, with scores of 67 percent and 70 percent respectively. Though these are also fairly high ratings, the two speakers do not have any consistent advantage over the US born speakers as a whole. The other bilingual speakers received somewhat lower scores, ranging from 60 percent for Ana, down to 0 percent for Jorge and Ramon, who were never given the same rating as the control group by any of the judges. This answers the third question raised above about the range of phonological nativeness found among US born speakers of Spanish. The most fluent of these young bilinguals are consistently ranked the same as native, monolingual speakers of Spanish by judges from the community. The least fluent among them are never ranked the same as a native speaker. All that remains is to determine, if possible, what non-linguistic variables correlate with these various levels of fluency.

The correlation of accent with social factors

In looking for social factors that might correlate with the nativeness of Spanish phonology among these bilingual speakers, I chose to explore two types of factors. To begin with, I looked at factors associated with language use and the language environment in the speaker's family. Secondly, I looked at social factors not specifically related to language. In the latter group I included the same general social categories that were associated with variation in English in Chapters 5 and 6 (sex, gang status and so on), as well as some other factors that might logically be related to Spanish use. As discussed in Chapter 2, the Latino family structure has an important role in the community and is different in some ways from that of Anglo communities, so I included among other things factors related to the sibling structure, as well as to contact with Mexico.

Factors related to language use and language environment

Table 7.4 presents the results of a series of one-way Analyses of Variance, with the accent rating score as the dependent variable, and various language-related factors as the independent variables. The first independent factor was whether the parents were monolingual or not, measured in two ways.[11] The first way (Monolingual Parent 1) involved three distinctions: both parents are monolingual, one parent is monolingual or neither parent is monolingual. The second (Monolingual Parent 2) collapsed these into two groups: (a) the speaker had at least one monolingual parent or (b) the speaker did not have a monolingual parent. Whichever way the variable was partitioned, this factor group showed a significant correlation with accent rating: the speakers with at

Table 7.4   One-way ANOVA results for family language use variables

Source	Sum-of-squares	DF	Mean-square	F-ratio	P
Monolingual parent 1 (both, one, none)	0.496	2	0.248	3.876	**0.04**
Monolingual parent 2 (yes or no)	0.495	1	0.495	8.16	**0.01**
Mom speaks English	0.495	1	0.495	8.16	**0.01**
Dad speaks English	0.121	1	0.121	1.676	0.214
One language per speaker	1.024	10	0.102	1.599	0.226

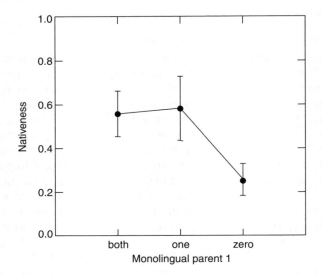

Figure 7.1   Means for phonological nativeness by monolingual parent (3 levels)

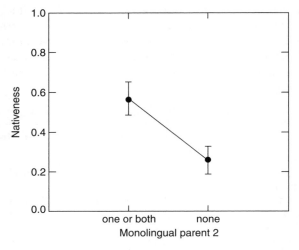

Figure 7.2   Means for phonological nativeness by monolingual parent (2 levels)

least one monolingual parent had higher accent ratings than those whose parents are both bilingual, as shown in Figures 7.1 and 7.2.

As was discussed earlier, in the case of many bilingual speakers their non-native fluency may be a result of language attrition rather than incomplete acquisition. The fact that having a monolingual parent improves fluency makes perfect sense in this context. Those children who are forced to continue using their Spanish with a parent who does not speak English have a better chance of avoiding deterioration in Spanish ability than those who can switch to English with everyone in their milieu.

I also looked at the speakers' mothers and fathers independently with respect to English fluency. In cases where the speaker had only one monolingual parent, it was always the mother. So, as the table shows, the effect of having a monolingual parent or not (Monolingual Parent 2) overlaps exactly with Spanish monolingualism in the mother. The effect of monolingualism in the father, then, overlaps with the difference between having one monolingual parent or two, and, as can be seen in Figure 7.1, this difference is not significant. The lack of additional effect for a monolingual father does not seem surprising in light of the fact that most of the Latino families I interviewed involved traditional gender roles, so that the mother spent much more time taking care of the children than the father.

The final language-related factor that I looked at was whether the speaker used both English and Spanish with the same individual or not. I selected this factor because of its role in Merino (1983), the study of Spanish loss discussed earlier. Merino found that the greatest degree of Spanish language attrition occurred among children who tended to use both English and Spanish with the same speaker. Those who generally used only one language or the other with a particular individual retained more Spanish, although as I mentioned, Merino did not indicate how many in this latter group used mostly Spanish with everyone, used Spanish and English about equally, or used only English to most people.

I used the data from Table 7.1, the summary of Spanish usage given earlier, to calculate a value for this factor. For the categories of mother, father, siblings, friends, grandparents and boyfriend/girlfriend, I counted the number of times the speaker reported using only one language with the people in question. I then divided this by the total number of personal categories for which I had data, yielding a percentage of the speaker's social circle with which the speaker uses only one language. These values ranged from 0 (for example, Jesus) to 100 percent (for example, Ana). As can be seen from Table 7.4, there is no correlation between this variable ('One language per speaker') and the accent ratings. I will discuss some possible reasons why this correlation was found in Merino's study at the end of the chapter.

General social categories, sibling structure, and ties to Mexico

Table 7.5 shows a series of one-way Analyses of Variance, again with the accent rating score as the dependent variable. The independent variables include those general social or demographic categories that were found to be significant in the analysis of variation in English, namely sex, gang status and social class. They also include some new variables that, in accordance with the literature and my own ethnographic study of the community, emerged as possible correlates of Spanish acquisition and maintenance. These are (a) the speaker's position in the sibling hierarchy ('Older siblings'), that is, whether he or she has several, one or no older siblings; (b) whether the speaker has any older siblings who were themselves born in Mexico or not ('Mexican-born siblings'); and (c) how often and how recently the speaker has visited Mexico ('Visits Mexico'). The value for this last category was a number from 0 to 4, which I assigned based on how frequently and recently the speaker visited Mexico. One variable that I considered but did not end up including in the statistical analysis was whether or not the speaker had family in Mexico, excluded because all but two of the speakers claimed that they did.

None of the usual demographic categories showed any significant correlation with accent rating, as can be seen in Table 7.5. In some ways, this result is not surprising, if the acquisition of Spanish by these speakers is treated as a normal process of acquisition beginning at birth, an assumption consistent with the acquisition history of the speakers. First language acquisition is usually considered an involuntary process, not affected by social factors at all.

Table 7.5   One-way ANOVA results for social categories and other variables

Source	Sum-of-squares	DF	Mean-square	F-ratio	P
Class	0.009	1	0.009	0.107	0.747
Sex	0.012	1	0.012	0.134	0.718
Gang	0.005	1	0.005	0.054	0.819
Mexican-born siblings	0.071	2	0.035	0.425	0.660
Older siblings	0.081	2	0.040	0.490	0.621
Visits Mexico	0.437	4	0.109	1.545	0.237

Given that these speakers are immersed in an English-speaking setting and have learned English natively, though, one might expect the process to have some parallels with second language acquisition as well. Theories of second language acquisition are divided in terms of the role they give to extra-linguistic factors. Flege's model of sound categorization does not include them at all. Schumann's acculturation model places a heavy emphasis on affective factors, but not on demographic categories such as gender. Looking at the particular social structures found in the Latino community, especially those related to family roles, I had predicted that gender might have some effect on fluency. Additionally, in studies of language attrition, it is affective factors that are usually found to be most relevant (for example, Major 1993), and there is good evidence in the history of at least some of these speakers to indicate that they learned and then lost Spanish. To the extent that the fluency ratings might reflect attrition, it seems to me that we might expect some correlation with social factors. Loss of a language, particularly where that language is part of the social context of the community, might be related to shifts in identity. I will return to this issue later in the chapter.

It was also interesting to discover that the factors of sibling status and contact with Mexico had no effect on the variable. There has been a great deal of discussion of the role of siblings in language acquisition in bilingual settings. Silva-Corvalán, for instance, says:

> The typical family situation is one in which the older child acquires only Spanish at home, and maintains a good level of communicative competence in this language throughout his life, with more or less attrition depending on a number of extralinguistic factors, while the younger children acquire both Spanish and English at home. These younger children are more likely to develop and maintain a contact variety characterized by greater distance from the norms of first-generation immigrants. (Silva-Corvalán 1994:10)

However, this study found no correlation between position in the sibling hierarchy and acquisition of Spanish. And while the presence of siblings born in Mexico would seem to assure that the individual had Spanish speakers of his or her own generation with whom to interact, this factor also shows no correlation with accent among this particular sample.

The speaker's degree of contact with Mexico was also not statistically significant in relation to the accent ratings. The probability of error for this variable was .237. Nonetheless, the mean accent ratings for each of the five Mexico groups increased in a linear fashion, with the lowest accent ratings for the '0' group (people who had never been to Mexico), and the highest for the '4' group (people who went very frequently, and had been there within the past year), as shown in Figure 7.3. It is possible that with a larger sample size this distribution might achieve statistical significance, so this variable is worth considering for future studies, though I will not discuss it further here.

Earlier, I noted that individual social factors such as gender did not seem to affect fluency. In some cases, though, interactions between variables can have a strong effect on the analysis of linguistic variation, as was shown in Chapter 5. For this reason, I used generalized linear models (with Spanish fluency as the dependent variable) to look for interaction effects among the factors discussed above, none of which had contributed a main effect to the analysis. The results of GLM estimates incorporating various cross-products of sex, gang and social class are presented in Table 7.6.[12] Most of these crossed factors show no effect on the dependent variable. However, the GLM analysis uncovered a significant interaction in how sex and social class were correlated with Spanish fluency. This effect is displayed visually in Figure 7.4. Interestingly, the working-class males and middle-class females received significantly higher accent ratings than the other speakers. Since these

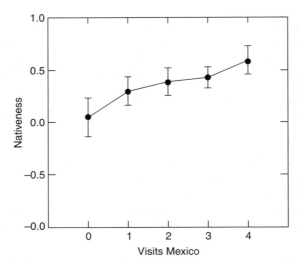

Figure 7.3   Means for accent nativeness by visits to Mexico (not significant)

Table 7.6 Generalized linear model results for the interactions of variables

Source	Sum-of-squares	DF	Mean-square	F-ratio	P
Gang*class	0.008	1	0.008	0.089	0.769
Gang*sex	0.010	1	0.010	0.111	0.743
Sex*class	0.331	1	0.331	4.777	**0.042**
Class*gang*sex	0.048	1	0.048	0.567	0.461

Table 7.7 GLM using the model 'Nativeness = Constant + SEX*CLASS + Monolingual parent 2' (Analysis of Variance)

Source	Sum-of-Squares	DF	Mean-Square	F-Ratio	P
Monolingual Parent	0.432	1	0.432	8.783	**0.008**
Sex*class	0.268	1	0.268	5.447	0.031
Error	0.885	18	0.049		

Dep Var: NATIVENESS; *N*: 21; Multiple *R*: 0.680; Squared multiple *R*: 0.463

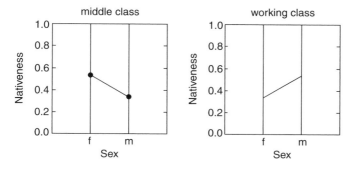

Figure 7.4 Accent nativeness and the interaction of sex and social class

two effects cancel each other out, no main effect was seen for either sex or social class. I'll return to possible explanations for this effect in a moment. Table 7.7 shows the generalized linear model for Spanish phonological nativeness, incorporating the effects of having a monolingual parent as well as the sex/social class interaction.

7.5   The gender/social class interaction and its influence on the acquisition of Spanish phonology

I mentioned above that the process of first language acquisition is not generally expected to correlate with social categories as sociolinguistic variables do. Such categories, as well as attitudinal factors, however, might be involved in attrition. Since there is good evidence that many speakers in this community may have experienced first language acquisition with subsequent attrition, it seemed somewhat surprising to me that at first none of the social factors appeared to correlate with fluency. The discovery of the 'hidden' correlation between the sex/social class interaction and accent rating suggests that social categories are in fact involved in the process of attrition, at least in this bilingual community.

Much more data on this effect would be needed before drawing any firm conclusions about why Spanish fluency patterns in this manner. However, it is possible that there is some parallel here with the interactions of sex, class and gang status seen in Chapter 5. In explaining the correlation of these factors with variation in English, it was proposed that the intersection of conflicting social norms in the community could be the source of the interactions and their linguistic effects. In particular, I discussed the presence of a 'toughness' norm associated with the working class, male gender and gang members, vs. a 'conservative' or 'conformity' norm associated with the middle class, female gender and non-gang members.

The speakers whose construction of identity included social categories from both the 'tough' and 'conservative' groups (such as middle-class gang members) were the most likely to emphasize their gender role linguistically with use or non-use of the variables (as was seen in Figures 5.11 and 5.16). I have referred to the complex category memberships that constitute the identities of these speakers as 'heterogeneous.' Among the 'homogeneous' groups, such as working-class gang members, there was much less linguistic differentiation by gender. In other words, the sociolinguistic variables in English are used more powerfully to signal gender by speakers who construct their identity and ethnicity with elements that reflect conflicting values of conformity or toughness. Whether this entails a higher or lower use of the variable depends on the values (conformity or toughness) associated with the specific variable and the identity of the speaker. Could this analysis be applied in some way to the accent rating data?

With respect to the interaction of sex and social class, the middle-class women and the working-class men preserve the highest levels of fluency in Spanish. These are the two homogeneous groups, as described above, which are consistent in stressing either toughness norms or conservative norms for gender and social class. The heterogeneous groups tend to have more Spanish attrition. In elementary school, when children are trying to work out their social and gender roles, the working-class girls may feel a pressure to be tough like their brothers, while still being 'good girls.' The resolution of these conflicts as part of identity construction may involve an unwillingness to speak Spanish, the low-prestige language. Similarly, middle-class boys who have been rewarded for 'good' behavior may find themselves needing to express their 'toughness' on the playground, and again, they may see speaking Spanish as socially unacceptable. On the other hand, the children with homogeneous social identities may be more secure in their language use generally, so that even if use of Spanish is somewhat stigmatized it may not be as likely to result in attrition or loss for them.

Relevant to this hypothesis is the case of a speaker I mentioned earlier, Paulina. Ofelia, Paulina's mother, describes a situation which seems to be fairly common, in which a school aged child refuses to speak Spanish and wants to speak only English. For Paulina, this occurred when she was in about the third grade. At first, Ofelia simply spoke to her in Spanish and accepted her daughter's responses in English, but she realized one day that she had not heard Paulina speak Spanish in a long time. She began to insist that Paulina speak to her in Spanish, but her daughter refused. Finally Ofelia asked directly why she would not speak Spanish, and Paulina told her that it was because all of the kids at school spoke only English. Ofelia insisted that it was important for her to know Spanish, and reminded her that the family made a trip each year to Mexico. She told Paulina that if she didn't speak Spanish, she would forget it and then she would be unable to talk with her grandmother and cousins. Paulina did begin speaking Spanish again. Some time after this, she admitted to her mom that some children at school had been making fun of the children who spoke Spanish. This story coincides neatly with the Merino study, which found that a sharp drop in Spanish language ability occurred between the third and fourth grades.

The stigmatization of Spanish in elementary school may be a significant factor leading to the loss of productive capabilities, particularly for some children. It should be noted that Paulina, who successfully passed through her period of schoolyard teasing and went on to become an extremely fluent speaker of Spanish, is female and middle-class, which is consistent with the explanation presented here about which children might be more resistant to social pressures toward loss of Spanish. Of course, this is a preliminary hypothesis which would require much more data before it could be confirmed. But even the suggestion that the same interactions of social factors might affect (a) a sociolinguistic variable in the dominant language, tied to regional sound changes, and (b) attrition of fluency in a minority language within the same community is an intriguing result. It highlights the fact that sociolinguistic studies in bilingual communities (beyond those focused on codeswitching or language shift) can contribute a great deal to linguistic theory.

At first, I was surprised that gang status had no effect on attrition, since it also forms part of the conflicting social norms pattern. But the crucial factor here is the age at which deterioration or loss of Spanish takes place. Merino has established this age experimentally at the transition from 3rd to 4th grade. At this age, children usually have not yet become involved with gangs. While there might be a few exceptions, in my interviews, speakers always mentioned middle school (grades 6 through 8) or junior high as the time when kids become interested in gangs. Therefore, the gang affiliation of the bilingual speakers now is not relevant to their Spanish fluency level, which may have been established much earlier.

7.6   Implications for theories of second language acquisition

One fact that has emerged clearly from this analysis is that learning Spanish from birth does not guarantee native-like fluency. The school data and interviews confirm that Spanish was the first language acquired in the home for almost all of these speakers, and yet their fluency ranges from native-like to very poor. If there were any lingering doubts about the extension of the Critical Period Hypothesis, found in Strozer (1994) and others mentioned above, they can now be discarded. Starting acquisition at an early age does not guarantee phonological nativeness.

Considering the data on language attrition, one might take the opposite approach and ask whether it is possible to attain native-like fluency in a language if one is born in a country where that language is a minority one. The answer is yes, as evidenced by speakers like Christian, Salvador and Paulina. Among the influences that favor fluency in Spanish in this community are having a monolingual parent and constructing one's identity from social categories that do not represent conflicting norms.

In addition, several studies (for example, Flege and Fletcher 1992; García and Cuevas 1995) have found that gender as a social factor did not correlate with degree of fluency. However, the results of this study suggest that gender in interaction with social class may be a factor. As was shown earlier, this interaction neutralized any effect of gender when it was analyzed independently. Therefore it is possible that the same effect was present in the other studies, but was not detected because interactions of social factors were not included in the models and the influence of gender was masked.

Finally, these data bear on the issue of whether a 'strategy of person' approach to bilingualism (in which each parent deliberately speaks only one of the two languages with the child) contributes to the success of acquisition of a second language in the home. Support for the success of this process is mainly anecdotal, and often attributed to a nebulous concept of making it easier for the child to separate the two languages cognitively. As I mentioned, Merino (1983) found a correlation between this factor and Spanish retention, while the present study did not. In my study, however, the presence of a monolingual parent (a factor Merino did not measure) emerged as relevant. One possibility might be that in Merino's study, the 'use of a single language' factor was tightly correlated with monolingualism on the part of one or both parents, and that this was the real source of the effect. In addition, there were native-like speakers in my sample, Salvador for example, who spoke Spanish with one monolingual parent and both English and Spanish with the other.

My data suggest that the supposedly positive results of the 'one-person, one-language' approach may be due to the fact that this system forces one parent to act as a monolingual in the minority language, that is, the language that is not the dominant language of the wider community. Bilingual parents who specifically adopt this approach are in essence simulating the presence of a monolingual parent in the household. However, if my hypothesis is correct, the same results in terms of acquisition should be obtained in households where the child uses only the minority language with one of the parents, and either both languages or also the minority language with the other parent.

If anything, it would seem advantageous for *both* parents to concentrate on speaking the minority language to the child, if this is feasible, in an environment where the surrounding community speaks a different language. Even the case of the second parent alternating between the two languages is simply like the case of Salvador, above, and should not be less effective than 'one-person, one-language,' if monolingualism by one parent is the true predictor of fluency. The only situation in which this would not be the case is if the previously mentioned 'cognitive advantage' of speaking only one language with each parent had some objective validity. However no scientific evidence for this effect has ever been offered, and I suspect it is a post hoc explanation for the success of the method, rather than an independent motivation for it. In sum, I believe that strategies of person are only more successful for households where the child could otherwise speak the majority language with every family member. Parents wishing to raise their child bilingual should assure that the minority language is spoken exclusively by at least one of them. Even then, social factors beyond their control may affect the child's ultimate fluency.

8
Language Attitudes

The study of language attitudes in a community can illuminate patterns of linguistic practice, especially those related to the construction and expression of identity. I introduced a number of questions about different ways of speaking and language varieties into the interviews. There were also numerous occasions when the speakers I talked to spontaneously brought up topics related to language, such as commenting on how other (non-Mexican) dialects of Spanish sounded. Language-related topics seemed to generate a great deal of interest among the CE speakers generally. In some ways, the attitudes of these young adults are surprising, and in other ways they match the attitude research that has been done in other communities.

Part I: Attitudes about Spanish

8.1 Using Spanish in the interviews

All of the conversations I had with students at Westside Park were begun in English (although some of the interviews with speakers from other networks started in Spanish). First of all, this is the language used for most purposes around the school, and therefore the most natural one to use in approaching students initially. But beyond this, I discovered immediately that the use of Spanish was not a neutral choice, and that the speakers often had great insecurities about their Spanish, which will be discussed in more detail below. I developed a series of steps for encouraging students to speak with me in Spanish, particularly if they seemed hesitant at first.

To begin with, even if I knew that an individual spoke Spanish, I always asked first. Whether or not one speaks Spanish can be a sensitive topic, and it might have been risky socially to just switch into Spanish. After they had affirmed that they did speak it, I volunteered that I grew up speaking Spanish, even though my Spanish was 'not perfect or anything.' This last point was crucial: I discovered almost immediately that many of these young adults are uncomfortable about how they speak Spanish and afraid that native Spanish speakers will laugh at them. I then asked if we could talk in Spanish for a while. If they were already looking uncomfortable, I phrased it as, 'Would it be all right if I asked you some questions in Spanish and some in English?'

In most cases, the students who were fluent were quite willing to speak Spanish. Occasionally someone might claim that they 'felt funny' speaking Spanish, or comment 'my Spanish is not too great.' In these cases I usually said that I understood and that sometimes I couldn't think of the word for something in Spanish. This is true, but besides that, it is exactly the complaint that I often heard from the students about their own Spanish. Most of them recognized (with a head nod, and so on) that this was exactly the problem. I then said that it was good for me to practice asking questions in Spanish, sometimes mentioning that I intended to interview some people who *only* spoke Spanish as well. Other times I commented that there was so much Spanish in LA and I felt that I should ask questions in Spanish about what it's like to grow up there. I suggested that I could ask them a few questions in Spanish, and if they felt uncomfortable we could switch back to English. Everyone agreed that this would be okay, and most were willing to continue in Spanish for a while.

I allowed my questions to include occasional English words where these seemed natural to me. Codeswitching is an integral part of Spanish as it is spoken in Los Angeles, and I wanted to present myself as someone local. I also wanted the students to feel that this was not a formal situation or a test, and that if they felt more comfortable using some English themselves, they could do so. The least fluent Spanish speakers often reached a point where they had trouble expressing something they really wanted to talk about, and then they would say, 'I don't know how to say it in Spanish.' I would assure them that it was okay to continue in English, and then they switched.

In a few instances, my impression was that the students were hesitant to speak Spanish with me because they perceived me as an Anglo and an outsider. The clearest example of this is Salvador, one of the most competent Spanish speakers in the study, as was seen from his accent rating scores in Chapter 7. When I asked if it would be okay for me to ask him some questions in Spanish, he said he felt 'weird' and added:

The only time that I speak Spanish really is when I'm at my house. Or like when I'm around people that speak Spanish you know, like – … say Dr Johnson [the principal] wants to start talking to me in Spanish or something, you know, I feel, you know like – I don't know. Out of place or something.

As was discussed in Chapter 1, there was evidence in the interviews that the students felt comfortable speaking with me, and that I had succeeded in establishing a participant role for myself in the school community. Nevertheless, I was, in at least some ways, an outsider, and it is impossible to know for certain the extent to which a particular student saw me as such. If for some students Spanish was not a language that they felt comfortable speaking with an outsider, the Spanish they spoke with me probably did not represent their vernacular style, even if their English was fairly natural. Nonetheless, most speakers seemed to relax as the Spanish part of the interview went on. After his initial hesitation, Salvador, for example, felt comfortable enough to talk about very personal topics in Spanish, such as some time that he had spent in jail, and he continued speaking Spanish for a long time, though I had explicitly said that he could switch back to English any time he wanted to.

The only speaker with a reasonable level of fluency who strongly resisted speaking Spanish was David. When I first asked David whether he spoke Spanish, he answered confidently, 'Yeah, fluent.' I then asked him a question in Spanish, which he answered in English. I continued to address him in Spanish, with him answering me in English; occasionally he would give a one- or two-word answer in Spanish, then go back to English. At one point I said explicitly '*Vamos a hablar en español*' ('Let's speak Spanish') with no effect whatsoever. A bit later, I requested directly that he speak to me in Spanish, again with no result. After a few minutes, I tried again, saying, '*Háblame en español!*' ('Speak Spanish to me!'). He answered, 'Or I could talk in both?' After this point there were a few longer turns by him in Spanish. Finally, I asked if he knew enough Spanish that it might help him if he were interviewing for a job. He answered confidently that he did, and I initiated a simulated job interview, which produced several consecutive turns in Spanish.

My insistence on speaking Spanish with David (which might superficially sound like a case of the interviewer badgering the informant) was a result of the unique nature of this particular interview. I treated all the speakers who expressed any hesitation about speaking Spanish with me in the most sensitive manner possible, although I did encourage them to try to speak some Spanish. I told them that my own Spanish was not 'perfect,' and asked their permission to try some questions in Spanish, stating explicitly that if they felt uncomfortable then we could switch back to English, because I did not want them to be uncomfortable. However, David did *not* express any hesitations about speaking Spanish. In fact, at one point in the interview he expressed pride in his own abilities saying that he spoke Spanish 'real good.' I could tell from a few turns that his abilities in Spanish were certainly good enough for the purpose of answering these questions, so that it was not limited ability that kept him from speaking with me.

Not only did he not say that he was uncomfortable, but also David's body language did not show any of the signs of discomfort that some other speakers, like Salvador, showed. When I asked if we could speak Spanish, he did not look embarrassed, look away, hesitate to answer or use hedges like 'well ...' or 'uh ...' He spoke to me confidently and enthusiastically – but mainly in English. He did take a few turns in Spanish, which again, seems to suggest a basic level of ability. David's behavior was unique among the speakers I interviewed. Once I had given an explanation of why I wanted to speak Spanish, even those like Sol with extremely low levels of competence struggled along for several minutes of answering questions in Spanish before switching back to English. Those with higher competence levels spoke in Spanish easily, for long stretches at a time. Why did David alone show such resistance to speaking Spanish?

A possible answer may be found in David's special social status. He is a *wanna-be*, the category used in the community for people who hang around with gangsters but are not yet members of the gang themselves, as discussed in Chapter 2. He is a *lame*, not only in the sense of anyone outside the well-defined peer groups (cf. Labov 1972a), but also in the further sense of being specifically rejected by the group of which he tries to claim membership, the Culver City gang. David is neither a member of the gang nor a person dissociated from gang activities. It would not be surprising to find this position of social insecurity coexistent with a high degree of linguistic insecurity. It was clear in the interview that David was trying to impress me with the supposedly dangerous life he led. Possibly he felt that he would not sound impressive in Spanish. As will be discussed in the following sections, there are many types of attitudes toward Spanish, but it continues to have lower prestige overall in the community than English does. Perhaps David does not want to be 'caught' speaking this low prestige language.

8.2   General attitudes about speaking Spanish

The attitudes toward Spanish and the use of Spanish among young CE speakers varied a great deal. Some of them felt that knowing Spanish was essential to their ethnic identity, while others emphasized that what matters is not speaking Spanish, but rather one's feelings about one's heritage. These attitudes were not simply reflections of the speaker's own level of Spanish ability. In fact, at times language attitudes show little or no correlation with use and ability. García and Cuevas (1995), for example, found no correlation between language attitudes and either Spanish use or Spanish ability among their group of second-generation 'Nuyorican' speakers, and neither did Zentella in the group she studied (1997:141). In general, the attitudes toward Spanish in the community as a whole are an important part of the language situation in Los Angeles, and should be examined carefully.

In discussing attitudes toward Spanish, I have given examples from individual speakers and identified their Spanish fluency level in most cases. There may be important differences in the attitudes of monolinguals versus bilinguals, for example, or even between someone who speaks Spanish fluently and someone who speaks it at a lower level of proficiency. In Chapter 7, quantitative, experimentally-based fluency ratings for all the speakers were presented and discussed; in this section I have simply provided short qualitative summaries of proficiency for individual speakers.

8.3   Self-evaluation and linguistic insecurity

As was mentioned earlier, some CE speakers expressed hesitation about speaking Spanish with me because they felt their Spanish was inadequate in some way. The following comments from various individuals illustrate this type of insecurity:

Sometimes my Spanish goes a little bit awkward.   (Jorge, 18)

It's weird because I know some of the words [in Spanish], but some of the words I don't understand.   (Magda, 19)

I speak a little Spanish, like to a point that I could get by, I guess, but I won't use proper grammar.   (Sylvia, 17)

Before I used to know perfect Spanish, everything, I knew. But when I talk Spanish now it's like I get confused.   (Rita, 17)

I know Spanish good, but not like great-great.   (Erica, 17)

Not surprisingly, these speakers were given generally low accent ratings (see Chapter 7). Marina, who received a higher accent rating, also mentioned not being able to find the right word in Spanish sometimes. In addition, when I asked her whether she and her friends ever spoke Spanish among themselves, she said they only did it 'once in a while,' and then added, 'I don't know, I think they're embarrassed to speak it.' People unfamiliar with bilingual communities may assume that all the bilingual speakers have about the same competence, but this is clearly not the case here. Embarrassment about use of Spanish is a factor that should be taken into account in discussing the language attitudes of Latinos in Los Angeles.

I did have some speakers who expressed pride in their use of Spanish. David, for example, said 'I'm good at Spanish, I can talk it real good,' though he also admitted that there are words he does not know. Marina, who lived in Mexico for a year when she was nine, told me proudly that she knows how to read and write in Spanish as well as English. When I asked Salvador if there was ever something he could say in English that he couldn't say in Spanish, he replied, 'No, I'm pretty good at saying stuff in Spanish and also in English.' It is interesting to note that this standard question in the investigation of bilingual communities ('Is there anything you can say in language X that you can't say in language Y?'), which is designed to elicit lexical items that have no precise equivalent in the other language, was always interpreted by my speakers as being about competence, again indicating how salient this issue is for them.

8.4   Attitudes about parents who speak Spanish: the language gap

Several speakers commented on the fact that their parents spoke only Spanish, usually in a way that expressed mild embarrassment or frustration. Ana, for instance, told me that she wished her mom knew more English for when monolingual English-speaking friends come over. Salvador said that he and his brother speak both Spanish and English with their dad, but only Spanish with their mom. He claims that 'she could [speak English], but ... we feel like we're not really communicating with her that- you know, that well.'

Another example of this type is Sancho. Sancho told me that he sometimes tries to speak English with his parents, but that they say they are too old to learn. Even more interesting, however, was his response when I asked him how he got along with his parents (at the beginning of the interview, when nothing about language had come up yet):

I like my parents, but um, sometimes we just don't, we don't really get along cause we don't talk to each other. [CF: mhm.] Cause I can't really explain to 'em how I feel in Spanish, [CF: mhm, oh that's interesting] and I would- and I wouldn't be able to explain to them in English. I don't know all the right words and I mean, every time I try to tell 'em something I get stuck.

Misunderstandings between non-native and native speakers have been studied from the perspective of second language acquisition, but the possibility of such misunderstandings arising within a single family has received little attention. Yet in a community like this one, where not all immigrants acquire English, while some children of immigrants lose their Spanish, such a situation is of course possible. Sancho's Spanish is actually fairly good, but he nonetheless feels that there is a language barrier between himself and his parents, as the passage above illustrates.

The attitudes reflected by these explicit comments about the drawbacks of monolingual parents were also sometimes found in more subtle implications. A large number of speakers brought up and stressed the fact that their parents spoke English, even when I had not asked about this. Interestingly, the monolingual or Spanish-dominant parents that I spoke with myself did not express any embarrassment over their lack of English skills. Esperanza, for example, cheerfully told me how well she gets along with her son's American girlfriend, even though the girl speaks no Spanish and Esperanza speaks almost no English. Esperanza also pointed out that when I was talking to her son Roberto (in English), she had come in and said to him in Spanish, 'Ask her if she wants something to drink,' forgetting momentarily that I spoke Spanish as well.

There was a comment from Jorge that suggested the possibility of other attitudes however. When I asked which language he spoke with his brothers and sisters, he said mostly Spanish and added as an explanation, 'for my mom can understand, for she won't feel guilty.' The meanings and usages of certain words in this community differ slightly from their use in Anglo dialects of English, and I am not entirely sure of the meaning of 'guilty' here. But my sense is that in this case it implies embarrassment, and in any event suggests possible insecurity about low English skills on the part of the parent.

Not all comments about Spanish-speaking parents were negative, especially when the parents had at least some competence in English. Sylvia, whose Spanish ability is somewhat limited, nevertheless considers the ability to speak Spanish with her mom as something unique that the two of them share. Sylvia's stepfather is Japanese, and I asked if he speaks Spanish. She said no, but that she and her mother do sometimes speak Spanish when he is around, adding 'we can't just, like, not speak Spanish anymore because he lives with us.' Of course, technically speaking they could if they wished, since Sylvia's mom speaks fluent English. What is highlighted here is the important symbolic value of the language that she and her mom share.

8.5   The importance of speaking Spanish to Mexican/Chicano identity

After discussing ethnic identity, I asked the speakers what things they felt were an important part of Mexican or Latino identity. I asked about eating certain foods, listening to certain kinds of music, and finally about speaking Spanish. Jesus pointed out very reasonably that 'some Mexicans don't like, you know like, *like* Mexican meals.' When I asked what he thought was important to being Mexican he mentioned simply 'being proud of what you are.' Erica and a few other speakers linked listening to music in Spanish with Mexican identity, although Erica in particular has little choice in the matter, since she hears it all day at her parents' restaurant.

Many speakers felt that speaking Spanish was important, much more so than particular foods or music, and this view was not necessarily related to their own level of Spanish competence. When I asked Erica, who was rated as not very fluent, whether she thought speaking Spanish was important to Mexican identity she replied, 'Yeah, I think-I think it's very important. Very. Cause, you know, you're Mexican, you have it in your blood.' Reina, a moderately fluent speaker, said that she believes speaking Spanish is important to being Mexican because there are people in the community who don't speak English and they need somebody to translate for them. She also told me with clear pride that all her brothers and sisters speak Spanish, and added as an explanation (jokingly), *¡Comemos mucho chile!* ('We eat a lot of chile!').

Christian, a highly fluent speaker, sees the importance of Spanish as pragmatic, more than symbolic. He says, 'You gotta know Spanish now... There's a lot of Latin people coming to this state and you need to know it.' Ricky feels not only that knowing Spanish is useful, but also that knowing additional languages, such as Chinese, would be even better. James, who speaks only English, shares the belief that speaking Spanish is important and says he regrets not being able to speak it himself. Paulina, who has a high level of Spanish competence, expressed surprise over the number of monolinguals in the community:

A lot of people don't know how to speak the language! Which shocks me, to see somebody with a last name like 'Lopez' or 'Bracamontes' or, that doesn't speak – you know?... But it happens!

Paulina indicates clearly that she thinks this is unfortunate. Her reference to 'the language' is also very revealing, highlighting the symbolic role that she accords to Spanish as the language tied to Latino ethnicity.

Several of the monolinguals mentioned their own experiences with others who criticized them, whether seriously or teasingly, for not knowing Spanish. Veronica gave the most complete explanation. I asked her about what ethnicity she considered herself to be, without mentioning anything about language, and she responded:

When people ask me [about ethnicity] I say Mexican but, but then they say, 'No you're not. You don't speak Spanish.' They, they just tease me to get me mad ... I guess a lot of people think if you don't speak Spanish you're not like full Mexican or whatever, but, but I *am*! I– I think so.

Amanda told me that most of the comments she gets are from guys, who say, 'you're a disgrace cause you don't know Spanish.' She defends herself, saying 'because I was never taught it!' In both these cases there seemed to be an element of teasing. Nonetheless, the teasing reveals an association in the community between speaking Spanish and ethnic identity.

There were also bilingual speakers who felt strongly that speaking Spanish was *not* an important part of ethnic identity. Avery, for example, feels the language has nothing to do with being Mexican. Salvador suggests, quite reasonably, that some people were never taught Spanish by their parents, despite being of Mexican descent. He says:

If they know Spanish and don't speak Spanish, that's one thing ... or if they never knew it, how could they speak it, know what I mean?... It's really the way they were brought up that counts.

Still, implicit in the first part of his statement is the suggestion that if one *does* know Spanish, speaking it is important in some sense.

An example of someone who knows Spanish but refuses to speak it came up in the interview with Mario. When I asked him if he ever spoke Spanish with his girlfriend he said, 'No, she d- speaks Spanish, I just never speak with her. I don't know, she doesn't like speaking Spanish.

She knows it, she doesn't like speaking it. Don't know why.' Note that Mario himself is a highly fluent speaker of Spanish, who spoke it easily and at length with me. Mario did not seem to associate anything negative with his girlfriend's reluctance. However, it confirms the fact that there are bilinguals in the community who choose not to speak Spanish.

Reina, who is less tolerant of this attitude than Mario, told me a story about her cousin that emphasizes the importance of speaking Spanish if one is capable of doing so. She mentioned her cousin, who used to live with them, so I asked if she and the cousin were close. Reina replied:

> I was at first . . . but then, um she- she changed. She started acting like she didn't know Spanish. [CF: Oh really?] And she came from Mexico, barely like, three years ago... and all of a sudden she changed, like, she started acting like she didn't know Spanish. [CF: Wow.] And she tried to act too American. [CF: Wow.] And I told, you know, I told her, 'What happened to you?' you know. [CF: That's too bad.] And, and then- then I told her, you know, I- know- it's not that I'm saying nothing- that there's nothing wrong with that, but, I mean, y- she- she would speak s- English to her mom, knowing that her mom didn't know English!

This story reveals how in the community, the use of Spanish vs. English can be seen as an expression of the assimilation/ethnic pride dichotomy discussed in Chapter 2. I should add that Reina's story actually ends with her fighting (physically) with her cousin over this issue. A similar current appears to underlie the comments of Erica:

> CF: Even if they're Mexican, some people don't speak Spanish.
> E: No! Some people are like that. I hate people like that, that are Mexican, and they try to act like if they don't know Mexican. So- but some of my friends that are Mexican, and- they don't know how to speak Mexican.

Again, there is a distinction drawn between monolinguals, for whom speaking Spanish is not a required part of ethnic identity, and bilinguals, who are socially sanctioned for refusing to use Spanish.

Perhaps as a result of these community attitudes, many monolinguals expressed a desire to learn Spanish. Tony, who has some comprehension but little productive ability, said that he is consciously trying to improve his Spanish by spending more time with his grandparents. Chuck is a particularly interesting case. He is a monolingual who is known among the other students as 'a Chicano activist' and has an extremely strong sense of his ethnic identity. He stated explicitly that he does not speak Spanish, although he claims to understand it, and I confirmed this with a few questions, which he mostly understood but was unable to respond to (for example, giving the correct number for his age). Showing his linguistic insecurity, Chuck says, 'I have like a fear of speaking Spanish because I can't roll my r's and I don't want to sound like a white boy'.

As might be expected from his strong ethnic stance, he nonetheless considers that speaking Spanish is important to being Chicano, and he expresses interest in improving his abilities, although he feels he cannot do so in his current social situation:

> I don't have the balls to, to try it out yet. Just, like, maybe when I'm out of here, but, not like- I- I wouldn't try to speak Spanish in front of my friends ... But like, I tried speaking Spanish before and I sucked.

At several other points in the interview, Chuck indicated an extreme sensitivity to the opinions of his friends, mentioning that they tease him for studying hard, and so on. He has many friends who speak Spanish (such as David and the four CC boys that I spoke with), but they seem to be intolerant of imperfect Spanish.

Since most of his friends are gang members, Chuck's comments may be relevant to the attitude of the gangsters toward Spanish. Interestingly, Santa Ana's (1991) study of Latinos in Los Angeles found monolingualism to be prevalent among the gang members he spoke with. He describes them as 'fiercely monolingual' and adds that 'one on one the gang members were diffident about Spanish and things Mexican' (1991:174). However, I did not find this to be the case at all in the region of Los Angeles where the interviews for this study were conducted. In fact, all of the present or former gang members I interviewed were bilingual, except for Patricia, Amanda, and James. These were the only three gang-affiliated speakers whose parents were born in the United States, so their monolingualism clearly has nothing to do with gang status.

Not only were most of the gang members bilingual, but they also tended to be very positive about the Spanish language and Mexican ethnicity in general. Christian, a core Culver City member, was cited above as saying that he felt that knowing Spanish was important. Sancho, also in CC, told me that he enjoys listening to Spanish music, and that he is accustomed to interpreting for his parents who do not speak English. As was reported in Chapter 7, however, there was no consistent correlation between Spanish fluency and gang membership, either positive or negative.

8.6   Parents' attitudes about teaching Spanish to their children

The parents of the young adults in the sample

When the young adults in my sample talked about their parents' attitudes toward speaking Spanish, there seemed to be a dichotomy between those who felt it was important for their children to learn Spanish and those who felt it could be detrimental to learning English. Ana, whose parents are in the first category, remembered that when she would come home from elementary school, her mother would sit down with her and teach her to read and write Spanish. Chuck, who was discussed above, also mentioned that his mother would like him to learn Spanish.

For some parents, assuring that their children would speak Spanish entailed some effort on their part. In Chapter 7, I discussed in detail the case of Ofelia, whose daughter Paulina began refusing to speak Spanish in about the third grade, due to teasing by monolingual English speakers at school. Ofelia insisted that Paulina speak Spanish, reminding her of the need to communicate with her monolingual grandmother in Mexico, and was ultimately successful. In my own case, I also passed through a phase of attempting to speak English at home, not because of any unpleasant experiences or teasing, but simply because I was often recounting school events which had taken place in English and found it easier to do this in the original language. Again, a direct insistence by my mother that I speak Spanish with her resulted in my ultimately attaining a high degree of fluency.

There are also a few cases of parents who refuse to teach their kids Spanish. Amanda's father was opposed to his children's learning Spanish, and spoke only English to them. Amanda's mother, who is Native American and does not speak Spanish, criticizes her husband for not having taught them Spanish when they were young, and Amanda herself regrets not learning Spanish. Similarly, Marina's father, despite speaking Spanish with the children when they were little, now insists that they speak English to him and to each other when they are around him, so that they will improve their English. Usually the reported motivation for not speaking Spanish to the children centers on the possibility that it will be detrimental to their English fluency; however it is possible that negative attitudes toward Spanish, from both inside and outside the community, also play a role. Of course the question of whether or not to speak Spanish to the children is not relevant for the many immigrant parents who are monolingual in Spanish, or who were monolingual at the time that their children were born.

The young adults in the sample as parents

I asked those of the young adults who were bilingual whether they would want to teach their own children Spanish. The response was uniform: all of them said that they wanted their children to learn Spanish. Even David, who was so reluctant to be interviewed in Spanish, said he would definitely want his kids to learn Spanish. When I asked Erica what she would like her kids to have as part of their Mexican identity (without mentioning language), she replied, 'Like, when I was born I learned how to talk Spanish before I learned how to talk English,' and said she would definitely teach her children Spanish. I asked Paulina whether it would be important to her to marry someone who was Latino. First she said yes, and then she said no, explaining that she really didn't care about the person's ethnicity, but would very much like them to speak Spanish so that if she had children, they could learn Spanish.

Christian expressed a very linguistically-enlightened point of view. He plans to teach his kids Spanish at home, and 'then as they go to school, they can learn English there.' He sees the value of knowing Spanish as pragmatic above all, a necessary skill in a state where it is so widely spoken. Even Sylvia, whose Spanish skills are mediocre, said she wants to try to speak Spanish with her kids (she was pregnant at the time of the interview). She is one of the people who expressed the opinion that speaking Spanish is an important part of Mexican ethnicity, because 'you have to know how to speak your language, I guess.' The term 'your language' seems quite significant here, paralleling Paulina's comment about 'the language' earlier.

Beyond the positive attitudes that most of my speakers had towards the idea of teaching children Spanish, I wanted to explore whether those of my speakers who already have children actually address them in Spanish. I had four speakers with small children of their own: Sol, Rita, Salvador and Marina. Sol is a very limited speaker of Spanish herself, and does not speak it with the baby or other family members. Rita, on the other hand, says she speaks both English and Spanish with her baby, and feels it is important that the baby learn Spanish. Like Christian, she seems to understand the usual patterns of acquisition; she says, 'English she's gonna learn in school; so I'll teach her Spanish at home.' I highlight this point because, as I mentioned earlier, many of the older parents in the community fear that teaching the children Spanish at home will have a negative effect on their English ability.

This type of speculation about language learning is actually fairly common in the community. Salvador, for example, talked about wanting his son, who is only 5 months old, to learn Spanish, but he wondered whether or not this would actually happen. He says:

> I'm not sure, I mean, how like, people, you know, learn to speak Spanish, the one- the ones that do. But I mean, I never went to school. Like, I really learned Spanish, you know, just by listening to my parents, when my parents, you know, talk in Spanish to me.

The mother of his baby is from Guatemala, and she and Salvador speak both English and Spanish with each other, although they do not live together. Marina's situation is similar, except that she and her boyfriend do live together. Her boyfriend is an immigrant from Mexico, and Marina told me they speak more Spanish than English at home, and use both in addressing the baby. Her baby is the only one of the four I've discussed who is old enough to be speaking herself (she is two years old), and Marina reports that the baby says some words in Spanish, but more in English. It will be interesting to see how the baby's two languages develop in the future.

Other cases of small children being spoken to in Spanish

In addition to the data from speakers who were parents, I had many speakers who talked about the children of friends, brothers and sisters, or other relatives. Chuck and his sister are both monolingual, but their mother speaks Spanish. Earlier I mentioned that Chuck's mother would like him to learn Spanish. She is also trying to teach it to Chuck's sister's child who is 17 months old. This seems to represent a fairly common pattern, where grandparents whose children are monolingual in English speak Spanish to the grandchildren. Sylvia, despite her own imperfect Spanish skills, tries to speak Spanish with her four-year-old nephew, but he refuses. She says that his grandfather speaks Spanish to him, but the little boy responds in English.

In Chapter 7, I discussed the fact that Avery speaks English with his older siblings, but Spanish with his baby sister, due to his perception that babies normally learn Spanish first, and English only when they get to school. It would be interesting to know whether this attitude is shared by others in the community. Even Avery himself shows some variation in this regard, since he speaks both English and Spanish to his girlfriend's young son.

8.7 Attitudes about other dialects of Spanish

I found a high level of awareness of non-Mexican dialects among my speakers. This is hardly surprising, since the population of Los Angeles includes people from all over the Spanish-speaking world, including large numbers of Cubans, Puerto Ricans and Central Americans from many countries. In all of the cases cited in this section, the speaker brought up the topic of other dialects without any prompt on my part. David, who had dated a Cuban girl, characterized Cuban speech as effeminate and mentioned some lexical items, including *gua-gua* ('bus'). Sancho is even more linguistically aware. In talking about Puerto Rican Spanish, he described the phonological alternation of /l/ and /r/, citing *mielda* for *mierda* ('shit') and *golda* for *gorda* ('fat') as examples. Interestingly, even Patricia, who is monolingual, has some awareness of dialect differences, and described Cuban Spanish as sounding faster to her. A majority of the comments I heard were at least mildly derogatory. My sense is that Standard (or even vernacular) Mexican Spanish is the prestige dialect in LA, and Caribbean and other dialects are lower in prestige.

Most of the speakers did not make any comment about my own dialect (Castilian). To some extent, living in LA had caused me to accommodate to a more general Mexican dialect in terms of phonology. However, an interesting situation came up during my interview with Marina. Just as we had begun to talk, the counselor came over from the office and asked if I could make a phone call for her to a Spanish monolingual parent. Marina came with me and overheard me speaking on the phone to the woman. When we resumed our interview she asked me, 'Are you American?' (meaning Anglo). I explained that my mother was Spanish and my father was 'American,' and that I had grown up speaking Spanish. We then spoke in Spanish for a large section of the interview. Much later, after we were again speaking English, I mentioned a friend of mine who is from Spain, and Marina said, 'I like the way you guys talk, Spain- you know, Spanish … yeah, Oh God!' I was not sure to what extent Castilian Spanish would be recognizable to speakers in Los Angeles, and I was interested to find that Marina not only recognized it (apparently) but also evaluated it positively.

Part II: Attitudes about codeswitching

The speakers in this sample did not seem to have a conscious awareness of Chicano English as a separate dialect in the way that some African-American English (AAE) speakers might. When I asked about 'how people talk around here' or when topics related to different styles of speaking came up, what most speakers brought up immediately was codeswitching. There does not seem to be a clear perception in the community of having a separate English dialect, apart from any use of Spanish, so I will begin by looking at the attitudes toward codeswitching among CE speakers.

The topic of codeswitching came up spontaneously in many interviews. In other cases I specifically asked speakers if they had ever heard anyone mix English and Spanish in the same sentence. Most speakers said that they themselves often do it. Reina attributes her own codeswitching to forgetting specific words, either in Spanish or in English, and refers to this way of speaking as 'taking turns.' When I asked Avery which language he used to talk with his school friends, he responded:

> Right here? I talk to them in Spanish or in English. I mix, like, you know [CF: In the same sentence?], yeah, you know, like everybody does, you know. They t- they put everything in like, English and Spanish the same sentence.

I asked his opinion about this way of talking, and he said 'it comes out all right.' Marta described a similar situation with respect to language use at home:

> In the house we talk both. And it's weird 'cause like we're talking English in a sentence, and then all of a sudden we put like Spanish into it. So it's like that in the house a lot ... People laugh but that's- I don't know, I'm just used to that so it's, it's normal.

It was clear from Marta's attitude and body language during this explanation (she was smiling, for example) that she had positive feelings about her family's use of codeswitching at home.

Codeswitching was a topic of interest not only for highly bilingual speakers, but also for those who were much less fluent. Sol, whose fluency is quite low, spontaneously offered the term *Spanglish* for this way of communicating, and commented that it was 'cool' and easier to

understand. Patricia, a monolingual, also told me that she could understand her friends when they spoke Spanish if they mixed in some
English. Apart from all the social significance of codeswitching, which
has been well studied and will not be looked at in detail here, there also
seems to be a perceived practical role for it in the community, in terms
of bridging the gap between proficient bilinguals and those who have
only a passive knowledge of Spanish.

Generally, the attitudes of the speakers toward codeswitching were
positive, and they often associated it in some way with ethnic identity. A good example comes from David, who said, 'Two languages
sounds better for us Mexicans.' He mentioned the movie *American Me*
as one of his favorites because the characters codeswitch. The same
point of view was expressed by Jorge, who is a competent but not
native-like Spanish speaker. When I asked him what he thought of
codeswitching, he replied, *Está bien, me gusta.* ('It's good, I like it.') He
added:

> Es que así nos- se hablan los Chicanos, los Mexicanos. Los que viven
> aquí. Como los de Mexico no hablan- no saben na' de eso, pero los
> que viven aquí sí hablan Chicano – 'Chicano language.'
>
> [It's like, that's how we- how the Chicanos speak, the Mexicans. The
> ones that live here. Like, the people in Mexico don't speak- don't
> know nothing about that, but people that live here do speak Chicano
> – 'Chicano language.']

There is a crucial ambiguity of meaning in the preposition *de* in the
third sentence. I have translated it as *in*, but it could just as easily have
been translated *from*. In the first case, the reference would be only to
people living in Mexico, but in the latter it could mean also
immigrants from Mexico living in the USA. This last interpretation
would be interesting in light of the many tensions that exist between
native born and immigrant Latinos in Los Angeles, suggesting that
native-born speakers see codeswitching as a linguistic way of setting
themselves apart.

One of the very few who expressed any reservations about
codeswitching was Salvador, a highly competent Spanish speaker. More
specifically, it is Salvador's father who disapproves of codeswitching,
and as Salvador reports, 'gets mad when you do that.' Interestingly, his
attitude is not based on linguistic prescriptivism, but rather on the idea
that codeswitching might be offensive to someone who does not speak

both of the languages, because 'they don't understand what you're say-ing.' I asked Salvador explicitly how he himself feels about it, and he says that he is 'used to it,' (meaning his father's attitude) and that he doesn't 'mix' anymore.[1] He then asked me, 'Why? You seen people that mix their Spanish with their English a lot?' I told him that I had, and that in fact my mother and I routinely did this at home. Salvador seemed slightly apprehensive that he might have offended me, and explained that his dad meant it more for 'out on the street,' and that he 'doesn't really get *real* mad.'

Interestingly, in an earlier part of the interview, Salvador had himself brought up the topic in a different form, referring not so much to codeswitching per se as to the advantages of having two languages available for interaction generally. He told me:

> I mean, it's easy, you know like, you know like, it's easier like when I'm talking to- speaking with someone that, that could speak English and you know understand Spanish also, cause, if I'm trying to say something and I can't f- you know, I don't know the word, or the word is like, it's like a real you know, like a real long word or something that you know, it's really not in your vocabulary? You can just tell them in Spanish and then you know if they know, they'll tell you or if they don't know, you know, they don't know what it means in Spanish, too. So it's- kind of makes it easier.

This view of bilingualism as an advantage for communication in the community generally is interesting, particularly since Salvador seems to be suggesting that his vocabulary might be larger in Spanish than in English.

As was discussed in the introduction, these younger speakers did very little codeswitching from English into Spanish, other than emblematic switches, either in the interview or around the school generally, despite their positive attitudes. There was much more switching when the language of the discourse was Spanish. To some extent, this might have been related to questions of fluency. Beyond this, I did not get any sense from them that codeswitching into Spanish carried the political sig-nificance that it had for the older speakers, who grew up in the 1960s and 1970s, during the first movements for civil rights for Mexican-Americans. The older speakers in the sample did much more codeswitching, over longer stretches, when the conversation was taking place in English.

Part III: Attitudes about Chicano English

8.8 Experimental evidence of language attitudes

Not much is known about attitudes toward CE specifically, as compared with AAE, for example; this is true both of attitudes from within the community and attitudes outside it. As was mentioned, the young speakers in my sample seemed to associate the characteristic 'way of speaking' in the community with codeswitching, and never discussed their own dialect of English apart from this context. This would be an excellent area for future studies to address, with matched-guise techniques and other experimental methods for evaluating attitude. One study of attitudes toward CE by people outside the community is mentioned by Baugh (1999:147). The study involves bidialectal and tridialectal speakers using CE, AAE or a standard variety to call about apartments advertised in the paper. Baugh notes that the preliminary evidence suggests that there is in fact a bias against CE, and that speakers of this dialect are often directed to lower income areas.

Much more study has been done of attitudes toward accented speech, that is, the non-native English of those whose first language is Spanish. In some cases it is possible that these studies actually are about reactions to CE; as I have discussed repeatedly, there is a long history in linguistics and other areas of failing to properly distinguish native CE and non-native learner varieties. For example, Ryan, Carranza and Moffie (1977) studied the reactions of 100 college students to taped English segments produced by Spanish – English bilingual speakers who represented 'a wide range of accentedness' (1977:269). They found that there was a strong correlation between perceived 'accentedness' and less favorable ratings on a number of scales, including pleasantness, friendliness, eventual occupation and fluency. However, they do not say whether any of the bilinguals are native speakers of English or not. The high ratings for some of these speakers on the 'unaccented' scale suggests that they might in fact be native speakers of CE, who happen to be bilingual. If so, this study provides interesting data on the perception of CE in comparison with non-native learner varieties.

Part IV: Attitudes as represented in the media

To some extent, attitudes toward CE can also be measured more indirectly. One way to do this is to look at the representation of CE in the media. For example, Peñalosa (1980) comments that 'a number of Chicano announcers and newscasters now appear on television in the Los Angeles area...but it is difficult if not impossible to detect any Spanish-accented characteristics in their speech' (1980:181). As noted in Chapter 1, I myself did not find this to be true any longer when I did my fieldwork in 1994. Newscasters whose phonology was non-native or typical of CE are now found on the local news broadcasts. This would seem to reflect a shift in attitudes toward CE, at least in the Los Angeles area.

Also, in many areas including Los Angeles, there is an increasing amount of broadcasting in Spanish, as well as local programs that are specifically designed to be bilingual. Such developments in and of themselves tell us something about language attitudes. The uses of language on these programs can be very enlightening. Where I live, in Los Angeles, there is a television station called KZLA, a *very* local station, that broadcasts programming of interest to the Latino population in the area. One of the bilingual programs on this channel features a hostess, Patricia, who introduces Spanish language music videos. She also takes requests from callers, discussing their preferences in music with them, as well as doing interviews with members of the audience in the studio and with some of the musicians whose videos are featured. She uses both English and Spanish for this purpose (and, to me at least, sounds very native in both). When she speaks English, it is clear from a number of phonological features that her native dialect is Chicano English. At the same time, there are features of her intonation and phonology that are strongly associated with the local California Anglo dialect. There is also a Spanish-language 'reality courtroom' type show, which features a judge who decides small civil claims. I heard a fair amount of codeswitching during an episode of this show that I watched, including some switching by the judge. These bits and pieces suggest that a larger study of CE and Latino speech generally on television would be fruitful.

8.9   The representation of the language of Mexican-Americans in feature films

In the next section, I will focus on the attitudes toward CE and the speech of Latinos generally as they are reflected in feature films with predominantly Latino casts. These films can reveal a great deal about how CE is viewed both by the dominant culture and by the Mexican-

American communities in which it is spoken, depending on which group had the larger role in the production of a particular movie. Additionally, although I will focus here only on the motion picture industry, further insights about how Chicano English and other aspects of speech among Mexican-Americans are perceived could be had from looking at works of literature, television programs, advertisements, popular music, and many other sources.

In terms of the representation of Mexican-Americans in the movies, I have chosen to begin with some relatively recent feature films which portray the lives of real or fictional Mexican-American characters. There are several good general studies available now of how Mexican-Americans are portrayed in films, such as Berumen (1995), and the excellent collection of articles *Latin Looks*, edited by Rodriguez (1997). These studies trace a number of the stereotypes that can be found in media portrayals of Latinos and Latinas historically. I do not know of any studies like these that look specifically at language issues, however.

Portrayals of the language of Mexican-American characters

In this section, I will discuss from a linguistic perspective five major films that feature predominantly Mexican-American characters and actors (although the overlap between these two categories is, perhaps unfortunately, not complete). I have chosen these films, released over a period spanning 15 years, because they all had a widespread distribution but are very different from one another in a number of ways. Because I am primarily interested in the linguistic image that reached the public, I selected the movies regardless of whether they were realistic in representing Latino communities or effective in furthering political and social causes. At some points, however, I will comment on these types of issues as well. Some questions one might ask about these portrayals of Mexican-Americans include the following:

- How is bilingualism, at community and individual levels, addressed? To what extent are characters shown as speaking Spanish, not speaking English, using different languages in different contexts, and so forth?
- To what extent is codeswitching portrayed as an integral part of how Mexican-Americans speak? How linguistically accurate is the representation of this phenomenon?

- What role does Chicano English play in portrayals of Mexican-American characters who might be expected to speak it?
- How often are Latino and Latina characters (especially older ones) portrayed as non-native speakers?

The films discussed are *Boulevard Nights* (1979), *Born in East LA* (1987), *La Bamba* (1987), *American Me* (1992) and *Mi Vida Loca* (1994). I will begin by briefly characterizing the representation of Mexican-American speech in each of the movies individually, and providing an excerpt of dialogue. Then I will look at them as a group and analyze the image of Mexican-American speech that they present. This is a general, qualitative analysis, addressing the types of questions raised above. However, quantitative studies of sociolinguistic variables in the portrayal of CE speakers on film could also be very interesting.

Boulevard Nights (1979) was one of the earliest feature films released by a big studio (Warner Brothers) to feature a predominantly Latino cast. The producer, director and writer were not themselves Latinos, though. The film was shot almost entirely on location in East Los Angeles, and revolves around a young Mexican-American auto shop worker, Raymond, who tries to get his younger brother out of a gang. It highlights themes of violence and revenge, and even though the main character is trying to work against the gang lifestyle, the film does not really present alternative models. Berumen (1995) notes:

> Education is never mentioned as being a viable option for reasonably persevering people such as Raymond and Shady... No alternatives are documented to demonstrate that Chicanos can be more than simply gang members and auto mechanics. (1995:170)

For exactly this reason, it evoked protests in many Latino communities where it was shown.

Many of the characters in *Boulevard Nights* are represented as speaking CE, although the varieties they use are sometimes more standard than what one would expect from real gang members, hanging out with each other. Ironically, Perozzi et al. (1984) note that one of the actors in the movie adopted a 'Chicano accent,' even though he grew up in the suburbs of Los Angeles and presumably spoke a variety indistinguishable from that of local Anglos. There is some use of codeswitching, as well as occasional use of Spanish by characters like the mother of the two boys. An excerpt of dialogue from *Boulevard Nights* appears below:

Cop:	You the brother?
Raymond:	Yeah.
Cop:	Sign. You better talk to this kid before he finds his ass in Quentin with the rest of his buddies. [Cop leaves]
Raymond:	What's the matter with you man?
Chuco:	He was a fucking cop, *ese*.
Raymond:	So what? He's right.
Chuco:	Ma, I'm so -
Carmen:	*No quiero oir nada.* [=I don't want to hear anything.]
Raymond:	What happened tonight?
Chuco:	11th street started it. The cops let us go. They don't know who did what.
Raymond:	Does 11th think you stabbed their homeboy?
Chuco:	That don't matter, does it?
Raymond:	C'mon inside.

Born in East LA (1987) was the first comedy to focus on life in the barrio. It had a certain advantage at the box office in that writer/director Cheech Marin had already made several successful movies. It is a difficult film to pigeonhole, in that it is full of tired (and potentially racist) stereotypes of the Mexican-American experience, but also tries to present social and political themes, by portraying the level of poverty in Mexico in a serious way. The basic story concerns a worker at an auto repair shop in East Los Angeles, who is caught up in an immigration raid and deported to Tijuana, and has a series of mishaps trying to return to the United States.

The English varieties represented in this movie for the characters who live in the USA are CE in their phonology, but have very little non-standard syntax. One might expect comedies to be more likely to feature vernacular dialects, although in Fought (2000) I did not find this effect for AAE dialects on film. But the main character of Rudy (Cheech Marin), despite having few non-standard grammatical features, does use exaggerated CE (or more precisely Sonoran) intonations with what appears to be a humorous intent. (This intonation is also used in an exaggerated way by non-native English-speaking characters from Mexico). Rudy also uses phonological features of CE such as stops for interdental fricatives and lack of glides. Significantly, he is portrayed as speaking very poor Spanish, and says explicitly to his mother at one point, 'Mom, you know my Spanish isn't that good.' Among the other characters there is a high representation of non-native English speakers, driven by the fact that much of the action takes place in Mexico, as well as a frequent use of Spanish, for the same reason. The non-native characters, such as José, below, are more likely to use non-standard grammar of the learner variety. Codeswitching in this movie is mainly of the 'emblematic' type. In fact, the use of words like *vato* or *órale* is specifically highlighted in a part of the movie where Rudy tries to train some would-be border crossers to pass as Americans, mainly by walking a certain way and using these terms. An excerpt of dialogue from this movie follows:

Rudy:	What're you looking at?
José:	A *pocho*. And a *pocho pendejo* at that.
	[=American asshole]
Rudy:	Yeah, who're you?
José:	*Me llamo José Negrón.* Welcome to the back of the bus.
	[=My name is...]
Rudy:	Yeah, well, I won't be here long. Soon as I get these fuckers to stop, I'm outta here.
José:	Oooo, good luck. These guys don't listen too good. *Sabes que la cagada que tienen en la cabeza les está tapando los oídos.* Maybe the shit they have in their head is clogging up their ears. [Exact translation of the Spanish sentence.]
Rudy:	Well, what happens next?
José:	We take a nap. And when we wake up, we'll be at the border. Then they take us off the bus. And then we buy a beer and figure out how to get back by Monday.
Rudy:	Shit.

La Bamba (1987) is an altogether different type of movie. According to Berumen (1995:213), *La Bamba* and *Born in East LA* (which was released the same year) are the two top-grossing films ever made about 'the Chicano experience.' If *Born in East LA* was criticized for presenting stereotypes of working class Mexican-Americans, though, *La Bamba* instead presented an arguably sanitized view of the same group. It is based on the true story of Richie Valens, a Chicano rock musician of the 1950s, killed in a plane crash with two other musicians when he was only seventeen. Berg (1997) raises some questions about this movie, noting:

There is a continuous tension in the film between Ritchie's attachment to his class, cultural, and ethnic roots on the one hand (his humble beginnings toiling in the fields, his devotion to his mother and his family, his discovery of his Indo-Hispanic lineage in Mexico) and his transformation into a nonthreatening middle-class American teenager on the other (his ignorance of Spanish, his decision to Americanize his name, his blonde Anglo girlfriend) ... Is such a story a demonstration of how quickly success follows acculturation? (1997:118)

Although most of the cast consisted of Latino and Latina actors, the title role of Richie was played by Lou Diamond Phillips who is Filipino-Hawaiian. The writer/director and the associate producer of the movie were Latino brothers (Luis and Daniel Valdez).

Even more than with *Born in East LA*, the varieties of English presented in *La Bamba* tend to be standard, almost Anglo-sounding dialects, with the occasional representation of imperfect non-native speaker English among some of the older characters. The assimilated view of language presented here mirrors the kind of acculturation themes that Berg discusses above. Although there is some codeswitching, there is relatively little use of Spanish in this movie as compared with some of the others, and in fact the character of Richie explicitly says, *Yo, yo no speako español* (a pidginized version of 'I don't speak Spanish'), which makes an interesting parallel with the comment above made by Rudy in *Born in East LA*. A couple of excerpts from *La Bamba* appear below:

Bob:	Mom, what the hell are you doing here?
Connie:	We came to work.
Bob:	Well I came to take you out of this dump.
Connie:	Not before we make some money. I mean honest money.
Bob:	Hey, hey, I've been working, okay, why can't you believe me for once?
Richie:	Mom, what's going on?
Bob:	We're getting out of this shithole tomorrow.
Connie:	Okay *mijo*, okay. [=son]
Connie:	Rosie, come stay with us sometime. Bob got us a big house in Pacoima, we could go visit LA.
Rosie's Dad:	Rosa, You're gonna be late for work.
Rosie:	My dad wouldn't like it.
Richie:	C'mon let's go.
Connie:	I love you *mija*. [=daughter]

Rosie:	Okay, bye Connie.
Connie:	Goodbye *mija*. [=daughter]
Rosie:	Richie.
Connie:	Bye Rosie.
Richie's little sister:	Bye! Bye!

American Me (1992) was directed by Edward James Olmos, who also starred in the movie. It is one of a number of movies that came out in the 1980s and 1990s which focus on violence and the gang lifestyle, following in the tradition of films like *Boulevard Nights*, and as such received a fair amount of criticism in the Latino community (Berumen 1995:238). It tells the story of Santana, whose family is victimized in the infamous Zoot Suit riots, and who becomes a gang member and eventually a leader in the Mexican Mafia. The film was shot in East LA, and featured Mexican-Americans in all the major roles. This movie was specifically mentioned by one of my speakers, David, 17, as a realistic portrayal of life for a Latino, and a movie he very much liked. Nonetheless, David's status as a 'wanna-be' gang member has certainly influenced his view, which may not be at all representative of other Mexican-American young adults.

The language in *American Me* is certainly affected by the gang theme. The varieties of English shown tend to be non-standard versions of CE, very different from those in *La Bamba*, for example. This 'tough' portrayal of Mexican-Americans as gang members is also reinforced linguistically by a much higher use of taboo language than in the other movies that have been discussed. The characters in this movie who are not gangsters are mostly non-native speakers. As was mentioned in the introduction, this type of pattern in films tends to reinforce the stereotype that CE is spoken by gang members, as well as the idea that other Mexican-Americans just speak 'broken' learner English. An excerpt of dialogue from *American Me* appears below:

Big Happy:	Can I talk to you, *ese*?
Santana:	Yeah c'mere. *¿Que trais, carnal?* [=What's up, brother?]
Big Happy:	You thinking of letting him in, *ese*? [=dude]
Santana:	I told you, he's my best crime partner.
Big Happy:	He ain't Mexican, *ese*.
Santana:	Yeah, but *¿sabes qué? Es mi hermano. Lo entiendes, menos? Órale.* So, homes, how's that leg? [=but you know what? He's my brother. You get it? Cool.]

JD:	Check it out, hard as a rock, *ese*.
Santana:	Shit homes, throw some shellac on it.
JD:	Shit, I'll still run your ass to the ground, *ese*.

Mi Vida Loca (1994) is the most recent of the movies discussed, and like *American Me* it focuses on the gang lifestyle. Neither the director nor the writer of this movie is Latino. The cast, on the other hand, not only consists entirely of Chicanos and Chicanas, but also features both actors and actual gang members in the various roles (Rodriguez 1997:182). The style of the movie is less scripted and artificial than usual, almost mimicking a documentary, and despite having a non-Latino writer, the representation of CE is fairly accurate. My students, mainly Anglos and African-Americans, often say that they adore this film, which in my opinion features a number of very tender and quite realistic moments. Again, however, the image of Mexican-Americans selected for the big screen is one of gang members, drugs, teen pregnancies and violence, and as such it cannot be said to be 'representative' of the experiences of Mexican-Americans who come from so many other types of backgrounds.

The varieties of English portrayed in *Mi Vida Loca* are definitely the closest to the actual varieties that I heard in my fieldwork. There is perhaps a quantitatively less frequent use of non-standard features than I would expect from the characters' backgrounds, but there are still plenty of the phonological and syntactic features of CE represented here. There is a significant amount of codeswitching. Also, younger speakers are sometimes portrayed as speaking Spanish, which in many other movies is associated exclusively with an older generation. In fact, some of the main characters in this movie clearly speak a native variety of English and a non-native variety of Spanish, which one does not often see on film, but reflects an accurate reality for many young adults in the Latino community of Los Angeles. An excerpt from *Mi Vida Loca* appears below:

Voice-over:	It seemed like she was gone forever when she went to the hospital to have Junior. When she came home, she didn't want to kick back at the market with everybody. She was tired all the time. I guess she was shining on Ernesto too.
Ernesto:	Hey Sad Girl, I wanna ask you something, What's up with, what's up with Mousie?
Sad Girl:	I don't know, I, she, you know, she's just really tired these days, I don't know.

Ernesto:	I call her, she won't return my phone calls, and my *abuela* tells me she don't wanna talk to me. [=grandma]
Sad Girl:	I don't know, you know, just hang in, give her a chance.
Ernesto:	Okay. Think I can call you sometime? Maybe just, just talk?
Home girls:	Let's go.
Sad Girl:	Yeah.
Home girls:	Let's go.
Ernesto:	Yeah.
Home girls:	Let's go.
Sad Girl:	I gotta catch up with my homegirls.
Ernesto:	All right.
Voice-over:	It wasn't like we planned it. These things never make sense when they come into your life. I think we just turned to each other because we missed my friend. I don't know, it just sorta happened.

In all of these movies, the language varies somewhat from one scene to another, so the excerpts represent one type of dialogue found in the film, though other varieties and styles may appear in other parts.

The image and language of Mexican-Americans on film

In this section I will discuss the general pattern of the portrayal of Mexican-American speech that these movies represent. Although I am looking at only five films, there is unfortunately not a very wide range of other films available featuring Latino casts, and these five are among the most commercially successful. So, whether this is good or not, these movies represent a big piece of the image of Latinos on film that the general public, in the USA and abroad, is receiving.

To begin with, the movies present a fairly realistic portrayal of CE, ranging from highly vernacular styles with a great deal of non-standard grammar (like Santana in *American Me*), to varieties that sound close to standard dialects in syntax, but have unmistakable CE phonological and prosodic features (like Rudy in *Born in East LA*). While this may not seem surprising, it would certainly be possible for films to inaccurately represent all Latino characters as speaking standard, Anglo-sounding dialects, or non-native speaker 'broken' English, for example. There are some characters who speak these other varieties in the films, but they are not disproportionately represented.

The films as a whole also gave a prominent role to codeswitching in the speech of Mexican-Americans, an element characteristic of real-life Latino speech in many communities. Even though the young speakers I interviewed did not do much codeswitching when speaking English, they talked about 'mixing' Spanish and English quite a bit, and seemed to see it as an important part of their community and identity. Also, codeswitching in both directions was very typical of the slightly older speakers. Although this fact may not be well understood by the general population, codeswitching does, of course, follow syntactic rules, like any variety of natural language (see, for example, Zentella 1997: ch.6). In the films discussed here, I did not hear any instances of ungrammatical codeswitching, which seems notable in and of itself. There was also very little in the way of 'broken' English. The character of Carmen in *Boulevard Nights* does say at one point, *Now, make turn*. But overall, the portrayal of the bumbling non-native speaker whose speech is full of ridiculous mistakes, which was quite frequent for Latino characters in movies of earlier decades (see Berg 1997), seems to have been mercifully eliminated from more recent productions.

Table 8.1 lists the main characters for each movie,[2] showing whether they are portrayed as speaking CE, a non-native speaker variety of English, Spanish only or a standard dialect of English. It also shows whether or not the character codeswitched. Table 8.2 gives the same information for the minor characters, grouped together by movie, and excluding characters of non-Latino ethnicities or without speaking roles. It also gives totals for major and minor characters. I was interested to discover how infrequently the major (and even minor) roles went to characters/actors over 40 years of age; for example, none of the movies featured a male over the age of 40 in a major role, and only two featured a woman over 40 in such a role. I suspect this is a characteristic of American film-making as a whole and has little to do with the representation of Mexican-Americans specifically. Also, men are represented with disproportional frequency over women. Of the major roles, 61 percent went to men, and an overwhelming 81 percent of the minor roles did as well, so that the Mexican-American image on film is much more likely to be a Latino face than a Latina one.

Possibly the most striking fact in looking at these tables is the extremely high percentage of main and minor characters who are represented as speaking CE (Which as I have used it here, encompasses speakers with CE phonology who used little or no non-standard grammar). The only clearly 'standard' speaker is Richie in

Table 8.1   Major Latino characters in five feature films

Movie/ character	Sex	Age	Standard	CE	NNS	Span only	Codeswitches?
American Me							
Santana	m	16–34		x			x
Mundo	m	15–33		x			x
Esperanza	f	19–53			x		x
Pedro	m	30		x			x
Paulito	m	3–21		x			x
Puppet	m	24		x			x
Little puppet	m	19		x			x
Julie	f	26		x			x
Neto	m	15		x			x
La Bamba							
Richie	m	16	x				
Bob	m	20		x			x
Connie	f	35			x		x
Rosie	f	18		x			x
Mi Vida Loca							
Sad Girl	f	18		x			x
Mousie	f	18		x			x
Ernesto	m	17		x			x
Whisper	f	17		x			x
Shadow	m	16		x			
Giggles	f	24		x			x
Baby Doll	f	18	x			x	
Big Sleepy	m	23	x			x	
Boulevard Nights							
Chuco	m	17		x			x
Big Happy	m	19		x			x
Raymond	m	22		x			x
Carmen	f	50			x		x
Shady	f	22		x			
Born in East LA							
Rudy	m	20s		x			x (teaching)
Oscar	m	20s		x			
Feo	m	20s		x			
Javier	m	20s			x		
Dolores	f	20s			x		

Table 8.2 Minor Latino roles in five feature films

	CE	NNS	Span only	Standard	Codeswitches?
Minor characters					
Boulevard Nights					
female < 40	4	0			
female 40+	1	1			
male < 40	17	8			
male 40+	2	0			
American Me					
female < 40	1	1			1
female 40+	1	1			1
male < 40	22	1	1		17
male 40+	1	1			1
Mi Vida Loca					
female < 40	3	2			2
female 40+	—	—	—		—
male < 40	10				6
male 40+			1		
La Bamba					
female < 40	3				1
female 40+	—	—	—	—	—
male < 40	2				0
male 40+		4	1		1
Born in East LA					
female < 40	—	—	—	—	—
female 40+	1				1
male < 40	2	3			4
male 40+		1			0
Major characters:					
(combined, all movies)					
female < 40 (*n* = 10)	8	2			7
female 40+ (*n* = 2)		2			2
male < 40 (*n* = 19)	17		1	1	14
male 40+ (*n* = 0)	—	—	—	—	—
Minor characters:					
(combined, all movies)					
female < 40 (*n* = 13)	10	3			4
female 40+ (*n* = 3)	1	2			3
male < 40 (*n* = 58)	53	4	1		35
male 40+ (*n* = 10)	2	6	2	2	

La Bamba, perhaps not coincidentally one of the few Chicano roles played by a non-Latino actor among these films. Interestingly, non-native English speakers in major roles were always shown as older characters, except in *Born in East L.A.* where a number of characters were actually living in Mexico. In the minor roles, one did occasionally find younger non-native speakers in movies such as *American Me* or *Mi Vida Loca*. Since there are a large number of young non-native speakers, immigrants from Mexico, in LA, one might say that this portrayal does not reflect the community accurately. On the other hand, some dichotomy and tension between native born and Mexican born Latinos exists, as was discussed in Chapter 2. It may be that these movies focus on US born characters and are not expecting them to have Mexican born characters as part of their social circles, unless these individuals are their parents or others from an older generation. Viewed from this perspective, the representation of non-native speakers can be seen as more realistic.

The percentage of characters who codeswitched was very high also, much higher than I would have expected. Even older, non-native English speakers, such as Raymond's mother in *Boulevard Nights* were shown codeswitching. Also, even when the variety portrayed was more standard overall, as might be said of many characters in *La Bamba*, some degree of codeswitching usually took place. Although the tables do not provide information about the relative amounts of codeswitching in the different movies, by far the most is found in the movies that focus on gang members, particularly *American Me* and *Mi Vida Loca*. The two movies with no connection to gangsters, *La Bamba* and *Born in East L.A.*, clearly have the least. In fact, the only codeswitching done by Rudy, the main character in the latter film, takes place when he is instructing a group of Asians and Native-Americans in Mexico on how to 'pass' as Chicanos. For instance, he trains them to say '*órale, vato*, what's happening?' ('Hey, dude ...'). It would be difficult to say whether the amount of codeswitching represented in these films is accurate (that is, similar to what one would encounter in a real community), since communities and individuals can vary so much on this dimension. Its high frequency, however, may reinforce the myth of CE as Spanglish that has been discussed.

Another element reflected in these films, and which is quite disturbing, is the large number of Latino characters who are gang members; of the 31 major roles in these movies, 16 are portrayals of gangsters. This is of course a reflection of the fact that three of the five movies described here have plots focused on the gang life. But

I selected these movies because of their wide distribution to the public, and as I mentioned there are regrettably few movies featuring predominantly Latino casts from which to choose. Also, the gang role effect is heightened somewhat by the fact that the movies with other themes, *La Bamba* and *Born in East L.A.*, assigned many more roles to characters of non-Latino ethnicities, especially Anglos. For example, in *Born in East L.A.*, second billing after Cheech Marin goes to Daniel Stern who plays an (American) Anglo living in Tijuana. The disproportionate representation of gang members as lead roles for Latinos presumably reinforces in the general public the sense that CE is spoken by gang members. Despite the ways in which these films do authentically represent Mexican-American speech – the large number of CE speakers using a range of styles, the frequency and natural representation of codeswitching, the lack of distorted stereotypes of non-native speakers – in another way they give an inaccurate perspective and reinforce existing myths.

9
Conclusions: The Future of Research on Chicano English: Where Do We Go from Here?

9.1   Conclusions

Much of our knowledge about sociolinguistic variation, particularly in the area of sound change, is based on studies of majority Anglo speakers in the USA, the UK and elsewhere. The research presented here, which focuses on a Latino community in Los Angeles, reveals patterns of language variation and change that are in some ways quite different from those found in majority communities. A close examination of such a different dialect and setting provides linguistic perspective, especially in terms of determining whether certain sociolinguistic patterns are universal, in other words properties of human language variation everywhere, or specific to particular types of communities. Both the fact that the community of Chicano English speakers is bilingual and the particular nuances of constructing one's ethnic identity as part of a minority group have implications for language use and language change, as has been shown in this study.

The history of CE is unlike that of any Anglo dialect in the USA. It grew out of a context where Spanish, non-native English and other varieties of English were all represented. The result is a dialect of English which shows significant influence from Spanish in the phonology (and maybe even an intonation pattern inherited from Nahuatl!), but surprisingly little direct Spanish influence in its syntax or semantics. The CE-speaking community is an interesting locus for the study of dialect contact. At least in Los Angeles, we find in CE the influence of both AAE (despite the fact that young Latino adults in this community tend to have little personal contact with African-Americans) and CAE (from which CE speakers have assimilated both discourse markers like *be all* and certain sound changes in progress, like /u/-fronting). All in all, a rich heritage for a dialect that is perceived by the public as an imperfect attempt at English.

If we turn to the area of sociolinguistic variation specifically, we find that, again, this community offers a new perspective on a number of issues. To begin with, it contradicts the common assumption in sociolinguistics that members of minority ethnic communities do not participate in the sound changes associated with the local Anglo population. CE speakers in Los Angeles do in fact participate in at least three such changes. Also, with respect to the correlation of social class with sound change, the CE speakers did not follow the curvilinear pattern that has often been found in Anglo groups. The construction of identity in this community involves a number of social factors and social roles that interact in complex ways. These complexities are reflected in the use of sociolinguistic variables by different speakers, and social class alone, apart from other factors, is not particularly illuminating or neatly patterned. Although quantitative sociolinguistic studies do often look for interactions between pairs of variables (such as sex and social class), I have rarely seen the possibility of three-way interactions explored. Yet in the current study, the interaction among three social factor groups yielded the most significant correlation with the data. In addition, this study confirms what sociolinguists have known for some time now: ethnographic research must be conducted alongside the linguistic research in order to understand the linguistic variation fully. Particularly in minority ethnic communities, labeling speakers with social class assignments or observing whether they appear to be male or female is insufficient.

Studying more than one type of sociolinguistic variable in the CE community also led to some useful results. Phonetic and syntactic variables are used differently to highlight the construction of identity in this community. Most young CE speakers sounded like the people they spent time with (as reflected in more or less use of the phonetic variables). Sisters of gang members, for example, sounded more or less like the gang members. But particularly among the in-between groups like taggers or people affiliated secondarily with gangs, the syntactic variables were used to highlight significant information about how the speakers saw themselves. The taggers, who saw themselves as tough like the gangsters, used more of the non-standard syntactic variable studied. The brothers and sisters of gangsters used much less of this variable, presenting themselves as different from the actual gang members. The other finding concerning the two types of variables was that the difference between monolinguals and bilinguals correlated with the syntactic variable but not the phonetic ones. It would be interesting to test this result in more communities and with more variables, since if it were replicated, this pattern would be highly relevant to linguistic theory.

Because of the crucial role of bilingualism in the CE community, historically and synchronically, the study has also addressed the issue of Spanish fluency. The second language acquisition literature has sometimes suggested that native-like fluency in a second language is guaranteed if acquisition begins before a certain age. The CE speakers in Los Angeles demonstrate clearly that this is false, since most of them began acquiring Spanish from birth, but as adults they cover a wide range of fluencies from native-like to negligible. The information available about the social context of the community supports the idea that this represents a pattern of acquisition with subsequent attrition or loss, rather than incomplete acquisition. An individual in a bilingual setting such as this one, then, may, but will not necessarily, acquire native-like phonological fluency in the home language, when this language differs from that of the wider community.

The factor that correlated most closely with Spanish fluency (in other words, the retention of Spanish) was having a monolingual Spanish-speaking parent. This result sheds some light on a theory often seen in the language acquisition literature: that a bilingual child's fluency in both languages will be improved if the parents each speak only one of the languages to the child. This study suggests that the best model for bilingual acquisition in a setting like Los Angeles is for at least one of the parents to speak only the minority language with the child, regardless of what the other parent and other family members do. In as much as the one parent – one language strategy inadvertently produces this effect, it will be successful, but not because of the separation of the languages as has been proposed.

Another factor that correlated with Spanish fluency was the interaction of sex and social class. Middle-class women and working-class men were more likely to maintain fluency in Spanish than speakers from other groups. This interaction of social factors forms a close parallel with the interaction of sex, class and gang status that was found to have an effect on the phonological variables. It is interesting to find the same identity-related factors playing a role in the sociophonetic variation associated with sound changes in English, and also in the very different kind of variation represented by the level of phonological fluency attained in Spanish.

The attitudes of the CE speakers in Los Angeles illuminate other perspectives on the linguistic situation. In some ways, speaking Spanish is valued, and young adults often articulated this view explicitly. But actual language use patterns suggest that Spanish is also stigmatized. Many CE speakers feel insecure about their command of Spanish. In fact the loss or attrition of Spanish in first-generation speakers can in some cases lead to a language gap within a single family and across a single generation. Some young CE speakers feel they cannot communicate well with their parents because their own Spanish is inadequate, and the parents' knowledge of English is too limited.

Similarly, with respect to codeswitching, these young adults almost unanimously expressed positive opinions, many of them identifying it as the characteristic way of speaking in their community. However, actual observation suggests that this is not a community in which codeswitching of the type often discussed in the literature, mixing large stretches from both languages to the point where it is difficult even to identify a 'base' language, is very common. In practice, many of the speakers used only emblematic switches when they were speaking English. They switched more when speaking Spanish, often to compensate for a lack of fluency, and it may be from this practice that the community's perception of codeswitching as prevalent arises.

These perspectives may be complemented by looking at attitudes from outside the community, about CE and the speech of Latinos generally. The few experimental studies that have been done suggest that CE is subject to the same prejudices and negative evaluations that affect most non-standard dialects. In terms of the representation of the speech of Latinos and Latinas in the media, the evidence is mixed. In some ways, the picture of language that is represented is more accurate than we might have expected, and in other ways it feeds stereotypical images and perpetuates myths such as the idea that CE is 'English with a Spanish accent.' If more Latino producers and writers are able to find a toehold in the movie industry, a wider range of images and linguistic portrayals may emerge in the future.

9.2 Future directions

Throughout this book I have given indications of areas where further research is badly needed. This has unfortunately been easy to do, because of the many areas of linguistic interest related to CE and Latino communities in the USA that remain unexplored. The field of sociolinguistics is a young one, and many dialects, such as CE, have barely (in all its meanings) begun to be studied in depth; without question, there are other surprising patterns and complex sociolinguistic interactions to be found in the myriad different ethnic groups across the USA that remain to be studied. It is my hope that researchers interested in dialects, sound change, ethnic identity, language contact, bilingualism and other sociolinguistic areas will use this book as a starting point for studying in depth the many topics I have not been able to cover here. What is it, then, that we sociolinguists need to do? Discussion of a number of directions follows.

Carry out more studies of the varieties spoken in Latino communities

A crucial need for linguistics is simply to have more studies of minority ethnic communities of all types, including Latino communities. I think it is particularly important to have *comprehensive* studies, ones which look at various aspects of the syntax, semantics and phonology of the community in question, while devoting sufficient time to the ethnographic groundwork needed to understand the social structure of the groups involved. Too often researchers take a narrow focus on a single salient variable and by doing so, fail to learn enough about the larger picture of language in that community.

Very little is known about sound change in minority ethnic communities. Presumably, on a phonetic level, sound change proceeds in the same way everywhere. But the way in which sociolinguistic variables are tied to social factors can be tremendously different from place to place, depending on how the speakers construct their identities and practice their social roles. For instance, in this study there was no 'curvilinear' pattern of social class associated with sound change, as has been found in many Anglo communities. What else might be different about the organization of sociolinguistic variables in African-American, Asian, Latino or Native-American communities across the country? How might gender, for example, function differently as a variable in communities of speakers from these disparate groups? If we wish to talk about sound change from a theoretical perspective, we must incorporate data from a variety of communities, rather than basing our conclusions mainly on studies of Anglo speakers in large, urban settings. We could also make better use of research from the other social sciences, particularly those that focus on the construction of ethnicity, gender, and other important elements of identity.

In addition, I believe we should not accept so readily the idea circulating in the literature that members of minority ethnic groups do not participate in the sound changes characteristic of Anglo populations in a particular region. There is now ample evidence, including the evidence in this study, that they sometimes do. Each community of speakers of Latino ethnicity (and of other ethnicities) where sociolinguistic research is conducted should be approached without preconceived notions based on studies of other groups. It is so early in the history of sociolinguistics as a field that we must be very careful about making sweeping, generalized claims, and in fact are better served by gathering up our tape recorders and our field methods (which themselves could use some improvement) and going out into communities of many different types, just to learn as much as we can.

An issue I think would be fascinating to explore is the relationship between variation in the two languages in a bilingual community. This type of research could be done in a Latino community, or in another bilingual setting. I don't know of any research on whether speakers who are dominant in one language participate in the sociophonetic variation typical of their weaker language. If they do, do the same social factors and patterns correlate with variables in both languages? The parallel found here between factors affecting /u/-fronting, for instance, and factors affecting fluency in Spanish suggests that this is a possibility worth exploring.

Finally, I have spent very little time here discussing regional differences in the varieties spoken by Latino speakers in different parts of the country. We need to know more about how CE differs from Puerto Rican English, for example. When I have heard Puerto Rican English speakers from New York, I would never mistake them for Latinos or Latinas from Los Angeles. Given that both dialects grew out of a similar contact setting involving the same two languages, it is theoretically intriguing to consider the sources of their differences. To me, one obvious source is the differences in the matrix dialects of the local Anglos, although this has not been discussed much, probably partly because of the mistaken conviction that African-Americans and Latinos never use any regional features. There are also differences in Mexican vs. Puerto Rican dialects of Spanish that might be traced into English as well. Furthermore, we know almost nothing about the type of English that is spoken in the large Latino communities that exist in places like Florida, Colorado or Illinois. Adding sociolinguistic data from these communities would enrich the field considerably and open up new theoretical insights.

Look at suprasegmentals

The area of prosody lags behind all the other areas in terms of sociolinguistic research and advances. This is true across sociolinguistics generally, not just in looking at CE. However, contact dialects like CE, which involve the intersection of prosodic patterns from two different source languages, have much to teach us about how intonation and other suprasegmentals work. Also, seemingly peripheral features such as clicks or creaky voice may turn out to have a more significant role than was previously thought, once they are studied in depth. With respect to CE, studying intonation is particularly crucial, in part because it is such a salient element of what speakers of other dialects hear (for example, what they may describe as a 'sing-song' pattern), even when there are few other phonological or syntactic features to mark a particular dialect as CE. Also, intonation differences between dialects can lead to mis-communication, just as they might with speakers of different language backgrounds.

Learn more about language attitudes

Language attitude studies are among the most valuable to the commu-nity because they help to identify linguistic prejudices that can have far-reaching consequences in the areas of education, employment, housing and so on. Studies of listeners' reactions to AAE, for example, have provided us with pertinent information about how AAE is per-ceived that can be applied to issues such as the misidentification of children as having speech defects when they are simply speakers of a non-standard dialect. We need comparable studies of reactions to CE. Since CE is also a non-standard dialect, we might expect the same kinds of negative attitudes that many members of society project onto AAE, for example. In addition, however, listeners evaluating CE may project the kinds of negative attitudes associated with non-native speakers, even when the person speaking is actually a monolingual native speaker of English.

In addition to matched-guise and other techniques that involve listener reactions, I think a great deal can be learned about societal atti-tudes towards particular dialects by studying the media. I have presented here only a brief, qualitative analysis of some feature films that feature Latino casts. The study of other areas of the broadcast media, such as newscasts, television programs and advertisements, could shed further light on how the speech of Mexican-Americans (or other groups) is perceived and portrayed. I cannot recall, for example, having ever heard CE of any type on a commercial, although I have, rarely, heard AAE. This is worth following up. Also, quantitative studies of films and television programs could be done, paying attention to sociolinguistic variables, in order to see how realistic media portrayals are in comparison with data on real communities of speakers.

In many areas including Los Angeles, there is also an increasing amount of broadcasting in Spanish, as well as local programs that are specifically designed to be bilingual, such as the program I mentioned in Chapter 8 that showcases Spanish language music videos. Both the use of certain varieties on these programs (Spanish, CE, codeswitching and so forth) and the language attitudes that seem to be reflected by the participants are of great interest. Is anyone on these programs ever berated for not speaking Spanish well, for instance? How 'local' does a program have to be before CE is used extensively by the host or hostess? In addition, media of other types could be fruitfully studied. In particular, the use of CE, codeswitching or Spanish in Latino/Solidur Mexican – American literature would be a rich area to study. Factors such as the age, gender or occupation of characters could be taken into account. Furthermore, the texts of many of these works also contain within themselves evidence of language attitudes, such as characters who are ridiculed for speaking broken Spanish, or who want their children to speak only English.

Conduct larger studies of bilingual acquisition

Many of the studies available on bilingual acquisition have focused on one or two children (usually those of the researcher). It would be extremely helpful to conduct large-scale, longitudinal research on acquisition across large sections of a bilingual community. To some extent, Zentella (1997) represents a study of this type, although her research focused on issues such as language choice and codeswitching, rather than on the details of acquisition of syntax and phonology. The fieldwork involved in a study of young bilingual children would probably be facilitated by the delight of parents in having someone entertain their children for a time, a factor that Zentella also mentions. And the benefits of such a study in helping us understand how two languages are acquired, stored and in some cases eventually lost, would be tremendous.

Get information about language in minority ethnic groups to a wider audience

I began this book with a list of the myths that circulate in the general public and even in some linguistic sources about language in Mexican-American communities. To me, the persistence of these myths reflects an enormous failure on the part of sociolinguistics to get scientific information from our field out to society as a whole. Medical researchers have disseminated the fact that smoking causes cancer and have banished the image of the Marlboro man; astrophysicists have convinced us that the stars we see with our own eyes may in fact have died millions of years ago. Why have we sociolinguists failed to make it understood by the general public that CE is not a deficiency and bilingualism is not a threat? Why do a majority of educators have so little idea of what non-standard dialects are and what they represent to their speakers? Sociolinguists, and particularly those of us who work primarily in minority ethnic communities must find a better way to get the word out. Many other sociolinguists agree with this view and are working towards this goal in communities across the country. As linguists we delight in the study of language as a subject of intrinsic interest to us. The natural fruition of all our data gathering, however, is a return of benefits to the communities we study and to our society as a whole.

Appendix A
Examples from Narratives, in IPA Transcription

Within the transcription, spaces do not mark pauses. A syllable-initial vertical tick indicates that the syllable following has a primary stress; a space is used to highlight this inconspicuous stress mark. The long single vertical stroke is a pause; the double stroke is a pause with terminal intonation. In these examples, that is a pitch rise before an abrupt fall. The values of the high central vowels transcribed [ɨ ʉ] are somewhat lower than the symbols normally indicate. Final consonants followed by an upper corner, e.g. [t˺] are 'unreleased', that is, coarticulated with a glottal closure released after the release of the oral closure. The preceding vowel often has creaky voice. The symbols [ɹ ɚ] represent the nonsyllabic and syllabic versions of 'American R'.

1 Reina

(A) [hiwəz ˈsposɨ ˈgoːtʰʉ | dʉwə ˈtɛstʰ ‖
hæɾə ˈbiðɛɹ ˈsɚʔn̩ ǀ ʔəm | ˈtʰɐjn̩ ‖
ʔən ˈhidn̩hævə ˈɹɐjt ‖]

He was supposed to go to do a test –
had to be there (at a) certain, um, time.
And he didn't have a ride.

(B) [hiz ˈwəkiŋwɨmɐj ˈdæd ‖ bə? ˈmɔm̩mɐj ˈdædɚ ˈkʰɐjnnəv |
lɐjk ˈskɛɹd | bikəzɨzɪntʰʉ ˈgæŋz ‖ biʔhiz ˈnɐʔlɐjk |
bi ˈfoɹlɐjkwn̩hi ˈjʉstʉgɪdɪn ˈtʰɹəbl̩əlɐt˺ ‖]

He's working with my Dad. But Mom and my Dad are kind of,
like, scared, because he's into gangs. But he's not like
before, like when he used to get in trouble a lot.

(C) [ˈwəɾijʉgɐjzdʊiŋtʰʉj ˈtʃɛðəɟɨ ˈno? |
ˈʔɔlijʉ ˈgɐjzɹaz ˈbɹɛðəzɨn ˈsɪstəz ‖]

235

What are you guys doing to each other, you know?
All of you guys are brothers and sisters.

2 Chuck

[wi 'wentʰʉə 'pʰɛɹɾi ‖ ʔæ 'nɛnegɐˀ 'bɹokn̩ əpˀ ‖
so 'wəɔɪdɹəŋkˀ ‖ ʔɛn | jɨno | wiɾon 'wɛnəgo 'hom ‖
wiwɚ| ʔɔʟ | jɨno | 'pʰəmp 'tʰəptɛnɛvɹiɹ̠ʰɪŋso |
wi 'wɛntʰɨðə 'bʉɫɨvɐɹdɪn | ʔɪ | ʔɪmmɐj 'hombojz 'tʰɹ̠əkˀ |
mɐjsɪsəz 'bojfɹ̠ɛn 'ʔækʃʉli ‖]

We went to a party, and then they got broken up.
So we're all drunk. And, you know, we don't want to go home.
We were all, you know, pumped up and everything, so
we went to the Boulevard in – in my homeboy's truck.
My sister's boyfriend, actually.

3 Rita

[ʔɛn 'ðɛn | ðɛɹwəzɨs | ðɪs 'gɐjɐjʉstu 'biwɪθ |
bə 'ʔɐjwəzn̩tˀ 'wɪθhɪmætˀtʰɛ 'tʰɐjm ‖
'ðɪswɨzlɐjkʰ | jɨnɐw | ʔŋ | ʔɪnno 'vɛmbɚ| ədi 'sɛmbɚ ‖
'hiʔəm | higɐʔ 'ʃɐtˀ kəzhi wəzɪnə 'bɪɹ 'ɹən | ʔɛnhi 'dɐjdɪn |
'ʔɪnstn̩tˀli ‖ ʔɪnə 'bɪɹ 'ɹən ‖

And then, there was this guy I used to be with,
but I wasn't with him at that time.
This was, like, you know, in November or December.
He, um, he got shot, because he was in a beer run, and he died in –
instantly. In a beer run.

Appendix B
Response sheet for the
Accent-rating Experiment

1. Esta persona me parece: (marque una)

———	———	———	———	———
muy simpática	un poco simpática	regular	un poco desagradable	muy desagradable

2. Cuando habla español, el modo de hablar de esta persona suena:

———	———	———	———	———
puro español	español bastante puro	un poco influido por el inglés	bastante influido por el inglés	muy influido por el inglés

3. Esta persona me parece:

———	———	———	———	———
muy inteligente	un poco inteligente	regular	no muy inteligente	no inteligente

4. ¿Dónde cree usted que nació esta persona?
   ——— en México
   ——— en México, pero lleva tiempo viviendo en Estados Unidos
   ——— en otro país Latino-Americano
   ——— en Estados Unidos

5. ¿Cuál cree usted que es la lengua materna de esta persona?
   español ———   inglés ———   otra lengua ———

6. ¿Cuál cree usted que es la raza de esta persona?
   hispana ———   morena (negra) ———
   blanca ———   de otra raza ———

Notes

Notes to the Introduction

1. Baugh (1984), for instance, entitled an early article 'Chicano English: The anguish of definition'.
2. This dialect is, of course, spoken by many people who are not Anglos. I have chosen this term, though, because the local regional dialect in an area is often associated with the majority white population, and speakers from ethnic communities where other dialects are spoken may be accused of 'sounding white' when they use the more general regional dialect.
3. There is more discussion of my fieldwork, and specifically of why I felt it would be helpful rather than problematic to work in the office, in Chapter 1.
4. See Mendoza-Denton (1999) for a more complete discussion of the classification LEP and other issues.

Notes to Chapter 1

1. A pseudonym
2. I use the term 'network' here in a very general sense, to mean a group of people in the community who all know each other at least casually, and have some social structure in common (church, school, community group and so on.). As will be seen later, these two larger divisions include smaller groups that fit the concept of network outlined in Milroy (1987).
3. I also interviewed some Anglo students, as will be discussed later.
4. In talking to the principal recently, she informed me that due to new district regulations, the racial composition of the school has changed significantly. There is now a much larger percentage of African-Americans, and a much smaller percentage of Latinos.
5. This is not just an assumption on my part, but rather a fact that was confirmed by my informants.
6. One interesting reflection of level of formality occurred in the interview with Oscar. Most of the students used the informal pronoun form *tu* ('you') when they spoke to me in Spanish. Oscar was one of the few who began by addressing me with the formal *Usted*, but he switched to *tu* midway through the interview.
7. For those who may not know, Phil Collins is a (fairly insipid, in my opinion) white pop singer whose music was popular in the 1980s.
8. For a full discussion of these concepts and their relation to sociolinguistic interviews, see Milroy (1987:47–9)
9. Mario, a former gang member, for instance, stated that his main problem in getting out of the gang was the information he had about drugs and illegal activities.

Notes to Chapter 2

1. I was also careful to exclude certain factors that might seem related to social class but are not good indicators in this community. For instance, a factor such as dressing in expensive-looking clothes, which might provide a clue to social

class in some Anglo communities, does not correlate well with social class among my speakers. It can even be misleading; some of the speakers who live in the Projects are among the best dressed students at Westside Park.

2. I have calculated social class only for the young adult speakers in my sample, among whom I will be analyzing linguistic variation, and not for the older speakers who will contribute primarily language attitude data, as well as a norm for the analysis of Spanish.

3. See Chapter 8 for more discussion of this.

4. For a comparison, see Taylor's (1993) *Girls, Gangs, Women, and Drugs*.

5. Some excellent reference works on gangs that can provide more detailed accounts of appearance and gang membership include Klein's (1995) *The American Street Gang*, and Vigil's (1938) *Barrio Gangs*. See also Mendoza-Denton (1997).

6. Richard, who is Anglo, had been a member of a gang in Pomona but it was in fact a Latino gang, and I believe he was the only Anglo.

Notes to Chapter 3

1. I am deeply indebted to John Fought for his collaboration with me on this chapter.

2. For example, some of his speakers raised unstressed /æ/ in a fronting direction rather than towards the /ə/ mean, as Anglos would.

3. I am leaving aside for now the question of /u/-fronting, which sometimes affects the nature of the nucleus.

4. Unlike many other dialects of English, California Anglo English does not have a contrast between [ɑ]and [ɔ] (the vowel found in *caught* in these other dialects).

5. For more on the stress-timed versus syllable-timed distinction, see Dauer (1983).

6. For those who may remember him, this is the pattern used by the infamous cartoon character, Speedy Gonzalez.

7. It is possible that the [o] substitution is really for [ɔ], although I have [ɑ] for *saw*, in my dialect, as I think most Californians do.

8. According to Quilis (1978), 79.5 percent of Spanish words have penultimate stress.

9. I included the diphthong /ow/ because of its particular role in California sound changes. I excluded schwa because of the separate issues involved in vowel reduction in Chicano English (Santa Ana 1991).

10. One feature not used by Amanda or other CE speakers was [ow]-fronting, an Anglo pattern that can be seen clearly on Helena's chart.

Notes to Chapter 4

1. The features of AAE have become part of the general body of knowledge in the field of sociolinguistics so I have not always cited specific sources. A good list of these features, however, can be found in Rickford (1999:4–9).

2. Also, Reina's example represents a somewhat different case in that it seems to be a translation not of a preposition per se, but of a Spanish verb, *bajar*, which when translated can yield the wrong preposition (or particle) in English.

3. Zentella (1997:130), however, observed this substitution of prepositions by Lolita, an English-dominant speaker in the New York Puerto Rican community she studied.
4. I am not ruling out their use in other dialects, though. A few of them, such as *kick it*, were definitely used by the Anglo speakers. Also, some of my Anglo students now claim to recognize *talking to* as a paraphrase of 'dating', although I have never heard any of them use it this way myself (and I do sometimes talk to them about their romantic lives, as well as overhearing many such conversations).
5. García (1984:90) also documents a usage of barely that emphasizes 'scarcity,' giving the example *I barely have two pieces*. I did not have instances of this usage among the young speakers I interviewed, although it is always possible that the right context simply might not have come up.

Notes to Chapter 5

1. As a side matter, I would like to see some evidence that 'American society' (and I would very much like to know who is being included here) lumps together these very disparate groups into a single 'sub-community.' I consider myself a member of American society, yet I do not view these groups in this way.
2. In common usage, a stereotype of teenage women from a northern suburban part of Los Angeles, perceived as talking with certain intonations and being obsessed with shopping; it has now spread as a stereotype applied to teenage women from many parts of California.
3. Although the individual vowel charts include tokens from various environments, for the statistical analysis, only tokens in the most favorable environment will be used.
4. See also the discussion of social class conflict in Chapter 2.
5. It should be noted that two types of raised /æ/ tokens could be heard among the speakers, (a) /æ/ with an inglide, similar to the tense /æ/ heard in many Anglo communities where raising is common (cf. Labov 1994:163), and (b) a more monophthongal /æ/, similar to /ɛ/, but typically less peripheral. Both types of /æ/ could be found in tokens from the same speakers. Since there was no apparent correlation of the two types with preceding or following environments, I did not distinguish them in the analysis.
6. A more complete analysis of /æ/-raising in an Anglo community can be found in Labov (1994, ch. 18).
7. Throughout this study, the threshold for significance is set at $p < .05$.
8. See also the discussion of 'non-conformity' in Labov (2001:512–18).
9. For more on this issue, see Chapter 2.

Notes to Chapter 6

1. I did not code for contact with the African-American community, since as discussed in Chapter 2, this factor did not play a significant role among these particular CE speakers.
2. For a complete discussion of the range of degrees of bilingualism among the speakers, see Chapter 7.
3. The numbers for the syntactic categories here are slightly different from those given earlier, because Table 6.4 includes speakers who never use negative concord, and these speakers were omitted from the run reported in Table 6.2.

Notes to Chapter 7

1. In fact, it might be appropriate to make a theoretical distinction between the type of switching that is related to lack of fluency, and the kind that is deliberate, even if not at a conscious level, chosen by the individual for the meta-message it conveys, or simply as an expected part of bilingual linguistic interaction in the community.
2. 'But I am the only one that came out *a musician.* My- all my brothers were into sports, basketball, baseball, *and everything,* and I couldn't do that. *I didn't like them.* I could, you know, play *and everything, but I liked the guitar more.'*
3. Of course this does presume that the parents are literate or have the assistance of someone who is literate. Mendoza-Denton (1999) has a more complete discussion of the survey.
4. I did not have access to the form for speakers from the main high school or the outside parent network.
5. There are a few low-fluency speakers for whom there was no BHS on file, such as Sol. Given that Sol's mother came to the USA as an adolescent, it is possible that Sol might be one of the few speakers who fall into the limited input category.
6. That is, 'dating'.
7. But compare Hill (1970) and Snow and Hoefnagel-Hohle (1982) for some evidence against the CPH, at least in its stronger versions.
8. See also Flege (1991); Flege and Fletcher (1992).
9. I began interviewing Carlos in Spanish, and was about to switch to English when his mother (who is monolingual) joined us, necessitating the continued use of Spanish. In several other visits to the house I was unable to connect with Carlos again, due to his very heavy work schedule.
10. A sample of the response sheet appears in Appendix B.
11. I discovered empirically that monolingual parents were always described by their children as speaking 'not much' English. Not a single person said that their parents *did not* speak English. Of course, most of these older speakers probably knew a few words in English after having lived in the USA for many years. But people described in this way differed clearly from those who were described as 'understanding English' or speaking 'some English,' and always turned out to be basically monolingual.
12. I also experimented with many other combinations such as sex*number of older siblings, but none of these were significant, and I have left them out of the table.

Notes to Chapter 8

1. I listened to earlier segments of the Spanish part of his interview and found that this is actually fairly true. Salvador did not switch as much as some of the other speakers did, at least in the interview situation.
2. I made a subjective judgment of which roles were 'leads' and which were minor.

References

Alcoba, Santiago and Julio Murillo (1998) Intonation in Spanish. In: Hirst and DiCastro (1998) pp. 152–66.

Anonymous (2001) Culver City CA Home Page (http://www.ci.culver-city.ca.us/cityinfo/).

Appel, Rene and Pieter Muysken (1987) *Language Contact and Bilingualism.* London: Edward Arnold.

Asher, James, and Ramiro Garcia (1969/1982) The optimal age to learn a foreign language. In: Steven Krashen, Robin Sarcella, and Michael Long (eds), *Child–Adult Differences in Second Language Acquisition.* Rowley, MA: Newbury House, pp. 3–12.

Bailey, Guy and Natalie Maynor (1987) Decreolization? *Language in Society* 16: 449–73.

Bailey, Guy and Erik Thomas (1998) Some aspects of African-American Vernacular English phonology. In: S. Mufwene, J. Rickford, G. Bailey and J. Baugh (eds), *African-American English: Structure, History, and Use.* New York: Routledge, pp. 85–109.

Baugh, John (1984) Chicano English: The anguish of definition. In Ornstein-Galicia (1984) pp. 3–13.

—— (1999) *Out of the Mouths of Slaves: African-American Language and Educational Malpractice.* Austin: University of Texas Press.

Berg, Charles Ramirez (1997) Stereotyping in films in general and of the Hispanic in particular. In: Clara E. Rodriguez (ed.), *Latin Looks.* Boulder, CO: Westview Press, pp. 104–20.

Berumen, Frank Javier Garcia (1995) *The Chicano/Hispanic Image in American Film.* New York: Vantage Press.

Bongaerts, Theo, Brigitte Planken, and Erik Shils (1995) Can late starters attain a native accent in a foreign language? A test of the critical period hypothesis. In: David Singleton and Zsolt Lengyel (eds), *The Age Factor in Second Language Acquisition: A Critical Look at the Critical Period Hypothesis.* Clevedon, Avon: Multilingual Matters pp. 30–48.

Brennan, Eileen and John S. Brennan (1981) Measurements of accent and attitude toward Mexican-American speech. *Journal of Psycholinguistic Research* 10: 487–501.

Butt, John and Carmen Benjamin (1988) *A New Reference Grammar of Modern Spanish.* London.: Edward Arnold.

Coleman, Richard and Lee Rainwater (1978) *Social Standing in America: New Dimensions of Class.* New York: Basic Books.

Dauer, Rebecca (1983) Stress-timing and syllable-timing reanalyzed. *Journal of Phonetics* 11: 51–62.

Delattre, Pierre, Carroll Olsen and E. Poenack (1962) A Comparative Study of Declarative Intonation in American English and Spanish. *Hispania* 45: 233–41.

Dorian, Nancy (1981) *Language Death: The Life Cycle of a Sottish Gaelic Dialect.* Philadelphia: University of Pennsylvania Press.

Duran, Richard P. (ed.) (1981) *Latino Language and Communicative Behavior.* Norwood, NJ: Ablex Publishing Corp.

Eckert, Penelope (1987) The relative values of variables. In: Keith Denning, Sharon Inkelas, Faye McNair-Knox and John Rickford (eds), *Proceedings of the Fifteenth Annual Conference on New Ways of Analyzing Variation*, Stanford, CA: Stanford University Department of Linguistics, pp. 101–10.

—— (1989) The whole woman: Sex and gender differences in variation. *Language Variation and Change* 1: 245–68.

—— (1991) Social polarization and the choice of linguistic variants. In: Penelope Eckert (ed.), *New Ways of Analyzing Sound Change*. San Diego, CA: Academic Press, pp. 213–32.

—— (2000) *Linguistic Variation as Social Practice: The Linguistic Construction of Identity in Belten High*. Malden MA and Oxford, UK: Blackwell Publishers.

Flege, James (1981) The phonological basis of foreign accent: A hypothesis. *TESOL Quarterly* 15: 443–55.

—— (1987) The production of 'new' and 'similar' phones in a foreign language: Evidence for the effect of equivalence classification. *Journal of Phonetics* 15: 47–65.

—— (1988) Factors affecting degree of perceived foreign accent in English sentences. *Journal of the Acoustical Society of America* 84: 70–9.

—— (1991) Perception and production: the relevance of phonetic input to L2 phonological learning. In: T. Huebner and C. Ferguson (eds), *Crosscurrents in Second Language Acquisition and Linguistic Theories*. Amsterdam: John Benjamins, pp. 249–89.

Flege, James, and K. Fletcher (1992) Talker and listener effects on degree of perceived foreign accent. *Journal of the Acoustical Society of America* 91: 370–89.

Flege, James, and J. Hillenbrand (1984) Limits on pronunciation accuracy in adult foreign language speech production. *Journal of the Acoustical Society of America* 76: 708–21.

Fought, Carmen (1997) *The English and Spanish of Young Adult Chicanos*. IRCS report 97–09.

—— (1999) A majority sound change in a minority community: /u/-fronting in Chicano English. *Journal of Sociolinguistics* 3(1): 5–23.

—— (2000) Language in the Media. Paper presented at University of California, Santa Barbara Linguistics Colloquium.

—— (2002) Ethnicity. In: J. Chambers et al. (eds), *The Handbook of Variation and Change*. Blackwell Publishers.

—— (forthcoming) California students' perceptions of, you know, regions and dialects? In: D. Preston and D. Long (eds), *Handbook of Perceptual Dialectology II*. Amsterdam: John Benjamins.

García, Maryellen (1984) Parameters of the East Los Angeles speech community. In: Jacob Ornstein-Galicia and Allan Metcalf (eds), *Form and Function in Chicano English*. Rowley, MA: Newbury House, pp. 85–98.

García, Ofelia and Milagros Cuevas (1995) Spanish ability and use among second-generation Nuyoricans. In: Carmen Silva-Corvalán (ed.), *Spanish in Four Continents: Studies in Language Contact and Bilingualism*. Washington DC: Georgetown University Press, pp. 184–95.

Gilbert, Dennis and Joseph Kahl (1993) *The American Class Structure: A New Synthesis*. 4th edn. Belmont CA: Wadsworth.

Godinez, Manuel, Jr. (1984) Chicano English phonology: Norms vs. interference phenomena. In: ed. by Jacob Ornstein-Galicia and Allan Metcalf (eds), *Form and Function in Chicano English*. Rowley, MA: Newbury House, pp. 42–8.

González, Gustavo (1984) The range of Chicano English. In Ornstein-Galicia (ed.), (1984) pp. 32–41.

Gorman, James (1998) Like, uptalk? In: Gary Goshgarian (ed.), *Exploring Language*. New York: Longman, pp. 568–70.

Guy, Gregory (1988) Language and social class. Language: The socio-cultural context. In: F. Newmeyer (ed.), *Linguistics: the Cambridge Survey, vol. IV*. Cambridge: Cambridge University Press, pp. 37–54.

Guy, Gregory, et al. (1986) An intonational change in progress in Australian English. *Language in Society* 15: 23–51.

Guzmán, Betsy (2001) *The Hispanic Population: 2000*. C2KBR/01–3. US Census Bureau.

Henderson, A. (1995) The short a̱ pattern of Philadelphia among African American speakers. *University of Pennsylvania Working Papers in Linguistics* 3: 127–40.

Hill, J. (1970) Foreign accents, language acquisition, and cerebral dominance revisited. *Language Learning* 20: 237–48.

Hinton, Leanne, Birch Moonwomon, Sue Bremner, Herb Luthin, Mary Van Clay, Jean Lerner and Hazel Corcoran (1987) It's not just the Valley Girls: A study of California English. In: Jon Aske, Natasha Beery, Laura Michaels and Hana Filip (eds), *Proceedings of the Thirteenth Annual Meeting of the Berkeley Linguistics Society*. Berkeley, CA, pp. 117–27.

Hirst, Daniel and Albert Di Cristo (1998) *Intonation Systems: A Survey of Twenty Languages*. Cambridge: Cambridge University Press.

Hollingshead, August de Belmont (1949) *Elmtown's Youth: The Impact of Social Classes on Adolescents*. New York: J. Wiley. Reprinted Belmont, CA: Wadsworth, 1993.

Keefe, Susan and Amado Padilla (1987) *Chicano Ethnicity*. Albuquerque: University of New Mexico Press.

Kent, Raymond and Charles Read (1992) *The Acoustic Analysis of Speech*. San Diego, CA: Singular.

Kerbo, Harold (1983) *Social Stratification and Inequality: Class Conflict in the United States*. New York: McGraw-Hill.

Klein, Malcolm (1995) *The American Street Gang: Its Nature, Prevalence, and Control*. Oxford: Oxford University Press.

Kvavik, Karen H. (1974) Research and Pedagogical Materials on Spanish Intonation. *Hispania* 59: 406–17.

—— and Carroll L. Olsen (1974) Theories and Methods in Spanish Intonational Studies. *Phonetica* 30: 65–100.

Labov, William (1966) *The Social Stratification of English in New York City*. Washington, DC: Center for Applied Linguistics.

—— (1972a) *Language in the Inner City: Studies in the Black English Vernacular*. Philadelphia: University of Pennsylvania Press.

—— (1972b) *Sociolinguistic Patterns*. Philadelphia: University of Pennsylvania Press.

—— (1990) The intersection of sex and social class in the course of linguistic change. *Language Variation and Change* 2: 205–54.

—— (1994) *Principles of Linguistic Change*, vol. 1: *Internal Factors*. Cambridge, MA: Blackwell Publishers.

—— (2001) *Principles of Linguistic Change*, vol. 2: *Social Factors*. Cambridge, MA: Blackwell Publishers.

Labov, William and Wendell Harris (1986) De facto segregation of black and white vernaculars. In David Sankoff (ed.), *Diversity and Diachrony*. Amsterdam and Philadelphia: John Benjamins, pp. 1–24.

Lambert, Richard and Barbara Freed (1982) *The Loss of Language Skills*. Rowley, MA: Newbury House.

Laver, John (1980) *The Phonetic Description of Voice Quality*. Cambridge: Cambridge University Press.

Lenneberg, Eric (1967) *Biological Foundations of Language*. New York: Wiley.

Lipski, John (1993) Creoloid phenomena in the Spanish of transitional bilinguals. In: Ana Roca and John Lipski (eds), *Spanish in the United States: Linguistic contact and diversity*. Berlin: Mouton de Gruyter, pp. 155–82.

Long, Michael (1993) Second language acquisition as a function of age: Research findings and methodological issues. In: Kenneth Hyltenstam and Ake Viberg (eds), *Progression and regression in language: Sociocultural, neuropsychological, and linguistic perspectives*. Cambridge: Cambridge University Press, pp. 196–221.

Macaulay, Ronald (2001) You're like 'why not?': The quotative expressions of Glasgow adolescents. *Journal of Sociolinguistics* 5.

—— (1976) Social class and language in Glasgow. *Language in Society* 5: 173–88.

Major, Roy (1993) Sociolinguistic factors in loss and acquisition of phonology. In Kenneth Hyltenstam and Ake Viberg (eds), *Progression and Regression in Language: Sociocultural, Neuropsychological, and Linguistic Perspectives*. Cambridge: Cambridge University Press, pp. 463–78.

Martin, Stefan and Walt Wolfram (1998) The sentence in African-AmericanVernacular English. In: S. Mufwene et al., *African-American Vernacular English: Structure, History, and Use*. London: Routledge, pp. 11–36.

Matluck, Joseph H. (1952) La pronunciación del español en el Valle de México. *Nueva revista de filología española* 6: 109–20.

—— (1965) Entonación hispánica. *Anuario de Letras*, Universidad autónoma de México 5: 5–32.

McLaughlin, Barry (1981) Differences and similarities between first- and second-language learning. In: Harris Winitz (ed.), *Native Language and Foreign Language Acquisition*. Annals of the New York Academy of Sciences 379.

Mendoza-Denton, Norma (1995) Gang affiliation and linguistic variation among high school Latina girls. Paper presented at NWAVE XXIV in Philadelphia.

—— (1997) Chicana/Mexicana identity and linguistic variation: an ethnographic and sociolinguistic study of gang affiliation in an urban high school. Stanford University dissertation.

—— (1999) Fighting words: Latina girls, gangs, and language attitudes. In: D. Letticia Galindo and María Dolores Gonzales (eds), *Speaking Chicana: Voice, power, and identity*. Tucson AZ: University of Arizona Press, pp. 39–56.

Merino, Barbara (1983) Language loss in bilingual Chicano children. *Journal of Applied Developmental Psychology* 4: 277–94.

Metcalf, Allan (1974) The study of California Chicano English. *International Journal of the Sociology of Language* 2: 53–8.

Milroy, Lesley (1987) *Language and Social Networks*, 2nd edn. Language in society, Series 2. Oxford: Basil Blackwell.

Moonwomon, Birch (1991) (æ) in San Francisco English. In: *Proceedings of the 17th Annual Meeting of the Berkeley Linguistic Society*, pp. 208–17.

Noland, D. (1991) A diachronic survey of English negative concord. *American Speech* 66(2): 171–80.

Ornstein-Galicia, Jacob (ed.) (1984) *Form and Function in Chicano English.* Rowley, MA: Newbury House.

Oyama, Susan (1976/1982) A sensitive period for the acquisition of a nonnative phonological system. In: Steven Krashen, Robin Sarcella and Michael Long (eds), *Child – adult Differences in Second Language Acquisition.* Rowley, MA: Newbury House, pp. 20–38.

Paradis, Michel and Yvan Lebrun (eds) (1984) *Early Bilingualism and Child Development.* Lisse: Swets & Zeitlinger.

Payne, Arvilla (1980) Factors controlling the acquisition of the Philadelphia dialect by out-of-state children. In: William Labov and David Sankoff (eds), *Locating Language in Time and Space.* Quantitative Analyses of Linguistic Structure, Series 1. New York: Academic Press, pp. 143–78.

Peñalosa, Fernando (1980) *Chicano Sociolinguistics: A Brief Introduction.* Rowley, MA: Newbury House.

Penfield, Joyce (1984) Prosodic patterns: Some hypotheses and findings from fieldwork. In Ornstein-Galicia (1984) pp. 71–82.

Penfield, Joyce and Jacob Ornstein-Galicia (1985) *Chicano English: An Ethnic Contact Dialect. Varieties of English around the World,* vol. 7. Amsterdam: John Benjamins.

Perozzi, Joseph et al. (1984) The right to have an ethnic accent: Some views of speech teachers and a speech therapist. In Ornstein-Galicia (1984) pp. 169–75.

Poplack, Shana (1978) Dialect acquisition among Puerto Rican bilinguals. *Language in Society* 7: 89–103.

——— (1980) 'Sometimes I start a sentence in Spanish y termino en español': toward a typology of code-switching. *Linguistics* 18: 581–618.

Preston, D. (1991) Sorting out the variables in sociolinguistic theory. *American Speech* 66(1): 33–56.

Quilis, Antonio (1978) *Curso de lengua española.* Valladolid, Spain: A. Quilis y C. Hernández.

Reiss, Albert (1961) *Occupations and Social Status.* New York: Free Press.

Rickford, John (1986) The need for new approaches to social class analysis in sociolinguistics. *Language & Communication* 6: 215–21.

——— (1999) *African American Vernacular English: Features, Evolution, Educational Implications.* Malden, MA: Blackwell.

Rickford, John and Faye McNair-Knox (1994) Addressee- and topic-influenced style shift: A quantitative sociolinguistic study. Reprinted in Rickford (1999) 112–54.

Rickford, John and Christine Théberge-Rafal (1996) Preterit had in the narratives of African American preadolescents. *American Speech* 71: 227–54.

Rodriguez, Clara E. (ed.) (1997) *Latin Looks.* Boulder, CO: Westview Press.

Ryan, Ellen, Miguel Carranza and Robert Moffie (1977) Reactions toward varying degrees of accentedness in the speech of Spanish-English bilinguals. *Language and Speech* 20: 267–73.

Sanchez, Rosaura (1982) Our linguistic and social context. In: J. Amastae and L. Elias-Olivares (eds), *Spanish in the United States: Sociolinguistic aspects.* Cambridge: Cambridge University Press, pp. 9–46.

Sankoff, Gillian and Pierette Thibault (1994) Réactions subjectives au parler français des jeunes anglophones à Montréal. Paper read at Second Language Research Forum.

Santa Ana, Otto (1991) Phonetic simplification processes in the English of the barrio: A cross-generational sociolinguistic study of the Chicanos of Los Angeles. University of Pennsylvania dissertation.

—— (1993) Chicano English and the nature of the Chicano language setting. *Hispanic Journal of Behavioral Sciences* 15: 3–35.

—— (1996) Sonority and syllable structure in Chicano English. *Language Variation and Change* 8: 1–11.

Saunders, George (1982) *Bilingual Children: Guidance for the Family*. Clevedon, England: Multilingual Matters.

Schlyter, Suzanne (1993) The weaker language in bilingual Swedish – French children. In: Kenneth Hyltenstam and Ake Viberg (eds), *Progression and Regression in Language: Sociocultural, Neuropsychological, and Linguistic Perspectives*. Cambridge: Cambridge University Press, pp. 289–308.

Schneider, E. (1989) *American Earlier Black English*. Tuscaloosa: University of Alabama Press.

Schumann, John (1978) The acculturation model for second-language acquisition. In: R. Gingras (ed.), *Second language acquisition and foreign language learning*, Arlington VA: Center for Applied Linguistics, pp. 27–50.

Scovel, Thomas (1969) Foreign accents, language acquisition, and cerebral dominance. *Language Learning* 19: 245–54.

Seliger, Herbert and Robert Vago (eds) (1991) *First Language Attrition*. Cambridge: Cambridge University Press.

Shuy, R., W. Wolfram and W. Riley (1967) *Linguistic Correlates of Social Stratification in Detroit Speech*. Final report, US Office of Education Cooperative Research Project No. 6–1347.

Silva-Corvalán, Carmen (ed.) (1994) *Language Contact and Change: Spanish in Los Angeles*. Oxford: Clarendon.

Smith, C. C., G. A. Davies and H. B. Hall (eds) (1988) *Langenscheidt's New Standard Spanish Dictionary: Spanish–English English–Spanish*. New York, Berlin, Munich: Langenscheidt.

Snow, Catherine and Marian Hoefnagel-Höhle (1982) The critical period for language acquisition: Evidence from second language learning. In: Steven Krashen, Robin Sarcella and Michael Long (eds), *Child-adult Differences in Second Language Acquisition*. Rowley, MA: Newbury House.

Stanford, Lin et al. (1982) First language retention and extralinguistic variables in immigrant bilingual children. *Selecta* 3: 67–72.

Stevens, Gillian (1986) Sex differences in language shift in the United States. *Sociology and Social Research* 71: 31–6.

Strozer, Judith (1994) *Language Acquisition after Puberty*. Washington DC: Georgetown University Press.

Stub, Holger (ed.) (1972) *Status Communities in Modern Society: Alternatives to Class Analysis*. Hinsdale, IL: Dryden Press.

Taylor, Carl (1993) *Girls, Gangs, Women, and Drugs*. East Lansing, MI: Michigan State University Press.

Thibault, Pierrette and Gillian Sankoff (1993) Diverses facettes de l'insecurité inguistique: Vers une analyse comparative des attitudes et du français parlé par des Franco- et des Anglo-montréalais. *Cahiers de l'Institut de Linguistique de Louvain* 19: 209–18.

Valdes, Guadalupe (1988) The Language Situation of Mexican Americans. In: S. McKay and S. Wong (eds), *Language Diversity: Problem or Resource?: A Social and Educational Perspective on Language Minorities in the United States*. Cambridge and New York: Newbury House.

Veatch, Thomas (1991) English vowels: Their surface phonology and phonetic implementation in vernacular dialects. University of Pennsylvania dissertation.

Vigil, James Diego (1938) Barrio gangs: Street life and identity in Southern California. Reprinted 1988, Mexican American monographs, no. 12. Austin: University of Texas Press.

Wald, Benji (1984) The status of Chicano English as a dialect of American English. In: Jacob Ornstein-Galicia and Allan Metcalf (eds,) *Form and Function in Chicano English*. Rowley, MA: Newbury House, pp. 14–31.

—— (1993) On the evolution of *would* and other modals in the English spoken in East Los Angeles. In: Norbert Dittmar and Astrid Reich (eds), *Modality in Language Acquisition/Modalité et acquisition des langues*. Berlin: Walter de Gruyter, pp. 59–96.

—— (1996) Substratal effects on the evolution of modals in East LA English. In: Jennifer Arnold et al. (eds), *Sociolinguistic Variation: Data, Theory, and Analysis: Selected papers from NWAV 23 at Stanford*. Stanford CA: Center for the Study of Language & Information, pp. 515–30.

Wallis, E. (1951) Intonational stress patterns of contemporary Spanish. *Hispania* 34: 143–7.

Wardhaugh, Ronald (1986) *An Introduction to Sociolinguistics*. Oxford: Basil Blackwell.

Weldon, T. (1994) Variability in negation in African American Vernacular English. *Language Variation and Change* 6: 359–97.

Wolfram, Walt (1969) *A Sociolinguistic Description of Detroit Negro Speech*. Washington, DC: Center for Applied Linguistics.

—— (1974) *Sociolinguistic Aspects of Assimilation: Puerto Rican English in New York City*. Washington, DC: Center for Applied Linguistics.

Wolfram, Walt and Clare Dannenberg (1999) Dialect identity in a tri-ethnic context: The case of Lumbee American Indian English. *English World-Wide* 20: 179–216.

Zentella, Ana Celia (1997) *Growing up Bilingual*. Oxford: Basil Blackwell.

Index